EQUAL RIGHTS

RIGHTS

THE
MALE
STAKE

EQUAL RIGHTS

Leo Kanowitz

THE MALE STAKE

University of New Mexico Press *Albuquerque*

Library of Congress Cataloging in Publication Data

Kanowitz, Leo.
  Equal rights, the male stake.

  Includes bibliographical references and index.
  1. Sex discrimination—Law and legislation—
United States. I. Title
KF4758.K36   342.73'0878   81-52056
ISBN 0-8263-0594-6 347.302878   AACR2
ISBN 0-8263-0595-4 (pbk.)

Contents

To
Libby

Preface

In recent years, American legal developments affecting all facets of sex discrimination have occurred with amazing rapidity. Despite the intense activity in this field, however, the fundamental issues confronting the courts, legislatures, and the American public have remained relatively constant: How demanding should the standards requiring equal treatment of the sexes be? Is preferential treatment for one sex (or gender) desirable or permissible to compensate for past social and legal discrimination against that sex (or gender)? Is the equal-rights movement one directed by women against men, or is it participated in by women and men to free both sexes from the burdens of past stereotypical thinking about their legal and social roles?

As explained in the first chapter, below, about two-thirds of this book is made up of previously published essays of mine, the remaining third consisting of matter that is published here for the first time. Because of the constancy of the underlying issues, I continue to hold the views expressed in the previously published essays.

Those portions of the book that have appeared in print before are identified by notes at the foot of the title page of the appropriate chapters. Those chapters that were originally published as separate articles over an eight-year period are not arranged in the order in which they first appeared. It should also be noted that the chapters that are based on previously published articles still refer to conditions that existed when the articles were originally written. Readers of the entire book, including the notes (which appear at the back), should have no difficulty discovering the few areas in which particular legal doctrines have been modified in the interim.

While this book was in press, several important developments were occurring in the courts and in the political arena. Those developments are discussed in a Postscript starting on page 145. Matters covered in that Postscript include the U.S. Supreme Court's decisions in *Michael M. v. Superior Court of Sonoma County* (a statutory rape law under which only males can be guilty does not violate equal protection), and in *Rostker v. Goldberg* (a male-only draft-registration requirement does not violate the Fifth Amendment's Due Process Clause), and the nomination by President Reagan of Sandra Day O'Connor to be the first woman member of the U.S. Supreme Court.

Many people have helped to bring this book into existence. I would like to express my appreciation to my students in the Sex Discrimination and the Law course that I have taught at my home institution, the University of California, Hastings College of the Law, and, as a Visiting Professor, at the McGeorge School of Law of the University of the Pacific and the Harvard Law School. The opportunity to test in the classroom some of the admittedly controversial ideas explored in this book has been extremely useful. I would also like to thank Dean Bert S. Prunty of the Hastings College of the Law for the support services and research facilities he has generated at the College and for his sympathetic encouragement of faculty research activities. My thanks also to Lovelle Stabler, Stephen R. Lothrop, and Beatrice Spelker for typing both the new and old matter contained in the book.

Portions of this book have previously appeared in volume 8 of the *California Western Law Review*, volumes 28 and 31 of the *Hastings Law Journal*, volume 3 of the *New Mexico Law Review*, and volume 6 of the *Hastings Constitutional Law Quarterly*. Permission of those journals to publish herein is gratefully acknowledged. I would also like to thank Marilyn Klinger of the California Bar, the coauthor of the article that appears as the Appendix, for permission to publish herein.

My greatest debt is to my wife, Elizabeth Kanowitz. Her encouragement and support, while she has been engaged in numerous interesting and important activities, within and outside the home, have been indispensable to my work in this and other fields.

1

Introduction

In two of my earlier books, *Women and the Law: The Unfinished Revolution* (1969) and *Sex Roles in Law and Society* (1973), I examined the history of sex discrimination in American law, and analyzed the defects in judge-made and statutory doctrine in this field. At the same time, both works proposed a variety of doctrinal reforms, especially in the employment-relations and constitutional-law spheres. In those earlier volumes, emphasis was placed on the injustices that American women had suffered as a result of legislative acts and decisions of courts and administrative agencies that accorded them less favorable treatment than men. Those books have often been relied upon by courts and legislatures in shaping new decisions and statutes that have ended many of the sex-based injustices of the past. They have also helped influence the United States Supreme Court to adopt new, more enlightened approaches to the constitutional-law aspects of sex discrimination, and have proved to be useful tools for those seeking to add the Equal Rights Amendment (ERA) to the federal Constitution.

A major impediment to the full realization of the goals set forth in the earlier books has been the widespread misperception that the political-social-legal movement for sex equality is exclusively a movement for women's rights. There have even been observers at various levels of American cultural and social life who have viewed the sex-equality movement as a movement by women against men. As a result, many potential male allies in this fundamental struggle for human rights have been unnecessarily prevented from playing the role they might otherwise have played had they understood the full dimensions of traditional sex discrimination in law and society—

and especially how men, like women, have been victimized by such discrimination.

Many of the goals of the women's movement can surely be achieved by the efforts of women themselves. At the same time, that movement's success can doubtless be hastened if men understand that those goals are compatible with their own ultimate interests and aspirations, and that their achievement can lead to greater personal freedom and fulfillment for both sexes.

To develop that understanding in both men and women is the aim of this book. About a third of its contents is published for the first time herein. The remaining two-thirds collects various of my previously published articles and testimony before committees of the United States Congress. The earlier pieces were written over a period of almost eight years, each in response to a discrete problem. When they first appeared, it was not contemplated that they might later be appropriately gathered in a single volume. Only recently has it become clear that, despite their diversity of subject matter, they revolve around a common unifying theme. That theme, as indicated by the title of this book, is the male stake in sex equality in the law.

Some men have always been able to escape the limitations of their own male backgrounds to embrace the idea of equality between the sexes. Such diverse historical figures as Aristophanes, Frederick Engels, John Stuart Mill, Henrik Ibsen, and the men who participated in the women's suffrage movement in the United States and other countries and in the current campaign for ERA ratification are only a few of those who come immediately to mind. Their reasons for supporting the sex-equality notion have not, however, always been the same.

A sense of justice coupled with the element of comic irony played significant roles in the insights developed by Aristophanes in his play *Lysistrata,* in which Sparta's women withheld their sexual favors to discourage their menfolk from engaging in the madness of war. By contrast, Frederick Engels, Karl Marx's friend and collaborator, saw the role of women in society as a reflection of the deficiencies of an economic system founded upon the private ownership of the means of production. John Stuart Mill's humanitarianism and the general philosophical premises of his essay *On Liberty* (that a society's organization must not be permitted to impede the maximum development of each of its members) were the foundations for the attitudes and positions in his book *The Subjection of Women*. And Henrik Ibsen, in his classic drama *A Doll's House*, clearly understood the denial of fundamental human rights that inhered in his contemporaries' relegation of women to an essentially ornamental role.

Examination of the activities and backgrounds of women's male allies in the struggle for the elective franchise and in the campaign for ratification of the proposed Equal Rights Amendment to the federal Constitution would reveal equally diverse perceptions, motivations, and goals. Some men engaged, or engage, in activities aimed at ending the unequal status of the sexes under the law because they abhor all forms of injustice. Others identify the interests of all people with the struggle for women's rights. Still others understand the many direct and indirect ways that men as well as women have been victimized by the arbitrary assignment of sex roles in law and society. And many men support the sex-equality movement for a combination of all these reasons, and for others as well.

In the following chapters, the reader will encounter a number of discussions of illustrative areas of the law in which men have been direct victims of sex-role stereotyping. The male's unique duty of compulsory military service, his primary obligation of financial support within the family, the preference for mothers over fathers in child custody disputes, and the absence of protective labor laws for men comparable to those that have long been in place for women are only a few examples of the many ways in which the law has disfavored men.

The ending of such antimale discrimination at the hands of the law—which would result from the achievement of a system of legal sex equality—would obviously produce an immediate and direct benefit for males. Their understanding of this possibility should, among other consequences, provide many men, who might otherwise be indifferent to or opposed to the ratification of the ERA, with a strong reason to support its passage.

Some ERA opponents have sought to justify their opposition to the amendment on the ground that the ERA, if adopted, would deprive American women of the "superior" position they now enjoy under the law. Though such claims are exaggerated, they contain an element of truth, as seen from the examples given above. There are three basic flaws in this position, however. One is that it assumes that all men—or all women, for that matter—will placidly accept a state of affairs in which women are accorded "superior" rights to men in any fields of the law. Another is its failure to recognize that a major vice of a "preferred" treatment for women by the law is its tendency to reinforce stereotypical notions about the proper role of women in society. And the third point—closely related to the second—is that it ignores the many ways in which women have been historically victimized by pervasive sex discrimination in law and society.

The abolition of profemale preferences in the law—in those areas where such preferences do exist—is, as already suggested, clearly a goal that would give males a direct and immediate stake in achieving a system of sex equality in legal doctrine. But such a direct and immediate stake in sex equality in the law and in social institutions is apparent for other reasons as well.

Anthropologists Geoffrey Gorer and Margaret Mead, as a result of their independent studies of primitive South Sea Island communities, came to remarkably similar conclusions. Their researches persuaded them that in societies in which sex-role stratification is blurred, that is, where no sharp delineation exists between male and female tasks, the tendency toward human aggression is less pronounced than in societies that sharply distinguish between the ideal characters of men and women. In the former societies, those in which sex roles are blurred, there is, in the words of Geoffrey Gorer, "no ideal of brave, aggressive, masculinity."[1] If such findings are valid, their implications for all of us—male and female alike—are immense. The tendency toward human aggression is at the core of numerous individual and social problems that plague us all. Marital disharmony, crime and delinquency, and many other individual and social disorders are traceable in large part to this tendency toward human aggression. They in turn radiate numerous other economic and governmental problems in their own right, ranging from a widespread sense of malaise among Americans to distortions in the allocation of the nation's limited financial and human resources.

In its extreme form, the tendency toward human aggression is expressed in the institution of war, that state of affairs in which the taking of human life, the most aggressive act conceivable, is not only permitted by governments and societies, but positively encouraged by them. That any war in the current era poses a substantial risk of destroying much of the world and its people because of the awesome weaponry available to nations that could easily become involved is a matter of common knowledge. The avoidance of violent solutions to international disputes has always been important. How much more so is such avoidance today in the light of the nuclear and germ-warfare arsenals stockpiled throughout the world. Whatever can be done to dampen the tendency toward human aggression these days would therefore appear to cry out imperatively for doing.

This is not to suggest that a one-to-one relationship exists between sex role stratification and international violence. The sources of international conflict are obviously many, varied, and complex. What is suggested is that, in addition to other approaches that have been tried over the centuries to dampen the tendency toward international violence, the approach of ending rigid sex-role stratification within the internal organization of nations is one that merits close attention. The ending of such stratification, if one can generalize from the findings of Mead and Gorer, should aid, to an extent yet to be determined, in reducing the possibility of violent international conflict, and, ultimately, the destruction of our planet.

Clearly, such a result would lie within the direct and immediate interest of all members of our society, male or female. The curbing of domestic antisocial behavior, reflecting the tendency toward human aggression, as in criminal and delinquent acts, also serves the interest of all who are potentially direct or indirect victims of such behavior—again, regardless of their sex.

Males thus have a direct and immediate stake in eliminating disadvantages they now incur, solely because they are males, at the hands of law and society. In addition, as members of the larger polity, they have much to gain from ending a system of sex-role allocation that may play a significant causative role in many of the longstanding problems of society that adversely affect all its members.

In some of what follows, I have criticized what, in my view, are mistakes and excesses of some elements of the "women's movement." Since few, if any, of us accept criticism dispassionately, it will not be surprising if those critical observations are not universally received in the spirit in which they are offered. Nevertheless, I deem it important to state precisely what that spirit is.

I happen to believe that the truth shall make us strong as well as free. Only by recognizing the obvious truth that some of its elements have committed errors and excesses that have tended to weaken the women's movement will its adherents forge the strength and unity that are needed to achieve all of that movement's legitimate goals.

It is because I firmly support the essential goals of that movement that I find it necessary to bring to the attention of its participants what have struck me as its shortcomings and failures. In many ways, the women's movement's shortcomings of the last two decades are insignificant when they are compared with its enormous successes during the same period. In less than twenty years that movement has been largely responsible for the new and more enlightened perception by the American people of the problem of sex-role allocation in contemporary American society, and for the enactment of progressive laws and the development of fresh judicial doctrine reflecting that new perception.

On the federal legislative level, the enactment of the Equal Pay Act of 1963, requiring "equal pay for equal work" regardless of the sex of the worker; the passage of Title VII of the 1964 Civil Rights Act, prohibiting sex-based employment discrimination by covered employers, labor organizations, and employment agencies; the enactment of the Education Amendments of 1972, outlawing sex discrimination in educational opportunity; and the promulgation of Executive Order 11246, as amended by Executive Order 11375, prohibiting employment discrimination on the basis of sex by those who contract with the federal government—all attest to the effectiveness and strength of the women's movement.

Similarly, on the federal judicial level, the U.S. Supreme Court's alteration of the standard by which sex-based classifications are to be tested for constitutionality, from the former "any-rational-basis" test under which sex-based classifications automatically passed constitutional muster, to the present standard, which requires such classification to be "substantially related to an important governmental objective," and under which few, if any, sex-based classifications will survive (at least as long as they are not justifiable as "benign" discriminations),[2] also reflects the strength and effectiveness of the women's movement in raising the consciousness about sex roles in all Americans. Similar enlightened and innovative legislative and judicial developments have, during this same period and for the same reasons, occurred at the state level in all fifty of the American states.

At the same time, one cannot help desiring a social and political movement that one admires, like one's loved one, to be free of imperfections. It is in this spirit that criticisms of some tactics or programs of certain elements of that movement are offered at various points throughout this book; and it is in this spirit that I hope they will be received and understood by its readers.

Above all, this book has been guided by three basic ideas. The first is that there are large numbers of American men who have not been—but should be and can become—active and enthusiastic supporters of sex equality under American law. The second is that this goal can be achieved in ways that are consistent with the fundamental principles of the women's movement. And finally, I firmly believe that in formulating specific programs to eliminate historical sex discrimination in the law, care must be taken to preserve and protect fundamental institutional values in American society—such as freedom of expression—values as precious, if not more so, to participants in the sex-equality movement as they are to other Americans.

2

The Male Stake
in Women's
Liberation*

"Why are you doing this?"

The question was asked of me in March of 1970 by a member of the New Mexico Senate Judiciary Committee. The occasion was my testimony in support of a bill that would finally give New Mexico wives the same power now enjoyed by their husbands to make a will of one-half of their community property, that is, the property owned in common by a husband and wife in New Mexico as a kind of marital partnership.

The senator's meaning was, at first, difficult to grasp. But his true intent soon became clear. He was simply perplexed—honestly and sincerely perplexed—by the prospect of a male (a married one at that!) supporting a bill that, *as he saw it*, would enrich New Mexico wives at their husbands' expense (but which, in fact, would merely have corrected a longstanding injustice suffered by wives in that state).

Like many other Americans today, both male and female, the senator apparently viewed the women's liberation movement as pitting women against men. In that context, males who support any or all of the goals of that movement are, at best, dupes of the enemy and, at worst, conscious traitors to their own kind.

His attitude is undoubtedly shared by many American men. Fear, anger, confusion, and anguish are only some of the negative male reactions to the women's liberation movement. Such reactions are not difficult to understand when one remembers that

*This chapter is a slightly revised version of an article entitled *The Male Stake in Women's Liberation*, 8 CAL. WEST. L. REV. 424 (1972) by Leo Kanowitz, copyright © 1972 by Leo Kanowitz.

many of the movement's participants have, with much justification, characterized men as the oppressor and women as the oppressed. People are not likely to feel comfortable in the shadow of an accusing finger.

The accusation, as I have suggested, is not without foundation. Few can doubt that ours is a male-dominated society; that women, though numerically a majority in the United States, constitute a sociological minority suffering disadvantages comparable to those endured by racial and ethnic minorities; and that in legal, political, employment, and social practices a male power structure reigns.

I am also convinced that, aside from its essential truthfulness, the characterization of the male as the oppressor has helped galvanize the women's rights movement.

How, then, can any male support such a movement? How could I have written my book, *Women and the Law: The Unfinished Revolution*, exposing arbitrary sex discrimination in American law? How can I support the proposed Equal Rights Amendment to the United States Constitution, which would remove any doubt that equal treatment under law without regard to sex is constitutionally commanded?

The answers to these questions are, at the same time, both simple and complex. Perhaps they will be of assistance to the many American males who, like the New Mexico senator, cannot conceive of men supporting the women's liberation cause.

There is one very obvious reason for men to support women's liberation—and that is a *hatred* of discrimination. Many Americans of both sexes *hate* discrimination when it is based on race. They *hate* it when it is based on religion, or national origin, or ethnic background. And they *hate* it when it is based on sex.

Americans are no longer puzzled by the prospect of white people combating discrimination directed at blacks, or Anglos speaking and writing against discrimination aimed at Chicanos or Puerto Ricans, or of non-Jews striking out at anti-Semitism. But for many people, the sight of males agitating for women's liberation still seems strange somehow.

In all these expressions of concern for a group to which one does not belong and whose welfare does not in obvious ways affect the person concerned, however, there are several common elements. One of the most important is the sense of fairness and decency, which, despite its being muted at times, is far from dead among Americans today. I am not referring here to the sentiment that might be described as maudlin do-goodism. What I am talking about is a basic revulsion against all forms of injustice, a concern for the welfare of others that American education aims to instill in all of us, the instinct which tells us that, though individual differences may justify separate treatment, the accidental fact of birth into a group whose skin color, nationality, or sex is distinctive does not justify such treatment.

This attitude is not limited to our time or country. Throughout history and in all lands, there have always been men outraged by society's relegation of women to an inferior social, legal, or political status. The Greek playwright Aristophanes, for example, reflected indignation at this state of affairs in his play *Lysistrata*. The English philosopher John Stuart Mill also championed the cause of women's freedom in the middle of the nineteenth century when he published his book *The Subjection of Women*—as have many other male writers before and since. And in England, the United States, and many other countries, thousands of men participated in the women's suffrage movement—picketing, demonstrating, and protesting in dozens of other ways so that women might share the political power previously monopolized by men.

But an abstract sympathy for the injustices suffered by others is not the only factor attracting growing numbers of men to the cause of women's liberation. With varying degrees of understanding, men have always been aware of their *direct* stake in the struggle for women's rights, that the liberation of women would lead inevitably to the liberation of men as well.

"What liberation of American men?" one might ask. How can one speak of men as the oppressor of women and, in the same breath, of the need to liberate men as well as women? The fact is, however, that in every type of discrimination and oppression, the discriminator suffers evil from the discrimination he or she practices. White people who discriminate against blacks on racial grounds, for example, develop guilt feelings, deprive themselves of the opportunity of developing personal relations with a large section of humanity, limit their educational experiences to contacts with one race, and conjure up fantasies about those they discriminate against.

In the case of male discrimination against women, comparable detriments to the male occur. But the price he pays for the luxury of feeling superior to women surpasses such indirect detriments. In thousands of ways, in law, social mores, employment pattern, and psychological health, males are *direct* victims, along with women, of a system that arbitrarily assigns roles on the basis of sex. This has long been recognized in Sweden, where many people now see the issue as one of a more rational and humane allocation of social roles without regard to sex rather than simply as one involving women's rights.

What, then, are some of the direct costs of male supremacy to the male? We all know, for example, that everywhere in the United States, when a man marries, he assumes the primary legal obligation to provide financial support to his wife and any children that may be born of this union. Such a scheme of legal regulation has been with us for a long time. Its implications are staggering. By the simple act of marrying, one human being, a male, is burdened with the awesome legal responsibility of financially caring for another human being who, before marriage, was deemed capable of providing that care for herself. True, this state of affairs reflects, among other things, society's expectations that children born of this union are best cared for by their mothers rather than their fathers (a presumption that also harms men, as we shall see), and the recognition that employment opportunity has never been equally available to women in our society. Still, the legal duty to support a wife does not depend in any state upon the wife's inability to earn her own living or on the presence of minor children of the marriage. Generally it is absolute, the wife having a corresponding duty to provide for her husband in a few states only in the exceptional case where he has been rendered incapable of doing so himself as a result of accident or illness.

What is more, this fundamental obligation is carried over in the support obligations imposed upon former husbands pursuant to divorce decrees. All too often, the amounts fixed for support in such decrees are too low to meet the actual financial needs of the ex-wife, as long as she is not gainfully employed, and too high as far as the ex-husband is concerned. The common result is to create

two financially needy families where one financially solvent family
had existed before.

This oppressive, one-sided support burden on American men
will surely have to be ended when true equality of employment
opportunity is achieved by American women. Support obligations
can then be evenly divided between husbands and wives, account
being taken of the incapacitating effects of illness, childbirth, or
agreements between the spouses modifying such obligations toward one another. The benefits to men of such changes in our law
of support would be direct, tangible, and substantial. Wives, too,
would achieve a large measure of economic independence as a
result of such changes and real equality of employment opportunity, ending the all-too-prevalent attitude among some men that
they have bought, or are buying, their wives because of their
financial contribution to the family. A further result, redounding to
the benefit of men as well as women, is that marital relationships
will flourish when the element of economic subordination has been
removed from them.

In most states, mothers are preferred over fathers as a matter of law
in custody disputes involving children of tender years. In rare
cases, a father is awarded custody. But the usual case awarding
custody to a mother ordinarily reflects arbitrary social presump-
tions about the respective roles of mothers and fathers in the up-
bringing of the children. Tacitly, at least, we have entrusted the
primary if not exclusive duty in this respect to mothers—to the
detriment of children, their fathers, and society as a whole.
Indeed, fathers are generally depicted by our communications
media—especially television situation comedies—as congenital
boobs, incapable of making meaningful decisions within the home.
Their primary, if not sole, family role is often expected to be that of
financial provider. Society apparently sees no contradiction therefore in permitting men to work unlimited overtime hours outside
the home, while simultaneously limiting the number of hours that
women may be required or permitted to work by employers more
concerned with profits than with human welfare.

Infected with the same bias, many men cannot conceive of a
law-imposed limit on the number of hours *they* may be permitted
to work outside the home. In part this explains why most efforts to
date to equalize the situation of the sexes insofar as state hours-

limitations laws are concerned have been directed at abrogating women's legislation rather than seeking to extend the benefits of such laws to men.

The net result in this realm, however, is that most young American children see relatively little of their fathers as compared to their mothers. Moreover, once they enter school, the contact of these children with women to the exclusion of men continues, since, because of our social mores, few men teach in kindergartens or primary schools. Thus, during their most impressionable, formative years, children, overwhelmingly exposed to the influence of women rather than of men, receive a completely distorted image of the universe. As part and parcel of this scheme of social expectations and legal regulation, men are deterred in countless ways from even trying to develop the intimate parental relationships with their children that are expected of mothers. Not only do children suffer from this state of affairs, but fathers, too, are deprived of some of the most rewarding experiences of parenthood, the mutual display of tenderness, affection, and love between parent and child. The goals of "women's liberation," when they are achieved, should change all that.

The price men pay for male supremacy is often their lives. "Women and children first," shouts the captain as the ship starts to sink. Perhaps this convention reflects the fact that, in its absence, women and children might be trampled in the rush for the small boats. Perhaps, insofar as children are concerned, it reflects the presumption that, if choices must be made, children are more worthy of being saved than adults, since so much more of their lives lie ahead of them. But in permitting women to go first, one can't help suspecting that chivalry, that ancient mask for economic and sexual exploitation of women, has been carried to an excess. To maintain the myth of the gallant, supreme male, the male under these circumstances is prepared to pay the ultimate price.

Then there is the matter of military service. Though it can be demonstrated that throughout the centuries many women have been as able as men to engage in the folly of war, male supremacy has led men to monopolize this madness for themselves. Our present requirement of compulsory military service is limited to men. Clearly, if the women who were capable of serving in the military were equally subject to the draft—a result that would probably be compelled, if the draft were not ended entirely, upon the addition of the Equal Rights Amendment to our Constitution—the statistical likelihood of individual men being drafted would be substantially decreased. Then, too, our nation's willingness to wage war for pointless causes might be modified.

In politics the demonstrated lower participation of women than men in the electoral process, largely induced by sex prejudice, has produced a government that is too often unresponsive to the needs of our nation's poor, oppressed, and victimized, since it is largely in this segment of our population that the greatest electoral abstinence is found. Consider also the damage to the nation caused by the subtle pressures limiting female elected representatives at all levels of government to a shamefully low number. The costs of such discrimination are borne by all of us—men and women—in the distorted allocation of priorities it produces.

The number of examples can be increased. In every sphere of human activity, the artificial and arbitrary assignment of roles on the basis of sex has caused misery and unhappiness to men as well as to women. Our ethos tells us that men are supposed to be aggressive sexually and women passive, that men are world-conquerors and women keepers of the hearth, men the doers and shakers of the universe and women their comfort and support. But in the depths of their beings, millions of individual men and women are neither physically nor psychologically constructed to perform as society expects. Indeed, it may be asked whether even a single individual exists whose personal makeup conforms to society's expectations with regard to his or her sex role.

This tension between society's expectations of people based on their sex and the real capacities, wants, and desires of individual human beings has burdened countless numbers of men as well as women with feelings of guilt, despair, and inadequacy. Millions of men and women are rendered incapable of relating to one another. The costs in human misery are incalculable. The by-products of such misery reach into every sphere of human activity, poisoning our lives, our environments, our futures.

The fact is that we are all in the same boat. The movement that is today known as one for women's rights or women's liberation will evolve, as it already has started to do in Sweden, into a movement that rejects all customs, institutions, laws, official and social practices that arbitrarily assign roles to human beings because of their sex and do not permit them to develop as individuals.

In such a movement, which is the natural and inevitable outgrowth of today's women's liberation movement, all of us, male and female, have a stake. The need is to start where "it's at" at this point in our history. By making common cause with the movement for women's liberation, men will come to understand that they too have nothing to lose but their chains.

3

"Benign" Sex Discrimination*

The decision of the United States Supreme Court in *Regents of the University of California v. Bakke*[1] left the constitutional fate of race-based "benign" discrimination unresolved. Although *Bakke* granted the relief sought by the plaintiff, admission to the medical school at the University of California at Davis, benign discrimination in the racial context was neither approved nor disapproved by a majority of the justices. Whether benign, compensatory, or preferential treatment by government is constitutionally permissible when it favors groups that have been victims of past societal and legal discrimination based on race is thus a question that will have to be determined in future cases.[2]

By contrast, in the realm of sex discrimination, the Court has to date approved and applied the principle of benign discrimination in at least three cases[3] and has approved, but found reasons for not applying, the doctrine in several others as well.[4] The thesis of this chapter is that, whatever the ultimate fate or propriety of "benign" discrimination in the racial area, it has no place in the realm of sex discrimination. The two phenomena differ in their legal and sociological dimensions in that men as well as women have been historical victims of severe and pervasive de jure sex discrimination, whereas, historically, white people have not been discriminated against because they are white. In addition, the dual aspect of any purportedly benign discrimination, that is, its inevitable tendency

*This chapter is a slightly revised version of part of an article entitled *"Benign" Sex Discrimination: Its Troubles and Their Cure*, 31 HASTINGS L. J. 1379 (1980) by Leo Kanowitz, copyright © 1980 by Hastings College of the Law. Reprinted with permission.

to impose burdens upon the class it seeks to aid, is much more pronounced in the realm of sex discrimination than in the area of racial discrimination.

Elimination of the benign-discrimination doctrine in the sex bias area would be consistent with the intended effect of the proposed Equal Rights Amendment to the federal Constitution,[5] as that intention is set forth by the amendment's most authoritative doctrinal supporters.[6] In addition, disapproval of sex-based benign discrimination need not deprive women of many of the special benefits they might enjoy under present or future law; it could, in most cases, simply mean that men too would enjoy those same benefits.

The dual aspect of laws that purport to accord preferential treatment to women often arises only because those laws do not apply to men as well. Once these mechanics are understood, it will become clear that courts as well as legislatures can be faithful to the principle of equal treatment without regard to sex, while preserving for women the benefits they may derive from laws designed to grant them benign or preferential treatment. One way courts can do this is through judicial restructuring of a statutory scheme, a device impliedly approved for use in appropriate circumstances by the United States Supreme Court in the recent case of *Califano v. Westcott*.[7]

THE EVOLUTION AND SCOPE OF THE SEX-BASED BENIGN-DISCRIMINATION DOCTRINE

In 1971, the United States Supreme Court, in *Reed v. Reed*,[8] invalidated as a violation of the Fourteenth Amendment's equal-protection guarantee an Idaho statute that preferred males over similarly situated females for appointment as administrators of decedents' estates. Although purporting to apply the "any-rational-basis" test that it long had applied in sex-discrimination cases, the Court, both in its result and in some of its language,[9] left the strong impression that it was applying a more stringent standard in judging this sex-based classification than any of the standards it had applied in the past.[10]

By 1976, a majority of the Court in *Craig v. Boren*,[11] striking down an Oklahoma statute that appeared to favor females over males,[12] openly acknowledged that a more demanding test was indeed to be applied to sex-based classifications challenged on equal-protection grounds.[13] Since *Craig,* "[t]o withstand constitutional challenge, . . . classifications by gender must serve *important* governmental objectives and must be *substantially related* to achievement of these objectives."[14]

The *Craig* test often is described as an "intermediate test,"[15] lying between the traditional rational-basis test of earlier cases and an "overwhelming-interest" test, long sought by sex-equality advocates, under which sex-based classifications could pass muster only if they were *necessary* to implement *overwhelming or compelling* governmental interests. Such a test has been applied when the interest being infringed by the classification is regarded by the court as "fundamental" or when the classification itself is regarded as "suspect."[16] The Supreme Court to date has held that classifications based on race,[17] national origin,[18] and alienage[19] are "suspect."

Despite strong efforts by litigants challenging official sex discrimination in recent years, they have been unable to convince a Court majority to adopt the "suspect" characterization for sex-based classifications. The closest these litigants have come was in *Frontiero v. Richardson,*[20] a 1973 case decided after *Reed* and before *Craig.* In *Frontiero,* four members of the Court opined that sex is a suspect classification because, like race, national origin, and alienage, it is an "immutable" characteristic and "frequently bears no relation to ability to perform or contribute to society,"[21] so that statutory distinctions based upon sex often have an "invidious" effect.[22] Four members of the Court do not a majority make. But because four other justices concurred in the judgment on other grounds, *Frontiero* struck down, as a violation of the equal-protection aspect of Fifth Amendment due process, a federal law that granted greater dependents' benefits to male members of the Army than to female members.[23]

Less than one year after the *Frontiero* decision, the Court decided *Kahn v. Shevin,*[24] the first modern[25] case to approve the benign-discrimination principle in the sex-discrimination area. In *Kahn,* a widower challenged as an equal-protection violation a Flor-

ida statute granting widows, but not widowers, a $500 annual proper-
ty-tax exemption. Writing for the majority, Justice Douglas, who
had on the previous day strongly rejected the notion of benign
discrimination in a racial context,[26] held that this patently sex-
based discrimination was permissible under what appeared to be a
"rational-basis" standard.[27] Justice Douglas and the five other members of the majority believed that the Florida legislature had been
aware of the generally lower economic opportunities available to
women than to men when it enacted the statute and had designed
the tax preference to compensate widows for such past and present
societal discrimination. In Justice Douglas's words:

There can be no dispute that the financial difficulties confronting *the* lone
woman in Florida or in any other State exceed those facing *the* man.
Whether from overt discrimination or from the socialization process of a
male-dominated culture, the job market is inhospitable to *the* woman
seeking any but the lowest paid jobs.[28]

Subsequently, in *Schlesinger v. Ballard*,[29] the Court applied the
same principle to uphold a federal statute that permitted women
naval officers to remain in the Navy longer than men without being
promoted.[30] This preferential treatment, concluded the Court in a
five-to-four decision, was designed by Congress to compensate
women naval officers for their reduced opportunity to demonstrate
their competence as a result of being excluded from sea duty[31]—an
exclusion not challenged by any of the litigants in the case.[32] In
Califano v. Webster,[33] the Court applied the benign-discrimination
rationale once again to uphold a method, since repealed, of computing women's Social Security retirement benefits so as to yield a
higher pension for them than for men with the same earnings
record.[34]
     Since adopting the benign-discrimination doctrine in the sex-
discrimination area, the Court has on several occasions refined the
method for determining whether a claimed benign sex discrimination is benign in fact. In *Weinberger v. Wiesenfeld*,[35] it invalidated
a Social Security Act provision that denied a surviving spouse of a
covered female employee with children a benefit that would have
been available to a similarly situated surviving spouse of a covered

male employee. Analyzing the statute as discriminating against the covered female employee in giving less protection for her survivors than it gave to survivors of similarly situated male employees, the Court first examined the statutory scheme and legislative history. It then concluded that Congress's *purpose* in enacting the statute was not, as contended by the government, "to provide an income to women who were, because of economic discrimination, unable to provide for themselves."[36] Rather, the statutory purpose was to permit widows, but not widowers, with minor children, "to elect not to work and to devote themselves to the care of children."[37] Finding that it "is no less important for a child to be cared for by its sole surviving parent when that parent is male rather than female,"[38] the Court struck down the gender-based distinction in the statute because it was "entirely irrational"[39] and extended the benefits of the statute to cover female employees.[40]

Most important for present purposes was the Court's observation that since the purpose of the statute "in no way is *premised* upon any special disadvantages of women, it cannot serve to justify a gender-based distinction which diminishes the protection afforded to women who do work."[41] Similarly, in *Califano v. Goldfarb*,[42] the Court rejected a claim that another provision of the Social Security Act[43] was designed to implement a benignly discriminatory purpose in favor of women, finding that the claim was merely an afterthought and had not entered into congressional consideration when the statute was enacted.[44]

Aside from rejecting, in *Goldfarb* and *Wiesenfeld*, post-hoc characterizations of sex-discriminatory classifications as benignly inspired and insisting upon proof of an original benign purpose on the part of the law-making authority,[45] the Court has more recently, in *Orr v. Orr*,[46] appeared to have severely narrowed the operational scope of the benign-discrimination doctrine. At issue in *Orr* was the validity of Alabama statutes permitting wives, but not husbands, to receive alimony.[47] Holding that the sex-based statutory scheme violated the Fourteenth Amendment's equal-protection clause, the Court, in an opinion by Justice Brennan, remanded the case so that the Alabama couts might determine whether the unconstitutional inequality was to be cured by allowing alimony to be awarded to husbands as well as wives, or by denying alimony to both groups.[48]

The Alabama appellate court had stated in *Orr* that "the Alabama statutes were 'designed' for 'the wife of a broken marriage who needs financial assistance.' "[49] Reading this as asserting a legislative purpose of "compensating women for past discrimination *during marriage,* which assertedly has left them unprepared to fend for themselves in the working world following divorce,"[50] Justice Brennan nevertheless did not undertake even the initial inquiry required in the face of a claim of benign discrimination, namely, to determine whether the intended beneficiaries of the classification had in fact been the victims of past discrimination.[51] In his view, even if past discrimination could have been demonstrated, there was still no reason for the sex-based rule, because the state already conducted individualized alimony hearings.[52] Since those hearings "can determine which women are in fact discriminated against *vis-à-vis their husbands,* as well as which family units defied the stereotype and left the husband dependent on the wife, Alabama's alleged compensatory purpose may be effectuated without placing burdens solely on husbands."[53] The inquiry not pursued in *Orr* because of the occurrence of individualized hearings was, in Justice Brennan's words, "whether women had in fact been significantly discriminated against *in the sphere* to which the statute applied a sex-based classification, leaving the sexes 'not similarly situated with respect to opportunities' *in that sphere.*"

These two limitations of the *area* in which data as to prior discrimination must be sought as an initial step in justifying a benignly discriminatory classification—coupled with Justice Brennan's earlier references to discrimination "during marriage"[55] and to whether women were discriminated against "vis-à-vis their husbands"[56]— suggest a conscious determination on the part of the Court majority to narrow substantially the scope of the benign-discrimination doctrine.[57]

THE EXISTENCE, AND SIGNIFICANCE FOR BENIGN DISCRIMINATION, OF PAST DISCRIMINATION AGAINST MALES

The impulse to narrow its scope undoubtedly reflects the dissatisfaction with the benign-sex-discrimination doctrine that has been expressed by members of the Court from the day it was first announced. Justices White[58] and Stevens[59] have come close to identifying what, in this author's opinion, is the doctrine's central defect.

And in *Orr*, Justice Brennan also identified some dangers in the doctrine,[60] expanding upon earlier observations of Justice Stevens. But no Justice, it is submitted, has ever seen the problem of benign sex discrimination in its full dimensions. The Justices' most serious error has been their failure to appreciate the extent of the societal and legal discrimination that males have suffered because of their sex and the significance of that discrimination for the benign-discrimination doctrine.

Two dissenting opinions were filed in *Kahn*. One, by Justice Brennan, in which Justice Marshall joined, objected to Florida's $500 annual exemption for widows not because widowers did not receive the same benefit, but because too many widows did. In Justice Brennan's view, the classification was constitutionally defective because of its overinclusiveness—it benefited rich widows as well as needy ones.[61] Had the statute been drawn more narrowly so as to exclude nonneedy widows from its coverage, it would have met with his approval, for "in providing special benefits for a needy segment of society long the victim of purposeful discrimination and neglect, the statute serves the compelling state interest of achieving equality for such groups."[62]

As for Mr. Kahn, the Florida widower who had sued to have the benefit of the statute extended to him, and his claim that the statute's major constitutional defect was its underinclusiveness in failing to grant widowers the same property-tax benefits it granted to widows, Justice Brennan's reply is especially significant. First he noted that "the statute neither stigmatizes nor denigrates widowers,"[63] a questionable proposition, especially when one considers the implications of the statute for the public perception of widowers who had been homemakers or otherwise dependent on their wives for financial support. He then added that, were widowers included, it "would not further the State's overriding interest in remedying the economic effects of past discrimination for needy victims of that discrimination. While doubtless some widowers are in financial need, *no one suggests that such need results from sex discrimination as in the case of widows.*"[64]

It is ironic, considering their usual alignment on issues of social concern, that a view similar to Justices Brennan's was reiterated by Justice Rehnquist, dissenting two years later in *Craig v. Boren.*[65] Justice Brennan's majority opinion in *Craig*[66] held that discrimina-

tion against males, as well as discrimination against females, because of sex was subject to heightened scrutiny under the Fourteenth
Amendment.[67] While appearing to concede in *Craig* that women
had been the historical victims of social and legal discrimination,
Justice Rehnquist insisted in dissent:

> Most obviously unavailable to support any kind of special scrutiny in this
> case, is a history or pattern of past discrimination, such as was relied on by
> the plurality in *Frontiero* to support its invocation of strict scrutiny.
> There is no suggestion in the court's opinion that males in this age group
> are in any way peculiarly disadvantaged, subject to systematic discrimina-
> tory treatment, or otherwise in need of special solicitude from the courts.[68]

Three members of the Court, Justices Brennan, Marshall, and
Rehnquist, thus have asserted categorically that males have not
been historical victims of sex discrimination. Justice Stevens also
has asserted that men as a general class historically have not been
the victims of sex discrimination.[69] Although no similar assertion
has been made by any other justice, that the others harbor such
views or at least assume the proposition to be true, is not unlikely.
This conclusion is warranted, among other reasons, by Justices
Stewart, Blackmun, Powell, Rehnquist, and Chief Justice Burger
having joined Justice Douglas's majority opinion in *Kahn*. A contrary implication is raised, however, by the position assumed by
several justices, including Justice Brennan himself, in the majority
decision of *Craig v. Boren*,[70] discussed below.[71]

As for Justice White, although his was the second dissenting
opinion in *Kahn*, and although he would have invalidated the statute because of its underinclusiveness in failing to cover needy
widowers,[72] he nevertheless did not dispute the expressed or implied views of the other Justices that men *as such* had not been
victims of past societal and legal discrimination.[73]

Justice White came tantalizingly close to seeing the defect of
benign discrimination when he stated in *Kahn* that "even if past
discrimination is considered to be the criterion for current tax
exemption, the State nevertheless ignores all those widowers who
have felt the effects of economic discrimination, *whether as a member of a racial group or as one of the many* who *cannot escape the
cycle of poverty*."[74] Nowhere, however, did he suggest that some,
perhaps many, Florida widowers may have felt the effects of an

economic discrimination that was directly and overwhelmingly related to discrimination they had previously suffered solely because
of their *sex*.

Only Justice Stevens, of all the members of the Court, has stated
positively that males have been the victims of *some* past sex discrimination, but even he has thus far not indicated an adequate
appreciation of the full extent of antimale sex discrimination or its
implications for the benign-discrimination doctrine. Justice Stevens's
recognition that sex discrimination has been a reality for males
appears in his concurring opinion in *Craig v. Boren*.[75] Agreeing
with the majority, although for somewhat different reasons, that
the equal-protection guarantee of the Fourteenth Amendment was
violated by the Oklahoma statute that permitted females between
the ages of eighteen and twenty-one, but not males in that age
bracket, to purchase 3.2 percent beer, Justice Stevens condemned
the classification, because, inter alia, "it is based on an accident of
birth [and] because it is a *mere remnant of the now almost universally rejected tradition of discriminating against males in this age
bracket . . . .*"[76] In a footnote to this reference to antimale discrimination, however, Justice Stevens emphasized that he was referring only to the long-standing disparity between the age of majority
for males and females.[77] In still another footnote, he stated categorically: "Men as a general class have not been the victims of the
kind of historic, pervasive discrimination that has disadvantaged
other groups."[78] Justice Stevens's recognition of a *specific* historical legal discrimination against males, although limited, is still the
only instance of a Supreme Court justice acknowledging that antimale
discrimination exists. Certainly, this acknowledgment is much more
forthright than the mere implication in the *Craig* majority opinion,
ambiguous at best because of the contrary implication in the *Kahn*
majority opinion, that males have been the historical victims of sex
discrimination. The implication in *Craig* arises from the majority's
subjecting what they characterize as an antimale discrimination to
a heightened level of scrutiny for equal-protection purposes,[79] over
Justice Rehnquist's strong objections that such heightened scrutiny
had previously been reserved for groups that have been the historical victims of discrimination.[80]

Thus, only one member of the Court, Justice Stevens, has expressly acknowledged the existence of a past legal discrimination

against males, but only in the very limited area of the longstanding
sex-based disparity in age of majority.[81] Justices Brennan, Marshall, and Rehnquist have categorically denied the existence of
social or legal antimale discrimination,[82] and even Justice Stevens
has rejected the idea that men as a class have been victims of
"historic, pervasive discrimination."[83] As seen from the conflicting
implications of *Kahn,* on the one hand, and *Craig* and *Frontiero,*
on the other, many of the other members of the Court, and at
times even Justices Brennan and Marshall, have emitted conflicting signals as to their views on this question.

What, then, has been the extent of legal and societal sex discrimination suffered by males? What are the implications of such discrimination for the benign-discrimination doctrine? And how does
sex discrimination differ from racial discrimination? Examining these
questions in reverse order, we observe first that, although sex and
race discrimination share many social and legal characteristics, they
also differ in ways that are crucial for the benign-discrimination
question.

The similarities between sex and race discrimination are probably best described in Justice Brennan's plurality opinion in *Frontiero
v. Richardson,* [84] which postulated a suspect classification analysis
for sex-based classifications. Suspect status, and the heightened
level of scrutiny it triggers, had previously been assigned by the
Court to classifications based upon race, alienage, and national
origin.[85] Comparing these various types of discrimination, Justice
Brennan sought to identify the characteristics that were common to
them and sex discrimination.

Sex-based classifications are like other recognized suspect classifications, Justice Brennan suggested, because in each, the classification is based upon a person's "immutable characteristics."[86] In
other words, one can no more change the fact that one is a male or
a female than one can change one's membership in the black race
or the white race, or one's nativity in Mexico, China, or France. A
second characteristic shared by classifications based on sex and
those based on race, national origin, and alienage, suggested Justice Brennan, is that the discrimination that has historically oper-
ated in these realms has been of an "invidious" character.[87]
"Invidiousness" in this context has been variously defined by different members of the Supreme Court.[88] In *Frontiero,* Justice

Brennan saw the invidiousness that linked sex-based classifications with suspect classifications, and differentiated them from such non-suspect statuses "as intelligence or physical disability," as residing in the fact that a person's sex bears "no relation to ability to perform or contribute to society . . . [thus] relegating the entire class of females to inferior legal status without regard to the actual capabilities of its individual members."[89]

To these shared characteristics can be added another similarity between race and sex discrimination, one that sets them apart from all other kinds of discrimination: members of both groups "carry an obvious badge."[90] An alien, an illegitimate child, or a person whose national origin is in a country other than the United States cannot by sight be distinguished from a citizen, a legitimate child, or an American-born person. Not so with a person who is black or one who is white; not so with a person who is female or one who is male. If the extremely rare instances of transvestism or sex-change operations are put aside, a person's race or sex is always immediately apparent. Among other consequences flowing from this special visibility in the case of race or gender is the increased difficulty of escaping from the destructive effects of societal biases about these statuses.

What then are the essential *differences* between discriminations based upon race and those based upon sex? With respect to race discrimination, no one can contend that white people have in the past been systematic victims of either social or legal discrimination because they were *white*. Many white people have no doubt been the victims of past societal discrimination because of their ethnicity or their religion, but they have not been discriminated against because of their race. Furthermore, to whatever extent white people have suffered from ethnic or religious discrimination, it has always been the result of societal behavior, that is, a de facto discrimination. It has never been a de jure discrimination; it has never been the result of state and federal laws or official practices of state and federal governments.

By contrast, a casual glance at the treatment males have received at the hands of the law solely because they are males suggests that they have paid an awesome price for other advantages they have presumably enjoyed over females in our society. Whether one talks of the male's unique obligation of compulsory military service,[91] his primary duty for spousal[92] and child support,[93] his lack of the same kinds of protective labor legislation that have traditionally been enjoyed by women,[94] or the statutory[95] or judicial[96] preference in child custody disputes that has long been accorded to mothers vis-à-vis fathers of minor children, sex discrimination against males in statutes and judicial decisions has been widespread and severe.

Moreover, to the extent that societal discrimination, as opposed to governmental discrimination, is a factor to be considered in determining whether a benign discrimination may appropriately be administered,[97] it is clear that males have been subjected to massive social and economic discrimination. The general social expectation that men will perform the breadwinner's role; the equanimity with which men's exclusive liability for military service is regarded by the general population, even during times of violent combat; the philosophy that a man's life is less precious than that of a woman, as expressed in the tradition of "women and children first" when ships are about to go beneath the sea; and the raised eyebrows at the prospect of a male who, breaking the shackles of his traditional sex role, determines to expend most of his daily energies in caring for his children and doing what have traditionally been regarded as wifely chores within the home, all suggest that men at all ages have been victims of virulent sex discrimination comparable to the kinds of discrimination that women as a group have suffered.

Herein lies the essential difference between the social and legal phenomena of sex discrimination and racial discrimination. Notwithstanding the similarities between them, in no kind of discrimination other than that based upon sex, whether it be racial, age, or religious, can the group that is alleged to be the beneficiary of such discrimination be so accurately described also as its direct victim.

The willingness of society and the legal system to subject males to the risk of early death, as seen in their exclusive draft and combat liability under federal law and in the social expectation that they will be the last to leave the ship, as well as the unwillingness to subject females to such risks, are also reflected in the male's role as the family's primary breadwinner. Although this role, thrust upon males by both society and the legal system, is changing somewhat, it is far from ended. Justice Stevens has indicated, imperfectly and indirectly, that he understands the relationship between the male's enforced role as family breadwinner and his shorter life expectancy than that of the female.[98]

In *Los Angeles Department of Water & Power v. Manhart*,[99] Justice Stevens wrote the opinion of the Court striking down as a violation of Title VII's prohibition against sex-based employment discrimination an employer's practice of requiring its female employees to make larger monthly contributions to its pension fund than its male employees. The employer sought to justify this practice by pointing to the female's higher average life expectancy. Exploring various reasons for this sex-based difference in life expectancy, Justice Stevens, after noting that sex-based differences in smoking habits might be a contributing factor, added: "Other social causes, such as drinking or eating habits—*perhaps even the lingering effects of past employment discrimination*—may also affect the mortality differential."[100]

Because Justice Stevens was exploring why women live *longer* than men, his reference to "employment discrimination" as a mortality factor clearly refers to discrimination *against men*. Conceivably, he might have been referring to racial, religious, or national-origin discrimination in the work place. Although both men and women would be prey to these discriminations, men presumably would have suffered greater overall effects of such discrimination because, in the past, they have substantially outnumbered women in the work force. There is, however, another possible meaning to Justice Stevens's linkage of the male's shorter life expectancy and employment discrimination. He could have meant—and he should have meant—that there is also a *direct sex-based discrimination* against males in the work place that plays a significant role in their lower life expectancy.

How many males, for example, died earlier than they otherwise would have only because they did not enjoy the same statutory protections as women?[101] How many men, unable to benefit from state laws that limited women's working hours and lifting requirements, and prescribed minimum wages for women only, had their health impaired by being forced by their employers to work excessively long hours, lift excessively heavy weights, under excessively onerous conditions, at whatever wage their employer was willing to pay?

Indeed, how many such men lived in Florida when *Kahn* was decided? Given the male's overall shorter life expectancy, the likelihood that a surviving spouse in Florida, or any other state, would be a widower rather than a widow was rather slim to begin with. If a male had lost his life in World War II or Korea or Vietnam, the relationship between his death and a sex-discriminatory law that, because it narrowed the draftee pool by excluding females, increased his chances of being selected by his "neighbors and friends" for hazardous military service would not be difficult to understand. Even among those husbands who died before their wives as a result of "natural causes," in how many instances were their earlier deaths hastened by their efforts not to disappoint societal and legal expectations about appropriate male behavior, brought about by social and legal institutions that locked both sexes into fixed, predetermined roles?

How many men, for example, were crushed both emotionally and physically by their striving to meet their exclusive legal obligation to provide for their wives' and children's financial needs? How many could not break the bonds of chronic unemployment because certain jobs—secretary, clerk-typist, airline stewardess, elementary schoolteacher, nurse, telephone operator—were regarded as unsuited for the male? How many qualified men were denied such jobs by governmental employers so that antimale discrimination, based on "archaic and overbroad generalizatations"[102] about the appropriate roles of men and women, transcended private, societal behavior and became de jure, state action? And how many men, although not having lost their lives in World War II, Korea, or Vietnam, returned from those wars psychologically, physically, and economically maimed because of a legal system that subjects males, and only males, to the duty of compulsory military service? In light of these and similar considerations, the Brennan-Marshall view that a more narrowly drawn *Kahn*-type benign-discrimination statute favoring needy widows would be permissible, although it did not include needy widowers because their need did not result from sex discrimination,[103] appears to have been adopted without adequate thought.

The Court's failure to understand the implications of past legal and social antimale discrimination for the benign-discrimination doctrine unfortunately has not been confined to the *Kahn* case.

That failure pervades every Supreme Court decision approving the benign-discrimination doctrine in the area of gender bias. Thus, in *Schlesinger v. Ballard*,[104] the Court upheld a law permitting women naval officers to remain in the Navy longer than men without being promoted, finding a benign purpose to compensate women for their reduced opportunity to demonstrate their competence as a result of being excluded from sea duty. As noted above, no one in the case challenged this exclusion.[105] Had women officers' exclusion from sea duty been challenged, it would have focused attention on the fact that men officers not only had an opportunity, but also were required, to participate in sea duty, and that sea duty is not an unmixed blessing. While sea duty conferred some advantages on males, such as permitting them to demonstrate their competence in a shorter time than women, it also subjected men to numerous disadvantages,[106] including the hardship of prolonged absences from shoreside friends and relatives and increased exposure to death and injury.[107]

Similarly, in *Califano v. Webster*,[108] the Court, by permitting women who retire at the same age and with the same earnings record as men to receive a higher Social Security pension, simply ignored the social and legal discrimination that men have suffered both within and without the employment sphere.[109] To the extent that a majority in *Wiesenfeld*[110] and a plurality in *Goldfarb*[111] would have been willing to approve the discrimination in those cases, had they been able to find a congressional purpose to prefer needy widows of covered male employees over needy widowers, they revealed the same inability to understand the existence and significance of past discrimination against males.

The recent case of *Personnel Administrator of Massachusetts v. Feeney*[112] further illuminates the major defect in benignly discriminatory statutes and official rules that purport to favor one sex while overlooking past social and legal discrimination against the other sex. In *Feeney*, there was a challenge, under the Fourteenth Amendment's equal-protection clause, of Massachusetts statutes that, using sex-neutral terms, gave military veterans an absolute preference over nonveterans for the most desirable civil service jobs. Although the negative impact of the preference was much more severely felt by women (more than 98 percent of Massachusetts veterans were male and only 1.8 percent were female),[113] a majority of the Court, applying the discriminatory-purpose test of *Washington v. Davis*[114] for alleged unconstitutional discrimination, held that no unconstitutional discrimination had occurred as a result of these veterans preference statutes.[115]

Justice Marshall, in a dissenting opinion joined by Justice Brennan, disagreed.[116] As he saw it, a purpose to discriminate against women in enacting and applying these statutes was readily discernible.[117] Having decided this, Justice Marshall, unlike the majority, reached the question of whether the discrimination was justifiable. Although he did not discuss the issue in precisely these terms, Justice Marshall was prepared to justify what he perceived as an antifemale, promale discrimination only if it was designed to compensate males, presumably for the past discrimination they had suffered as a result of being exclusively liable for compulsory military service, and then only if an appropriate standard of justification had been met by the statutes.[118] Justice Marshall's failure to discuss explicitly the past antimale discrimination inherent in an all-male draft resulted from his conclusion that his test, which appears to be a blend of the intermediate and overwhelming-interest tests,[119] was not met by the statutes. To the extent that the statutes' goals were "important," he asserted, they could be achieved by alternative methods less drastic than an absolute job preference for veterans, which he perceived as essentially an absolute job preference for males. Had Massachusetts adopted less drastic alternatives, such as an absolute preference for a limited duration or merely a point preference rather than an absolute preference, Justice Marshall made it clear that he would approve the scheme despite his earlier conclusion that it in fact discriminated against women.[120]

Two important points emerge from the Marshall-Brennan dissent in *Feeney*. The first is that benign discrimination in the gender area is a two-way street. Had the state chosen less drastic ways to be discriminatory, Justices Marshall and Brennan would have upheld the discrimination although, as they saw it, it favored males and disfavored females. Second, in *Feeney*, Justices Marshall and Brennan were prepared to approve promale compensatory discrimination without considering the full implications of past discrimination against women,[121] just as in *Kahn* they had previously approved profemale benign discrimination without considering the implications of past antimale discrimination.[122]

It is clear from the *Feeney* dissent that the exclusive draftability of men—and not just the hardships of military services—justifies in Justices Marshall's and Brennan's opinion what they regard as a discrimination favoring men over women, rather than one favoring veterans over nonveterans of either sex. Women have never been subject to the draft. While they have been spared the hazards and burdens of military service, they have also been deprived of any benefits that might flow from being drafted. such as job training, employment opportunities, veterans' benefits, and the like. For the draft, like other laws that apply only to one sex, is a dual-aspect law. In indicating a willingness to uphold some forms of veteran's preference as a benign discrimination designed to compensate male veterans for the sex discrimination inherent in their military experience, Justices Marshall and Brennan thus overlook the implications of antifemale discrimination *in the very sphere* of the alleged benign discrimination, not to speak of the generalized past discrimination against women in American law and society.

Feeney is the rare case in which benign discrimination is discussed, or at least hinted at, by members of the Court as compensation for past antimale discrimination. In all the other Supreme Court cases in which the doctrine has been applied, it has been in the context of compensating women for past discrimination. As discussed earlier,[123] in none of these cases had the Court ever indicated an understanding of the existence of past social and legal discrimination against men.

If and when the Court finally acknowledges the full extent of past antimale discrimination, what should this mean for the benign-discrimination doctrine? An answer to that question can be found in a footnote to Justice Brennan's plurality opinion in *Frontiero v. Richardson*,[124] which foreshadowed the benign-discrimination doctrine ultimately approved in *Kahn* and applied in other cases. In that footnote, Justice Brennan stated:

It should be noted that these statutes [giving male Army personnel greater dependents' benefits than female personnel] are not in any sense designed to rectify the effects of past discrimination. . . . On the contrary, these statutes seize upon a group—women—who have historically suffered discrimination in employment, and rely on the effects of this past discrimination as a justification for heaping on additional economic disadvantages.[125]

In every Supreme Court case of benign discrimination favoring women including *Kahn, Ballard,* and *Webster,* that discrimination also has disfavored men.[126] In essence, in each of these cases, reliance has been placed on past discrimination against men "as a justification for heaping on additional economic disadvantages."[127] This practice was specifically disapproved in Justice Brennan's *Frontiero* footnote,[128] and has been disapproved by the Court in other contexts.[129] Recognition of the past discrimination against men—pervasive, de jure, and societal discrimination—should therefore lead to the abrogation of benign discrimination that purports to favor women. Conversely, the longstanding discrimination against women in law and society should dampen any tendency to justify benign discrimination favoring men (such as was reflected in Justice Marshall's dissent in *Feeney*).

Some will no doubt question whether any account should be taken of the implications of past antimale discrimination for profemale benign discrimination. They will point out that ours has been a male-dominated culture, that males have always been able to change the laws on the draft, spousal and child support, protection in the work place, and the like. In short, they will say that males have not been a "discrete and insular minority,"[130] powerless to alter the past discrimination against them. They will argue that the discrimination against men was thus not "invidious"[131] and that it therefore should not be taken into account in assessing the propriety of preferential treatment for females, who were in fact politically powerless with not even the right to vote until 1920.[132]

There are several answers to such contentions. First, whether past discrimination against men has been invidious is irrelevant to this chapter's central thesis. That thesis is not that the benign-discrimination doctrine should be extended to men because they have been victims of past discrimination. Rather, what is urged is that past discrimination against men is a sufficient reason for denying benign, compensatory, or preferential legal treatment to women—just as past discrimination against women should be a sufficient reason for denying benign discrimination in favor of men.

Second, despite the apparent political and practical power of men to have at any time changed the situation, men have been victims of past invidious discrimination. Appearances here simply do not match reality. Our nation has always needed an armed force to defend it, for example, but until recently, it was inconceivable to anyone, male or female, that the duty of military service should, or could, devolve upon women as well as men.[133] Centuries of sex-role allocation, based on "habit, rather than analysis,"[134] simply disabled Americans of either sex from restructuring the duties of military service, family support, and protections in the work place so as to permit men and women to share the burdens and benefits of social existence more equitably. Viewed in this light, the apparent power of men to change their sex-based roles in the past can be seen as being more theoretical than real. In this respect, men were as powerless as any other discrete, insular minority; past discrimination against them was invidious in every sense of the word.[135]

Recognition of these realities of male powerlessness is, moreover, implicit in Justice Brennan's majority opinion in *Craig v. Boren*.[136] *Craig*, it will be recalled, upheld a heightened level of scrutiny—the "intermediate" test—for what was characterized by the majority as antimale discrimination. The majority did so over the protest of Justice Rehnquist, who, citing the celebrated *Carolene Products* footnote,[137] argued that such active review had always been reserved for groups that had been discriminated against *and* had been members of a discrete, insular minority. Although Justice Brennan's opinion ignored these arguments, his approval of heightened scrutiny of antimale discrimination represents a tacit acknowledgment of the actual past powerlessness of males to break the bonds of inherited sex-role stereotyping.[138]

In sum, a major reason for ending sex-based benign discrimination is the record of past legal and societal discrimination against men. No Supreme Court Justice has indicated that he understands the dimensions of such past antimale discrimination, and several appear to be totally oblivious to it. In addition, no member of the Court has ever considered the significance of past discrimination against one sex for a doctrine that permits law-based discrimination that favors the other sex.

A second major reason for abrogating the benign-discrimination doctrine in the gender area, as the following section demonstrates, is that laws that purport to grant preferential treatment to one sex also impose direct burdens or detriments on members of that same sex.

PERVERSE EFFECTS OF BENIGN DISCRIMINATION

In 1964, the statutory age of majority for most purposes in Illinois, as in many other states, was eighteen for women and twenty-one for men.[139] In permitting a female to engage in unfettered buying and selling and other commercial activities three years earlier than a male, the Illinois statute clearly granted the former a benefit.[140] At the same time, the lower age of majority frequently represented a burden or detriment for females. Thus, in the 1964 case of *Jacobson v. Lenhart*,[141] the Illinois Supreme Court upheld against an equal-protection attack the earlier termination—because of the running of a limitations period—of a female's right to sue on a tort claim, which reflected the differences in the ages at which females and males attained majority. To the extent that many young people needed protection against acquiring oppressive obligations, because of their lack of discretion and knowledge of business matters, the female's lower age of majority also meant that the state was offering this protection to young men between the ages of eighteen and twenty-one, but not to young women in the same age bracket. A nineteen-year-old male who entered into a disadvantageous contract could in most instances disaffirm that contract before reaching the age of twenty-one, but a nineteen-year-old female would be bound by that contract.

The female's lower age of majority thus confers an advantage or benefit on women while also imposing a detriment, burden, or disadvantage upon them. It is, in other words, a dual-aspect law, its dual aspect arising primarily from the fact that similarly situated men and women are accorded differential treatment.

Another useful way of visualizing the law's dual aspect—one that will be important when the cure for an unconstitutional sex-based inequality is considered—is to look upon it as two separate laws enacted in the guise of a single law. One of the two laws confers the advantage on women mentioned above. In effect, it states: women, but not men, between the ages of eighteen and twenty-one, shall have the right to engage in business, commercial, property, and other legal transactions to the fullest extent permitted to any person subject to the laws of this state. The other unstated, but implied, separate law creates the disadvanage. It states: men, but not women, between the ages of eighteen and twenty-one, shall be protected against imposition by third parties.

In 1905, the United States Supreme Court, in *Lochner v. New York*,[142] invalidated a New York statute that limited working hours of men and women bakery employees to ten a day, holding that the statute violated the freedom of contract impliedly guaranteed to an employer and its employees by the Fourteenth Amendment's due-process clause. But three years later, in *Muller v. Oregon*,[143] the Court held that due process was not violated by an Oregon statute limiting women's working hours in certain enterprises to ten hours a day. Although not discussed in precisely these terms, the Oregon law was perceived by the Court as a species of benign discrimination, designed to compensate women for the past discrimination they had suffered at the hands of nature (their generally frailer physiques than men's and their childbearing functions)[144] and of society (their inability to assert themselves as well as men in the market place).[145]

There is no doubt that the women-only hours-limitations law in *Muller*, in one of its aspects, conferred a positive benefit on women. As a result of such laws, which soon were enacted in other states on a "half-a-loaf" theory[146] because of the *Lochner-Muller* sequence of decisions, female, unlike male, workers did not have to fear being forced to work unwanted overtime hours. Because of these laws, employers either would not ask females to do so, or, if they did, female workers could refuse the request with relative impunity. By contrast, a male risked being discharged or otherwise disciplined if he refused his employer's request or demand that he work over-time hours. Working women covered by such laws thus could spend part of their days with their families and children;[147] they also had more time than men for leisure, recreation, rest, the life of the mind, or any other endeavor they wished to pursue.

Once again, the laws which so clearly benefited women also burdened them in ways they did not burden men.[148] One probable effect of these laws was to discourage employers, whose operations occasionally or frequently required employees to work overtime, from hiring women, since they were prohibited from permitting or requiring those women to work the needed overtime. A major impact of the women-only hours-limitation laws was thus to reduce women's employment opportunities. Moreover, those women who desired overtime work for the extra compensation such work might yield were also denied this opportunity by women-only hours-limitation laws.[149]

Before we examine the resolution of the problems created by the dual aspect of a purportedly benignly discriminatory law, it is again important to visualize the hours-limitations law for women only, though a single law in form, as two separate laws in effect. One is a genuinely protective, benefit-conferring law for women. It states, in effect: women, but not men, have a right to refuse to work more than ten hours (or eight, or whatever the limit may be) a day. The other, burden-imposing law, for women, states: employers must not hire women, though they may hire men, for any jobs requiring occasional, or any, work in excess of ten hours a day; and men, but not women, are permitted to earn, over their regular daily wages, any extra compensation they may derive from overtime work.

In approving the overtime restrictions for women employees in *Muller*, the Supreme Court focused entirely on the law's beneficial aspect and ignored its detrimental aspect, which severely damaged women in the work place. The Court has dealt similarly with every law that it has approved as being benignly discriminatory toward women. In each instance, it has seen only the law's beneficial aspect and has ignored its detrimental aspect.

In *Califano v. Webster*,[150] for example, the Court approved, as benign discrimination, the more favorable Social Security pension benefits accruing to women than to men who retire at the same age and with the same earnings records. Entirely ignored by the Court was the fact that this disparity tended to induce more women than men to retire early and that knowledge of this tendency could discourage an employer from hiring women.[151]

Similarly, the approval by the Court in *Schlesinger v. Ballard*,[152] on benign-discrimination grounds, of a strict "up or out" system for male Naval Officers, and a guarantee for female officers of thirteen years before mandatory discharge for failure to be promoted, entirely overlooked one detrimental impact on women of such a differential. Females were rendered ineligible for severance pay for a longer period than males, an issue raised by a female officer in a post-*Ballard* federal court case, *Two v. United States*.[153] Nor did the Court in *Ballard* take into account another detrimental impact of the policy upon women: the easing of pressure on their superiors to promote them precisely because women officers could stay in the service two years longer than men without being promoted.

Even in *Kahn*, where the widows-only tax exemption was perceived as conferring a benefit on women—at least on that portion of the population of women who were widows—the law also disfavored women. For example, those women who died before their husbands and who, during their lifetimes, were concerned with how their surviving husbands might fare financially in their struggle for existence, received less favorable treatment as a result of this purportedly benign discrimination than did men who were concerned about how their widows might fare.[154]

The dual aspect of a benignly discriminatory law, that is, its imposition of a burden as well as the conferral of a benefit on the group it seeks to assist, often affects the same women in both aspects. This is the case with laws that prescribe women-only maximum working hours, minimum wages, more favorable retirement benefits, and other protective laws in the employment sphere. In those instances, the laws' dual aspects stem principally, if not entirely, from their exclusive applicability to women.[155] At other times, as in the *Kahn*-type tax preference, however, the dual aspect of a law is present because the legislature or the court, or both, have focused their attention on only one part of the group, and not another.[156]

In *Duley v. Caterpillar Tractor Co.*,[157] for example, the Illinois Supreme Court upheld a more favorable survivor's benefit for widows than for widowers under the Illinois Workmen's Compensation Act.[158] In effect, it found in the gender differential a benignly discriminatory purpose to favor widows because of a "rational difference" between the sexes "based on the disparate earning power of men and women."[159] Totally ignored by the court, however, were the adverse effects upon another group of women—covered women employees—caused by this sex-based disparity in a law purportedly designed to help women. In granting widows greater benefits than widowers, the Illinois Workmen's Compensation Act, like

similar laws in other states,[160] deprived women workers of the
family protection accruing from their employment that it provided
to covered male employees.

This detrimental aspect, for women, of a law granting widows
greater benefits than widowers was recognized by a majority of the
Supreme Court in *Weinberger v. Wiesenfeld*[161] and by a plurality
of the Court in *Califano v. Goldfarb.*[162] At the same time, other
parts of the opinions in those cases suggest that the Justices understood neither the dual aspects of a benignly discriminatory law nor
the perverse results that can flow from focusing on only one of
those aspects in isolation.

In both cases, the government argued unsuccessfully that Congress had had a benign purpose when it enacted the disputed
provisions, namely, to compensate widows of covered employees
for past discrimination against them and for the generally greater financial needs of widows as compared to widowers. The government
failed only because the majority in *Wiesenfeld* and the plurality in
Goldfarb were not at all persuaded that this had been Congress's
purpose. Presumably, these Justices—in both cases through an
opinion by Justice Brennan—were prepared to validate such benign discrimination had they been convinced that Congress's purpose in fact had been benign. Indeed, in both cases Justice Brennan
embarked upon an elaborate exploration to determine whether
Congress's apparent preference for widows had a compensatory
purpose or was merely an "archaic and overbroad generalization"[163]
about sex roles, or as stated in Justice Steven's concurring opinion,
was "the accidental by-product of a traditional way of thinking
about females,"[164] the result of legislative "habit, rather then analysis."[165]

Having characterized the fundamental discrimination in both
cases as directed against covered women employees, Justice Brennan could hardly have maintained that it was also benign toward
those same covered women employees. In seeking to determine
whether Congress might have had a benign purpose to benefit
needy widows, therefore, the *Wiesenfeld* majority and *Goldfarb*
plurality were prepared to permit a large group of women (covered
employees) to be deliberately, seriously, and discriminatorily injured by the federal government for the sake of assisting another
group of women (surviving spouses of covered male employees).[166]

More recently, in *Orr v. Orr*,[167] in which the Court invalidated a one-way alimony statute on equal-protection grounds, Justice Brennan noted that had the statute in *Orr* been upheld it would have produced "perverse results."[168] Because only the financially secure wife whose husband is in need would be advantaged by the discrimination, the classification would generate "additional benefits only for those it has no reason to prefer."[169] It is submitted, however, that the results are even more perverse where a classification inflicts damage upon those it intends to benefit. This would have been the result in *Wiesenfeld* and *Goldfarb* had Justice Brennan and his colleagues been persuaded that Congress's purpose had been to prefer widows over widowers.[170] It has in fact been the result of every purportedly benign-discriminatory statute or rule that has been upheld by the Court. Such perverse results have been caused by the dual aspect of these discriminatory laws and the Court's failure adequately to recognize their dual nature or its significance for the benign-discrimination cases it has decided.

Blindness to the dual aspect of benignly discriminatory laws has, of course, not been total. Limited recognition that a benignly discriminatory law can injure the group it seeks to aid does appear in Justice Brenann's *Orr* opinion. He notes there, for example, that "classifications which distribute benefits and burdens on the basis of gender carry the inherent risk of reinforcing the stereotypes about the 'proper place' of women and their need for special protection."[171] But the reinforcement of stereotypical notions about the sexes, while an important consideration,[172] is in a relative sense the conferral of a vague, indirect, and remote burden. Far more serious, and thus far entirely ignored by the Court, are the direct, severe, and immediate burdens imposed on one sex by the laws that purport to grant that sex special benefits to compensate for past discrimination.

Finally, it should be noted that just as the legal and social phenomena of racial and sex discrimination were distinguished earlier, insofar as the impact on the allegedly dominant group in each realm was concerned, so, too, is there a fundamental difference between the dual aspects of benignly discriminatory laws in both areas. Racial minorities can of course suffer adverse effects from a discriminatory law or official practice designed to compensate them for past discrimination. But such adverse effects would be limited

4

Remedying Sex Discrimination*

In addition to the common characteristics described in the previous chapter, the three modern benign-sex-discrimination cases decided by the Supreme Court—*Kahn, Ballard,* and *Webster*—share other important features. In each, the plaintiff was a male. In none, did the male plaintiff seek to have the Court deprive women of the benefits accorded them by the respective laws in question: the tax exemption in *Kahn;* the thirteen-year discharge-free period in the Navy, despite the failure to be promoted in the interim in *Ballard;* and the exclusion of three low-earnings years in computing Social Security retirement benefits in *Webster*. Finally, in all of these cases, the male plaintiffs sought to have the benefits of these laws extended to them.

That the courts have the power to extend legislatively created benefits to a group or class not intended to have been benefited by the legislature is by now abundantly clear. In the sex-discrimination cases themselves, the Supreme Court has done this on numerous occasions in recent years. Thus in *Frontiero v. Richardson,*[1] upon finding an unconstitutional sex-based inequality in allowances for Army dependents, the Court extended the right to receive the benefits to women.[2] Similar extension remedies were approved in *Wiesenfeld*[3] and in *Goldfarb*[4]—in the latter case notwithstanding the enormous additional financial burden this imposed on the federal government.

*This chapter is a slightly revised version of part of an article entitled *"Benign" Sex Discrimination: Its Troubles and Their Cure,* 31 HASTINGS L. J. 1379 (1980) by Leo Kanowitz, copyright © 1980 by Hastings College of the Law. Reprinted with permission.

The judicial extension of benefits to a group that a legislature or court had deliberately excluded, based on a finding of unconstitutional underinclusiveness of a classification, is, moreover, not a recent innovation. In the 1968 case of *Levy v. Louisiana,*[5] the Court found that the State's denial of a right to an illegitimate child to sue for its mother's wrongful death, while according that right to a legitimate child, denied the former equal protection. The Court cured the inequality by extending the right to the illegitimate child rather than by taking the right away from the legitimate child. As early as 1872, the Court, in *Railway Co. v. Whitton,*[6] found that the Judiciary Article of the federal Constitution had been violated by a territorial legislature's law that, by limiting wrongful death suits to the territorial courts, denied plaintiffs the right to sue in the federal courts. In that case too, rather than invalidating the legislatively granted right to sue in the territorial courts, the Court extended it to the federal courts despite the legislature's intention not to permit suits in such tribunals.[7]

Perhaps the most succinct statement of the principles that should govern a court's decision whether to abrogate or extend a statutory benefit on the ground that the class to which it applies is underinclusive appears in the opinion of the New Jersey Supreme Court in *Schmoll v. Creecy.*[8]

[T]he question is whether the Legislature would want the statute to survive, and that inquiry cannot turn simply upon whether the statute, if adjusted to the constitutional demand, will cover more or less than its terms purport to cover. Although cases may be found which seem to speak in such mechanical terms, we think the sounder course is to consider what is involved and to decide from the sense of the situation whether the Legislature would want the statute to succumb.[9]

In most cases in which courts have been faced with the "extension-abrogation" choice, the guiding principle has thus been to implement a presumed legislative choice. Stated differently, the question has been, What would the legislature have preferred had it known that the classification it created would be held invalid because of its underinclusiveness? Would it have preferred to achieve the required equality by taking the benefit away from the group to which it had granted the benefit or by extending the benefit to the group from which it had been withheld?

The Supreme Court has not always directly confronted the extension-abrogation question in sex-discrimination cases. Nevertheless, its extension remedies in *Levy, Whitton, Frontiero, Wiesenfeld,* and *Goldfarb* have all implicitly been based on presumed legislative intentions. This implication is especially clear in the last three cases, in each of which the Court extended the respective federal benefits despite the government's protests that this would impose substantial burdens on the federal fisc.

The Court's implied assessment of presumed congressional intention on abrogation versus extension of the federal benefits in *Frontiero, Wiesenfeld,* and *Goldfarb* is also borne out by its differing behavior in *Orr v. Orr*[10] and *Stanton v. Stanton.*[11] In the last cases, state law had conferred certain benefits that the Court held to be unconstitutional because the benefited class was underinclusive. In *Stanton,* it was the benefit[12] of an earlier age of majority for females than for males. In *Orr,* it was the benefit of alimony rights for wives, but not for husbands. In both cases, the Court did not decide the question of extension or abrogation. Rather, it remanded each case to the state courts so that those courts could make the decision.

The Court's different treatment of federal and state laws, with respect to determining the proper tribunal to decide the extension-abrogation issue, is merely a specific application of the familiar principle that the Supreme Court is the final arbiter of the meaning of federal laws. This role, with respect to state laws, is performed by the states' highest courts. Just as courts often decide what a legislature meant by language it used in a statute, so in resolving the extension-abrogation issue, courts decide what the legislature meant, that is, what it would have intended with respect to extension or invalidation, if its legislatively created classification were to be held unconstitutional because of its underinclusiveness.

How an underinclusive classification is to be remedied will thus be decided by the federal courts if the classification is created by federal statutes or by federal common law. By contrast, the same issue with respect to classifications created by state law will be decided by the state courts. In still a third category, special problems arise with respect to the extension-abrogation issue where state law has created the classification, but the issue arises in a case within the exclusive jurisdiction of the federal courts. This problem most often arises when state "protective" labor laws are challenged in federal court as violating the command of Title VII of the 1964 Civil Rights Act[13] that employers, inter alia, not discriminate against employees and prospective employees on the grounds of sex. The exclusive jurisdiction of the federal courts over Title VII actions requires that the federal courts, when they find that the state law violates Title VII's equality principle, also decide in the first instance whether the state legislature would have preferred to extend the benefit of the state law to men or to take it away from women.[14]

It is highly probable, therefore, that had the Supreme Court rejected the benign-sex-discrimination doctrine, it would have extended to the male plaintiff the benefit of the thirteen-year protection against mandatory discharge previously enjoyed by female naval officers in *Ballard* rather than take that benefit away from female naval officers. Similarly, the Court would have extended to the male plaintiff in *Webster* the more favorable method of computing Social Security retirement benefits, which Congress itself did shortly after *Webster* arose.[15] In those cases, abrogation of the benign-discrimination doctrine would have represented no loss for women who had previously profited from the beneficial aspects of those laws. They would have retained those benefits while men, too, would have enjoyed them. Because those laws also imposed a burden or detriment on women primarily as a result of their non-applicability to men, the extension to men of these laws' beneficial aspects would also have removed their burdensome or detrimental aspects from women.

A different issue arises with respect to the disputed tax preference for women in *Kahn*. There the tax preference was state-created. The question of its extension or abrogation would, therefore, have had to have been decided by the Florida Supreme Court. Unlike the task thrust upon the Utah court in *Stanton* and the Alabama court in *Orr,* which involved assessing legislative intentions about restructuring rights and obligations between private parties and which appeared to require immediate resolution, the task in *Kahn* would have appeared to involve divining legislative intentions about restructuring governmental largesse toward private parties. Were *Kahn's* tax preference to be extended to widowers it might cost Florida an undetermined, but substantial, sum of money in lost tax revenues. If the Florida Supreme Court acted as other state courts have acted in comparable circumstances, there would be a strong possibility that it would invalidate the tax preference for widows rather than extend it to widowers. Had the Florida court chosen this course, its actions would have been contrary to those of the United States Supreme Court. That court, as we have seen, has extended benefits to the group from which they had been unconstitutionally withheld,[16] despite a far greater financial cost to the federal government, absolutely as well as relatively, than the cost Florida would incur were the widow's tax preference to be extended to widowers.[17]

State courts,[18] and some lower federal courts in Title VII cases,[19] have been much less willing than the Supreme Court to extend benefits to a class excluded by the legislature whose intentions they have been authorized to ascertain. These courts have often asserted that to extend these benefits to a group deliberately excluded by the legislature would constitute judicial usurpation of the legislative function. What these courts fail to recognize is that the decision to take the benefit away from the class the legislature intended to benefit—when that benefit can be preserved by extending it to the group the legislature had originally excluded—is analytically no more nor less a judicial usurpation of the legislative function than the extension itself.

Recognition of this principle is, moreover, implicit in the recent Supreme Court decision in *Califano v. Westcott*,[20] in which the Court not only extended a benefit to an excluded class, but implied that under some circumstances a court might restructure a statute[21] to have it conform to constitutional requirements, though finding those circumstances to be absent in *Westcott* itself.

The facts in *Westcott* were relatively simple. Federal law provided benefits to families whose dependent children were deprived of support because of their father's unemployment, but denied benefits in the case of the mother's unemployment.[22] The Court, on the basis of the *Craig* test, held that this gender-based classification violated the equal-protection aspect of Fifth Amendment due process. But because no party had argued that nullification of the program was the proper remedial course, the Court majority, in an opinion by Justice Blackmun, stated that it would be inclined to consider that issue only if the power to order extension of the program were clearly beyond the constitutional competence of a federal district court.[23] That no such remedial incapacity existed was strongly suggested, noted Justice Blackmun, by the Court's previous decisions, which routinely had affirmed district court judgments ordering extension of federal welfare benefits.[24]

Although no party in *Westcott* had opposed the extension prinicple, one, the Commissioner of the Massachusetts Department of Public Welfare, who administers the act in that state, had sought to have the extension by the district court take a particular form. In his view, it was proper to permit either a mother's or a father's unemployment to qualify a needy family for benefits, but only if the parent in question could show that he or she was both unemployed *and* the family's "principal wage-earner."[25]

The statute, of course, said nothing about the unemployed father having to be the family's principal wage-earner to qualify the family for benefits when he becomes unemployed. Neither did the statute state anything about qualifying families if the mother becomes unemployed. Yet the majority, as we have seen, had no difficulty in effectively rewriting the statute to make it conform to constitutional requirements by extending benefits to families in which the mother is unemployed. This result was reached partly because no party had raised that issue, but also because of a discerned congressional intention that the unconstitutionality should be cured by extending the benefits, as evidenced by the strong severability clause in the Social Security Act and the hardship that would be imposed, were the program simply nullified, on families Congress plainly meant to protect.[26]

Nevertheless, the majority in *Westcott* referred to the particular form of extension urged by the commissioner, in contrast to the simple extension that it approved, as a "restructuring" of the act.[27] Significantly the majority rejected the proposed "restructuring" in *Westcott*, not because it disapproved of the idea of restructuring in principle, but only because it found restructuring to be inappropriate under the circumstances of *Wescott* itself.[28] If the commissioner's "model" of providing benefits to only those families in which the unemployed parent of either sex was the principle wage-earner had been adopted, it would have meant cutting off benefits to some needy families already receiving benefits "merely because the unemployed father cannot prove 'bread-winner' status."[29]

The Court also indicated that this type of restructuring, even more than when a court extends a benefits program to redress unconstitutional underinclusiveness, "risks infringing legislative prerogatives."[30] In contrast to mere extension, which has "the virtue of simplicity," the "principal wage-earner" solution "would introduce a term novel in the [Aid for Dependent Children] scheme, and would pose definitional and policy questions best suited to legislative or administrative elaboration."[31] Therefore, "any fine-tuning of . . . coverage along 'principal wage-earner' lines is properly left to the democratic branches of the Government. In sum, we believe the District Court . . . adopted the simplest and most equitable extension possible."[32]

From the Court's language and its disposition of the restructuring issue in *Westcott*, it can be concluded that extension of a benefit to an excluded class, even if it involves the restructuring of a statute, is more likely to be approved by the Court the simpler and more equitable that extension or restructuring appears. As will be demonstrated below, some forms of extension or restructuring of benefits which at first glance appear to be far from simple turn out upon closer examination, and especially with the aid of the dual-aspect analysis proposed in chapter 3, to be simple and equitable in fact.

In a series of cases, federal courts have struck down, as violations of Title VII's equality principle, a variety of state protective labor laws that, as written, applied only to women workers. As indicated earlier, the prototype of such laws had been upheld as a benign discrimination by the 1908 Supreme Court decision in *Muller v. Oregon*.[33] Among the types of laws that have been invalidated in recent years as a result of Title VII have been those that prohibit an employer from permitting only women workers from working more than a given number of hours in a day,[34] those requiring daily overtime pay for women workers only,[35] those imposing maximum hour limitations for women workers only,[36] those limiting the weights only women workers can be required to lift in the course of their employment,[37] and those requiring seats at work and periodic rest and meal periods for women workers, but not for men.[38]

In only one case, *Potlatch Forests, Inc. v. Hays*,[39] did a federal district court, whose decision was affirmed by the Eighth Circuit Court of Appeals,[40] uphold such a law, even though it had been enacted by the Arkansas legislature to require that only women workers be paid time-and-one-half their hourly rate for hours worked in excess of eight in one day. The *Hays* court harmonized the women-only overtime pay law with Title VII's requirement of sex equality in employment by extending the benefits of the law to male employees, rather than by taking it away from female employees.

Implicit in *Hays* was the court's understanding that the Arkansas legislature would have preferred such a result had it known that its women-only overtime pay law would be invalidated because of its inconsistency with Title VII.[41] Shortly after the *Hays* decision, however, the Arkansas Supreme Court, which as noted earlier is the final arbiter of the meaning of Arkansas law, including the presumed intention of the Arkansas legislature on the abrogation-extension issue, held in *State v. Fairfield Communities Land Co.*,[42] that the Arkansas legislature had not intended to benefit men. Totally ignored by the Arkansas court was the question implicitly resolved in *Hays*. That question was not what the Arkansas legislature's original intention had been with regard to covering men under the statute. The original intention was clear from the fact that the statute covered women employees only. Rather, the question to be resolved was what the Arkansas legislature had intended— or would have intended, had it thought about the matter—as to whether the benefits under the statute should be extended to men or taken away from women, if the statute in its original form were held to be unconstitutional or violative of a federal law because of its benefited group's underinclusiveness.

Had the Arkansas court pursued that inquiry, it could reasonably have concluded that the Arkansas legislature would have preferred the extension of those benefits to male workers over their being taken away from female workers. Among other reasons, the court could have concluded that the 1915 Arkansas statute,[43] like the post-1908 protective labor laws of many other states that applied to women workers only, had not been applied by the legislature to men primarily because the legislature had not believed that it could validly enact such a law to benefit both sexes. This had been the message of the *Lochner-Muller* sequence of United States Supreme Court decisions in 1905 and 1908.[44] In *Lochner*, the New York legislature's efforts to enact hours-limitation laws that would protect both men and women workers had been invalidated by the Court as a violation of the liberty of contract guarantee it found implicit in Fourteenth Amendment due process. But in *Muller,* due process was held not to be violated by a law that limited the working hours of women workers only. Many women-only protective laws were later enacted by the states[45] despite any wishes their legislatures, like the New York legislature in *Lochner,* might have had to benefit both sexes. Although in 1917 the Court held in *Bunting v. Oregon*[46] that an hours-limitation law for both sexes would be constitutional, by then inertia and habit had kept many women-only protective laws unchanged and permitted other women-only laws to be subsequently enacted.[47]

The historical genesis of many women-only protective labor laws, the responsibility of courts to assess presumed legislative intention with respect to invalidation or extension if a law is declared invalid because of the underinclusiveness of the group it seeks to benefit, and the equal intrusion into the legislative domain whether a court decides to invalidate the law or to extend it to the excluded group, all suggest that the result in *Hays* was more sound than the one reached by the Arkansas Supreme Court in *Fairfield Communities Land Co.*[48] These considerations also suggest that in the case of a daily-overtime-pay law or minimum-wage law for women only, the proper remedy is to extend the benefit of the law to men rather than to take it away from women. In the language of *Westcott,* extension would be both simple and equitable,[49] since it would not deprive any woman employee of benefits she had enjoyed under existing law. To the contrary, because of the dual aspects of such laws, their extension to men would not only give men the same benfits that had previously been enjoyed by women only, but would also relieve women of the detrimental effects of such laws that had previously burdened them.

Extension of such laws to men, it is submitted, would not be inequitable to employers, although extension might cost them more for both overtime work and higher wages for men who had been earning less than the state law's minimum wage for women. That such extension is reasonable is demonstrated by the government regulations that have for many years increased their cost of doing business. Also, the effect of the *Lochner-Muller* sequence upon the enactment of such laws suggests that employers had become the unintended beneficiaries of these laws, to the extent they were not required to pay male workers the same minimum wage or overtime pay as female workers. In addition, the alternative to extending overtime and minimum-wage benefits to male workers is to take them away from women workers, that is, to invalidate the law.[50] Were this to be done, it would create another windfall for employers who, until the law's invalidation for underinclusiveness, at least had been required to pay women workers the minimum wage or overtime pay prescribed by the statutes. Finally, even after the benefits of such laws were extended to men, employers could still seek further restructuring of the laws by their respective legislatures—although concededly the burden of disturbing the status quo would then be on the employers rather than upon those who desired to maintain the benefits for both sexes.[51]

Extension to males of overtime-pay or minimum-wage laws that as written apply to women only, rather than invalidation of these laws, thus would appear to be the proper remedial course. There are two types of women-only protective labor laws, however, that would present special problems were they simply extended to male employees. They are laws prohibiting employers from permitting or requiring women employees to work more than a given number of hours in a day and laws prohibiting an employer from permitting or requiring women employees to lift objects weighing more than a given number of pounds, either repeatedly or on a single occasion, in the course and scope of their employment.

Were employers who had been prohibited from permitting women to work overtime now also to be prohibited from permitting men to work overtime, as a result of the law's extension, two results would ensue. Men, like women, would enjoy the benefits of such a law. If they wished, they could safely refuse their employer's request or demand that they work overtime. Like women, they would have more time for pursuits beyond the work place. The problem, however, arises because many men have grown to depend upon the opportunity to work overtime as a means of making ends meet or of improving their living standard. Also, many employers at times require some overtime work to be performed by their employees. Were the overtime prohibition simply extended to men, men would be deprived of the overtime-pay opportunity, employers would be disabled from satisfying the needs of their enterprise, and women who wished to work overtime to maintain or improve their living standard would continue to be denied that opportunity.

A similar problem results if a women-only weight-lifting restiction is simply extended to men. If an absolute thirty-five-pound limit that applies to women is extended to men, for example, many objects that have to be lifted in the course of employment will simply not be lifted manually, although many individual men and women are capable of lifting such objects without harming themselves.

One obvious way to resolve the difficulties created by the statutory or constitutional requirement of sex equality and the negative effects of either invalidating or extending these laws is for the legislature that enacted them to undertake the necessary restructuring to preserve the benefits while simultaneously removing the burdens for both sexes. This can be done in the area of hours-limitation laws by enacting the principle of voluntary overtime. If employees of both sexes had the right to work overtime, as well as the right to refuse to work overtime, this goal could be met. In being permitted to work overtime, both men and women could earn the income they need to maintain or improve their living standard. In having the right to refuse to work overtime without being punished by their employers, men and women workers who wished to pursue family, personal, recreational, cultural, and educational interests, or simply rest, could do so. This solution has been recognized in a proposed amendment to the federal Fair Labor Standards Act that is supported by the American Federation of Labor–Congress of Industrial Organizations.[52]

A weight-lifting restriction can be dealt with in a comparable manner. A legislature can restructure the law so that it protects both sexes, but does not completely hobble an employer who needs certain objects weighing more than a specified weight lifted by its employees. Such a solution is found in the Georgia rule promulgated by the Georgia Commissioner of Labor, protecting both sexes, that provides: "Weights of loads which are lifted or carried manually shall be limited so as to avoid strains or undue fatigue."[53]

Although legislative power to effect such change is undoubted, invoking legislative, as opposed to judicial, aid presents a major difficulty because any person or group that seeks to have a legislature change the status quo bears a heavy burden. The question

then becomes, Upon whom should that burden be cast? It is in the
light of this problem that the possibility of judicial restructuring of
the laws assumes major importance. It is true that regardless of
how the courts resolve the question of invalidation or extension,
the legislature retains the last word. Still, the problem of overcom-
ing legislative inertia remains, making the allocation of this burden
crucial.

Westcott's implication that *judicial restructuring* of a legislative
scheme to cure its unconsitutionality (or invalidity under a statute)
is permissible if it can be done simply and equitably thus assumes
special importance. That a court can do this in remedying a state
hours-limitations or weight-lifting law that by its terms applies to
women only is illustrated by the 1971 decision of the Ninth Circuit
Court of Appeals in *Rosenfeld v. Southern Pacific Co*.[54]

In *Rosenfeld,* the defendant employer had refused to hire any
women for a certain job because, among other reasons, the job
required the lifting of weights in excess of what California law
permitted for women,[55] and occasional work days of more than ten
hours, which another California law prohibited an employer from
permitting or requiring women employees to work.[56] Finding that
such laws were inconsistent with Title VII's command of sex equality in employment, the court concluded that the employer's policy
was "not excusable under . . . the state statutes" and upheld the
judgment for the woman plaintiff who had been discriminated against
because of her sex.[57] Significantly, however, the court added the
following observaton: "We leave undecided the questions of this
kind which may arise concerning the varying employment policies
of other employers under circumstances unlike those of the present case".[58]

What, then, was the precise effect and scope of the *Rosenfeld*
decision? Although the court did not discuss the dual aspect of the
laws in question, its careful limitation of what it was deciding suggests that it took into consideration, or at last was aware of, that
dual aspect. One effect of the hours- and weight-limitation laws in
Rosenfeld was to deny women equal employment opportunity with
men. Another effect of the hours-limitation law was to deny women
the same opportunity as men to earn overtime pay. These effects
reflected the laws' burdensome or detrimental aspects. As suggested earlier, those detrimental aspects can be thought of as being

embodied in separate and distinct statutes.[59] Accordingly, the only issue confronting the *Rosenfeld* court was the validity of those detrimental aspects or, in other words, the validity of the implied separate statutes embodying those detrimental aspects. The court's ruling that the employer could not rely on those statutes to deny the plaintiff the same job opportunity that it granted to men went only that far and no farther. The court itself acknowledged this narrow scope when it limited its holding to the precise situation in the case.

After *Rosenfeld* was decided, had a California male employee sought to have the beneficial aspect of the hours- or weight-limitation laws, that is, the benefits of the implied separate statute, applied to him, nothing determined in *Rosenfeld* would have precluded the same court from granting such relief. Having dealt only with the burdens of those laws, *Rosenfeld* decided nothing about the beneficial aspects of those laws or the implied laws embodying those separate aspects.

A court presented with a male employee seeking to have the benefit of the hours-limitation law extended to him could well have decided to grant the remedy for the reasons suggested in connection with the extension of minimum-wage and overtime-pay laws: the distortion of the original purpose of state legislatures to protect members of both sexes against working unwanted overtime hours by the *Lochner-Muller* sequence[60] and the fact that invalidation of the protective law is as intrusive of legislative function as is the extension of its benefits to men.[61]

A similar conclusion could be reached by a court if, following *Rosenfeld,* a male worker had sought to benefit from the weight-lifting restriction that had previously applied to women workers only. His claim of course would be that *Rosenfeld* had decided only that the weight-lifting law could not be relied on by the employer as an excuse for denying women equal job opportunities, that is, that *Rosenfeld* dealt only with the law's detrimental aspects or with the implied separate statute embodying those detrimental aspects. The case did not hold that women employees could not continue to benefit from the implied separate beneficial statute by being able to refuse with impunity to lift weights in excess of the maximum allowed by the statute, or that those beneficial aspects could not be extended to men. Because a simple extension of the weight-lifting restriction to men could produce unforeseen hardships on employers by preventing them from requesting any employee of either sex to lift certain weights, extension of that restriction, while simple, might not prove to be as equitable to all concerned as would be a judicial restructuring of the weight-lifting statute. Were the court to restructure the statute so that it protected members of both sexes from lifting weights that caused undue strain or fatigue, as in the Georgia provision cited earlier,[62] it would have removed the detriment in *Rosenfeld* and preserved the benefit in this subsequent case in a manner that can be seen to be both equitable and simple.

In California, the locus of the *Rosenfeld* decision and of other cases invalidating women-only protective labor laws for being inconsistent with the Title VII, the problem of remedial choice has been largely mooted by subsequent state legislation and administrative agency action that, by and large, has extended prior women-only benefits to men. Thus, as a result of this legislative-administration action, male employees in California are now equally entitled with women to the same minimum wage, to seats at work and periodic rest periods, and to protection against lifting excessive weights.[63] Significantly, however, the California Industrial Welfare Commission has not promulgated any new work orders limiting the working hours of either men or women workers. The *Rosenfeld* decision would thus appear to have had the practical effect of depriving women workers of the hours-limitation protection as well as relieving them of its burden, although the case addressed only the burden aspect of those work orders. In large part, this result may be explained by failure of the California legislature and the state's Industrial Welfare Commission to understand the narrow nature of the *Rosenfeld* holding.

Nevertheless, the analysis suggested above should give the California Industrial Welfare Commission and the California Legislature a basis for reevaluating their post-*Rosenfeld* treatment of the hours-limitation question for both sexes. Furthermore, in those states that have not dealt with the apparent judicial invalidation of hours or weight-lifting limitations, courts and legislatures can still restructure statutes or rules embodying such limitations so as to make their truly beneficial aspects apply to both sexes. Enactment at the state level of statutes embodying the principle of voluntary overtime, as proposed for the federal Fair Labor Standards Act,[64] would be one way in which this could be done. And in numerous other areas, aside from state protective labor laws, the "restructuring"[65] proposed herein is a technique that is readily available. .

Unfortunately, the technique of judicial, or even legislative, extension of the beneficial aspects of laws and invalidation of their detrimental aspects—whether applied in separate proceedings or in a single proceeding, or treated as a simple extension or invalidation, or as an equally simple restructuring—is not available for every law that has a dual aspect. The obligation of compulsory military service, for example, is, as has been shown, also a dual-aspect law. The benefits military service confers include job training at government expense, employment opportunity, and veterans' benefits ranging from preference for government employment to educational and home-loan support under the G.I. Bill of Rights. Its detriments are equally obvious. Persons involuntarily inducted into the armed forces not only have their lives and careers disrupted by being removed from family, friends, and civilian jobs, but they face extraordinary risks of injury or death in the performance of their military duties. There is no way, moreover, to eliminate these detriments; they inhere in the nature of military service.[66]

For too long, the burden of compulsory military service has been cast exclusively on the male members of our society. Thus far, the exclusion of women from this civic duty has not been justified by the courts as benign discrimintion. Rather, the courts have upheld this exclusion based on the prevailing constitutional tests under which sex discrimination was assessed. All the cases upholding a male-only draft against constitutional challenge[67] were decided, however, before the *Craig* intermediate test for gender discrimination had been promulgated by the Supreme Court.[68] It is doubtful that the male-only obligation of compulsory military service can survive the *Craig* intermediate test.[69] The danger is that exclusion of women from the draft, should a draft become necessary, will be sought to be justified as benign discrimination.

To uphold exclusion of women from compulsory military service on benign-discrimination grounds would, for all the reasons examined earlier, be erroneous. It would ignore the effects of widespread societal and legal discrimination against males, and the detrimental aspects, for women, of being excluded from the draft.

In this limited realm, however, there is no way to both preserve the benefits and remove the burdens of the draft for both sexes. When the draft becomes sex-neutral in its operation, the effect will necessarily be to confer on both sexes the burdens as well as the benefits of compulsory military service.

The development of a sex-neutral draft, as well as the abrogation of the benign-discrimination doctrine itself, which has been the principal corrective proposed herein, can have positive effects on the development of constitutional principles affecting governmental sex discrimination. While its impact on Equal Rights Amendment ratification is difficult to measure, it should influence Supreme Court decisions in sex-discrimination cases brought under existing constitutional provisions. Abrogation of the benign-discrimination doctrine should increase the likelihood that a Court majority could be persuaded to treat gender as a suspect classification. Even if this did not occur, it would be much more difficult for the Court to find that any governmental gender-based classification has passed the intermediate test of *Craig*. In effect, if not in theory, the *Craig* intermediate test is likely always to produce the same results as the overwhelming-interest test that would be applied were sex classification held to be suspect.

In sum, in the overwhelming majority of cases, abrogation of the benign-discrimination doctrine in the sex-discrimination area would not cause women to lose the benefits they now derive from laws that are justified by that doctrine. Those benefits would simply be enjoyed by men as well as women. At the same time, abrogating the benign discrimination doctrine would also remove from women the detrimental burdens imposed upon them by the laws that purport to discriminate in their favor. Above all, eliminating the benign discrimination doctrine would signal a recognition of a major fact too long ignored—that, as a result of centuries of sex-role streotyping, men as well as women have been victimized by legal and social institutions.

CONCLUSION

In the decade of the 1970s, the United Stated Supreme Court made giant strides in response to claims of unconstitutional sex-based discrimination. Although the Court has not yet agreed to treat gender classifications as suspect—a development devoutly to be desired—it has subjected such classifications to the heightened level of scrutiny required by the *Craig* test.[70] The practical effect of applying that test, under which a gender classification will satisfy the equal-protection guarantee only if it can be shown to be substantially related to an important governmental interest, will be to invalidate practically all gender classifications that would have satisfied the Court's former "any-rational-basis" test in this area—all, that is, except those classifications the Court finds to have been created for a benign or compensatory puspose.

The benign-discrimination exception to the *Craig* test has undermined the Court's basic human rights achievement in the sex discrimination decisions of the 1970s.[71] Except for some contrary intimations of a willingness to apply the benign-discrimination exception to men in the Marshall-Brennan dissent in *Feeney*,[72] the exception has been applied only in cases in which the classification appears to favor women. As demonstrated, such classifications also inevitably disfavor women in important respects, because both sexes are not sought to be benefited by the law in question.

The most important shortcoming of the Supreme Cort's benign-discrimination doctrine in the area of gender bias has been the Court's failure to understand the scope and extent of past and present official discrimination against males. Not surprisingly, this shortcoming is shared by many members of the public who have come to think of the political and social movement for equal rights without regard to sex as essentially a movement for women's rights.

Although the injustices perpetrated upon women by the American social, political, economic, and legal systems have been severe— indeed, outrageous[73]—men have been equally powerless victims of sex discriminatory laws, official practices, and social mores. The heightened level of scrutiny approved in *Craig*, to be applied where males allege their victimization by a sex-discriminatory law, is implicit recognition of this fact. The Court, however, has failed to face up to these implications of *Craig*.

The movement for equal rights without regard to sex is understood by most of is participants as a movement for human rights. In their efforts to achieve ratification of the proposed Equal Rights Amendment and to convince the Court to raise still higher the level of scrutiny applicable to gender classification under existing constitutional provisons, equal rights advocates understand the fundamental goals of the movement to be the ending of law-imposed sex-role stratification, and not just of the stereotyping of women's roles. The right of all individuals, male or female, to realize their fullest potential as human beings, without governmental interference resting on gender-based assumptions about their attributes, is what the equal rights movement is all about.

The benign-discrimination doctrine has been substantially narrowed since it was first formulated in *Kahn v. Shevin*.[74] *Wiesenfeld*[75] and *Goldfarb*[76] make it clear that the "benign" purpose must have been behind the statute at the outset; otherwise the doctrine will not be applied. *Orr*[77] represents a further retrenchment: if the benign purpose can be achieved without a benign preference, i.e., by individualized hearings, the doctrine will not apply, and if the benign purpose is not designed to compensate for past discrimination "within the sphere" of the benignly discriminatory statute or rule, a further reason exists for not applying the doctrine.

Although the Court has narrowed the circumstances under which it will apply the benign-discrimination doctrine, it has not repudiated it, and the doctrine undoubtedly still has a substantial field in which to operate. If the Court entirely abrogates the benign-discrimination doctrine in the gender bias area, as proposed herein, most of the truly beneficial aspects of benignly discriminatory laws (which also have detrimental aspects) can be preserved for women by various judicial techniques. Even if the courts fail in an individual cases to invoke such techniques and instead invalidate benignly discriminatory laws in their entirety, legislatures can still restructure such laws in ways that will confer their beneficial aspects on both sexes. In most cases, judicial or legislative extension of benefits to the gender previously excluded from sharing in these benefits will in itself remove the law's detrimental aspects, or at least its most detrimental features.

Finally, it is to be hoped that, for the reasons advanced herein, the Court will soon come to understand that the benign-discrimination doctrine in the gender-bias area is an illusion, that it is inconsistent with, and undermines, the Court's positive achievements elsewhere in recent sex-discrimination cases, that it reflects an inadequate understanding of the political and social striving for equality without regard to sex, and that the doctrine should be repudiated in is entirety.

5

The Equal Rights Amendment and the Overtime Illusion*

As a citizen, a lawyer, and a law professor, I have been deeply concerned for a number of years with the status of women in the United States, or more precisely, with the question of sex roles in our society—as this question has come to be more accurately designated in Sweden. Since 1965, I have studied this question to determine the role that has and can be played with respect to it by our legal institutions. The results of those studies were published in my book *Women and the Law: The Unfinished Revolution.*[1] In *Women and the Law*, I explore major aspects of the legal status of American women and analyse some of the social causes and effects of sex-based discrimination in American law. Among the subjects examined are abortion, prostitution, marriageable age, age of majority, married women's names, support obligations within the family, divorce, special criminal penalties for women, jury service rules, domiciles of married women, marital property regimes in the common law and community property states, and contracts and torts of husband and wife.

Much of the book, however, deals with the law affecting women's employment in the United States, particular attention being paid to the Equal Pay Act of 1963 and to the history and effects of the prohibition against employment sex discrimination in Title VII of the 1964 Civil Rights Act. In addition, *Women and the Law*

*This chapter is a slightly revised version of the author's testimony before the U.S. Senate Judiciary Committee, September 11, 1970. The full text of the testimony is printed at Hearings Before the Committee on the Judiciary, United States Senate Ninety-First Congress, Second Session on S.J. Res. 61 and S.J. Res. 231, Proposing an Amendment to the Constitution of the United States Relative to Equal Rights for Men and Women 161–93 (September 9, 10, 11, and 15, 1970).

explores in considerable detail the principles of American constitutional law affecting this area of human rights.

Rather than recapitulating the contents of *Women and the Law,* or even its exposition and analysis of persisting sex-based discriminatory legal rules and official practices, I refer you to the book itself—although I am sure that many instances of such discrimination have already been brought to your attention. But I would take this occasion to repeat the hopes I expressed for the book in its Preface.

"Perhaps," I wrote, "an awareness of the many areas of sex-based legal discrimination, whose continued existence this book seeks to identify, will stimulate, first, courtroom and legislative attacks upon those disparities or injustices, then, a much-needed national examination of the respective roles of the sexes in every sphere of American life, and finally, the active and continuing participation of all Americans in bringing about the needed changes."[2]

My investigation in this field has persuaded me that many irrational and harmful distinctions continue to be made in the legal, political, and social treatment of the sexes in our country, that the resulting injustices have impeded our development as a nation, and that they have led to much personal unhappiness for American men as well as women.

By relegating women to special tasks, by perpetuating ancient myths about the alleged physical and psychological limitations of women, we American men have subjected ourselves to an awesome burden. For the doubtful joys of feeling superior to women, we have paid a terrible price. Not only have we suffered with respect to uneven laws in the field of support obligations within the family, child support and custody awards in divorce proceedings, and the frequent lack of protective labor legislation where such legislation exists for women, but our insistence that men and only men are entitled to be society's doers and shakers has led to our dying from eight to ten years earlier, on the average, than the women of our country. Perhaps even more important is that, because of arbitrary social and legal distinctions, both men and women are often prevented from relating to one another as people, as fellow members of the human race.

So, when I speak or write of the need to erase sex-based discrimination in American law, I am moved not only by the desire to end the injustices that American men have perpetrated upon our nation's women, but to end those we have imposed upon ourselves as well.

But recognizing that sex discrimination pervades American law and that it is pernicious does not tell us how best to bring about the needed changes. It is to this question—and specifically to whether the constitutional amendments proposed in either Senate Joint Resolution 61 or in Senate Joint Resolution 231 are appropriate steps to that goal—that I would now address myself.

Before I explain my reasons, however, let me state my position on these two proposed amendments. First, I support the Equal Rights Amendment as worded in Senate Joint Resolution 61. Second, I oppose the amendments to that Amendment that are set forth in Senate Joint Resolution 231.

Third, I should also like to discuss what I believe is the core question in the controversy over the Amendment's desirability, namely, the issue of state protective labor legislation. As I shall explain, I believe that much of the discussion of this question is at cross-purposes, that it proceeds from a basic fallacy in the thinking of proponents as well as opponents, and that if it can be cleared up, the spectacle of otherwise natural allies opposing one another may disappear. Finally, I would be glad to try to respond to any questions the Committee might care to ask about other aspects of this subject.

SENATE JOINT RESOLUTION 61

Senate Joint Resolution 61, if adopted and ratified by the requisite number of state legislatures, would add a new article to the United States Constitution, to take effect one year after the date of ratification. The crucial language of that proposed new article reads: "Equality of rights under the law shall not be denied or abridged by the United States or by any State on account of sex. Congress and the several states shall have power, within their respective jurisdictions, to enforce this article by appropriate legislation."

I had occasion to consider the present desirability of such a constitutional amendment in *Women and the Law*. Writing in 1969, I suggested that many proponents of the Equal Rights Amendment

were mistaken in their belief that the United States Supreme Court
and lower state and federal courts had in the past held existing
provisions of the United States Constitution, in particular the Fifth
and Fourteenth Amendments, inapplicable to women.

"The fact is, however," I wrote, "that the courts have not done
this at all. Instead, they have generally held that existing constitutional provisions do apply to women, but that within the limits of
those provisions, women in many situations constitute a class that
can reasonably be subjected to separate treatment."[3]

I also suggested that the adoption of the Equal Rights Amendment would not fundamentally change the picture. "While the
proposed amendment states that equality of rights shall not be
abridged on account of sex," I wrote, "sex classifications could
continue if it can be demonstrated that though they are expressed
in terms of sex, they are in reality based upon function. On the
other hand, under existing constitutional provisions, particular classifications of men and women that cannot be shown to be based upon
function, are vulnerable to attack—as has already been demonstrated in some lower state and federal courts with respect to
discriminatory laws in the realm of jury service, differences in
punishment for identical crimes, right to sue for loss of consortium
and the like."[4]

This last reference was to a series of recent cases in which sex-
based discriminatory legal rules had already been struck down by
various courts as violating the equal-protection clause of the United
States Constitution's Fourteenth Amendment. (*E.g.*, *White v. Crook*,
251 F. Supp. 401 (1966); *Robinson v. York*, 281 F. Supp. 8 (1968);
Owen v. Illinois Baking Corporation, 260 F. Supp. 820 (D.C. Mich
1966); *Clem v. Brown*, 3 Ohio Misc. 167, 207, N.E. 2d 398 (1965);
etc.)

I also suggested that "as some of these cases make their way to
the Supreme Court, the Court, influenced by the reasoning of the
opinions below and perhaps more responsive to the present sociological climate surrounding the question of women's legal status
than it has been in the past, may drastically revise its prior approach to determining the kind and extent of official sex discrimination that is allowable."

I continue to hold these views. I believe that there is a very high
degree of probability that the United States Supreme Court, when

it next confronts an equal-protection or due-process challenge to a sex-discriminatory law, will drastically modify the undifferentiated principle originally enunciated in the 1908 case of *Muller v. Oregon*, 208 U.S. 412 (1908) that "Sex is a valid basis for classification"— a principle I described in *Women and the Law* as being "often repeated mechanically by the courts without regard to the purposes of the statute in question or the reasonableness of the relationship between that purpose and the sex-based classification."[5] Indeed, I suggested, "[t]he subsequent reliance in judicial decisions upon the *Muller* language is a classic example of the misuse of precedent, of later courts being mesmerized by what an earlier court had *said* rather than what it had *done*.[6]

But if I believe that the Equal Rights Amendment would not achieve anything that could not be achieved by the courts in interpreting existing constitutional provisions, the question arises as to why I am supporting the Equal Rights Amendment at this time, especially since my position on the Amendment has heretofore wavered between mild opposition and lukewarm support. The answer is simple. Although I still believe that there is a very high degree of probability that the Supreme Court will perform as I hope and expect in this area, there is no guarantee that it will do so. Moreover, I now believe that it is necessary for all branches of government to demonstrate an unshakable intention to eliminate every last vestige of sex-based discrimination in American law. The adoption of the Equal Rights Amendment at this time would give encouragement to the many American women and men who now see the need for substantial reform in this area. Finally, should the next few years bear out my prediction that the Court will soon begin to interpret existing constitutional provisions so as to eliminate irrational sex discrimination in the law, no harm will have been achieved by the presence of the Equal Rights Amendment. Indeed, many examples can be cited in which laws and official practices may violate more than one constitutional provision at one time.

Moreover, should the Supreme Court not respond as I have suggested it ought to in this area, then the need for the Equal Rights Amendment will have become manifest. The time that will have been gained by sending it on its ratification road immediately will be precious.

There is one word of caution I would add at this point, however. Congress, if it adopts the proposed Equal Rights Amendment, as I hope it will do, should make sure that the record discloses that it does not thereby intend to discourage the United States Supreme Court from interpreting existing constitutional provisions—and especially the equal protection clause of the Fourteenth Amendment—so as to eliminate every sex-based discrimination in American law that cannot be sustained by overwhelming proof of functional differences between men and women.

I say this because there is a very real danger that if this is not done, the adoption of the Amendment at this time will ultimately represent a defeat rather than a victory for those of us who seek the eradication of irrational sex-based distinctions in American law and society. In the absence of such a clarifying declaration in the legislative history, the Court, when faced with an equal-protection or due-process challenge to a sex-discriminatory legal rule of official practice within the next few years, may be prompted to reason as follows: since a coordinate branch of the federal government, the Congress, has deemed it necessary to adopt the Equal Rights Amendment, then it must have believed that existing constitutional provisions were inadequate to provide the needed relief in this area. Though such a view is not determinative, it is at least persuasive. As a result, deferring to Congress's apparent wishes in this respect, the Court could withhold any modification of the *Muller* principle and simply await the ratification of the Equal Rights Amendment before providing the needed relief in this area.

The problem of course is that one cannot be sure that the Equal Rights Amendment will be ratified by the requisite number of state legislatures. Even if it is eventually ratified, this may occur many years from now. In the meantime, many litigants, both men and women, seeking to prevent unreasonable discrimination based upon sex, may find that no redress is available from the courts.

I am aware of course of the decision in *Gray v. Sanders,* 372 U.S. 368, wherein the Supreme Court at page 379 invoked the Fifteenth Amendment's prohibition against voting denials based on race and the Nineteenth Amendment's similar prohibition of denials based on sex to sustain a challenge to a county-unit voting system that was based on the Fourteenth Amendment's equal-protection clause. *Gray v. Sanders* is no guarantee, however, that the Court would act the same way under the circumstances we are currently concerned with. For one thing, *Gray* was decided *after* the ratification of the Fifteenth and Nineteenth Amendments, while the fear that I have expressed concerns the Supreme Court's response while the ratification of the proposed Equal Rights Amendment would still be pending. For another thing, the *Gray* decision did not require the Court to overrule or substantially modify any of its recent decisions. But if the Court were to do as I hope and expect it will with respect to equal-protection and due-process challenges to sex-based legal discrimination, it would have to drastically modify several decisions that were rendered as recently as 1961 (*Hoyt v. Florida*, 368 U.S. 57) and 1954 (*Goesart v. Cleary*, 335 U.S. 464).

For these reasons, I believe it is of crucial importance that Congress, in adopting the proposed Equal Rights Amendment, make clear its hope and expectation that forthcoming decisions of the United States Supreme Court will soon transform that Amendment into a constitutional redundancy.

Finally, before moving on to the proposed amendments to the Amendment that are contained in S.J. Res. 231, let me make one more observation. Some proponents of the Equal Rights Amendment are undoubtedly convinced that its adoption will inevitably revolutionize judicial attitudes about sex roles in our society. Some opponents of the Amendment are equally convinced that its adoption will introduce chaos, uncertainty, and confusion in our law and judicial processes.

My most recent studies in this area have persuaded me that neither view is correct. I have just returned from a seven-month sabbatical leave in Europe. While there, I began an examination of law-based sex discrimination problems in France, West Germany, Switzerland, England, Denmark, and Sweden.

My study is still incomplete and it will be some time before I shall be able to publish my conclusions. For the moment, however, I think I can say with some assurance that the experience of the West German courts in interpreting a similar constitutional provision ("*Manner und Fraunen sind gleichberechtigt*," translated as "Men and women are equal before the law," Art. 3, sec. 2, Constitition of the German Federal Republic) demonstrates two important points. One is that our courts will face no extraordinary difficulties in dealing with the Amendment. The other is that the Amendment will not of itself represent a cure-all for the myriad problems of sex discrimination. For as I suggested in *Women and the Law*, even after the adoption of the Equal Rights Amendment, "the crucial factor will continue to be the responsiveness of the judiciary to the social impulse toward equality of treatment without regard to sex."[7]

But in contrast to my former position, when I believed that, for *tactical* reasons, efforts to secure passage of the Amendment ought to be abated in favor of vigorous challenges under existing constitutional provisions, I now believe, for the reasons advanced earlier in these remarks, that, provided the adequate legislative history is made, passage of the Amendment at this time could do no harm and possibly could do much good.

SENATE JOINT RESOLUTION 231

Let me now turn my attention to Senate Joint Resolution 231. That Joint Resolution, introduced as a substitute to Senate Joint Resolution 61, would change the proposed Equal Rights Amendment in several respects. First, it would place a seven-year limitation on the ratification process. Second, the Amendment would become effective two years after ratification rather than one year after ratification, as proposed in S.J. Res 61. But most important, it would qualify the basic declaration of equality contained in S.J. Res. 61 by adding this second sentence:

This article shall not impair, however, the validity of any law of the United States or any state which exempts women from compulsory military service or which is reasonably designed to promote the health, safety, privacy, education, or economic welfare of women, or to enable them to perform their duties as homemakers or mothers.

As indicated earlier, I recommended the rejection of S.J. Res. 231.

First of all, I oppose the seven-year limitation on the ratification process. It is to be hoped that the basic Equal Rights Amendment, as worded in S.J. Res. 61, will be ratified long before seven years have passed. But should that not be the case, I can see nothing that will be gained by imposing such a time limit—especially if, as I have suggested, the legislative history will clearly show Congress's hope and expectation that the Supreme Court will in the meantime render the Amendment unnecessary.

Second, while there is some merit to the idea that the state legislatures and Congress should be given more than one year to enact appropriate implementing legislation, a one-year period would be adequate since both state and federal legislatures would have had time to prepare for their work while the ratification process was still pending.

My most severe reservations about S.J. Res. 231, however, go to the language in the second sentence of the first section that would qualify the basic declaration in favor of equal treatment in the law without regard to sex that is contained in the first sentence of that section. I suggest that there are serious questions about the *meaning* of the second sentence. And even if the meaning of it can be ascertained, I fear that the interpretation probably intended by its sponsor would render that language objectionable to me as being incompatible with the needs of our society and the basic goal of equal treatment under law without regard to sex.

In ascertaining the meaning of the second sentence, I think it is important to note first the provision that it qualifies. That provision states, "Equality of rights under the law shall not be denied or abridged by the United States or by any State on account of sex." Then comes the sentence in question, which states that the Article shall not impair the validity of certain kinds of laws currently assumed to benefit women in a variety of ways.

One possible interpretation, resulting from this juxtaposition of the two sentences, would be as follows: since the first sentence guarantees equality of treatment without regard to sex, and since the benefits presumably flowing to women from certain laws are held inviolate in the second sentence, then the only way to achieve the equality of treatment guaranteed in the first sentence is to extend those benefits to men. Under this construction, since women's present exemption from compulsory military services is to be preserved, the constitutional command of equal treatment can be obeyed only by extending the exemption to men. This would render unconstitutional our Selective Service law, which applies to men only. While, personally, I would have no objection to such a construction of this language, I wonder if this would be acceptable to the Resolution's sponsor.

A similar analysis can be offered of the remaining language of the second sentence, i.e., up to the beginning of the last clause. For it is not only women who have an interest in laws designed to promote their health, safety, privacy, education, or economic welfare. Men are equally interested in being protected by government in these areas. A reasonable reconciliation of this language with the command of the first sentence would be to read it as requiring the extension of the benefits of such laws to men. Indeed, if this is intended by this language, I could support it—although, as I will explain, the Equal Rights Amendment, as worded in S.J. Res 61, achieves this same goal and is preferable.

The last clause of the second sentence raises some difficulties, however. It states, "or to enable them to perform their duties as homemakers or mothers." Here the extension approach is clearly not intended. Though it is possible to think of men performing the function of homemakers, it is a little difficult to conceive of them as mothers in a biological sense. Moreover, this last clause would appear to lend constitutional dignity to the social presumption that the highest, if not the sole, life's work for women is that of wife and mother.

The apparent intention of this last clause provides a key, I believe, to the probable meaning and intention of the rest of the language in the second sentence. That is, rather than intending these benefits and protections to be extended to men, the Amendment's sponsor apparently intends, by the language of the second sentence, to preserve these for women alone. Not only would this represent a nullification of the spirit and intent of the proposed Equal Rights Amendment as worded in S.J. Res 61, but it would be a substantial step backward from the encouraging recent trend of decisions in the state courts and lower federal courts.

Even if S.J. Res 231 is intended to embrace the possibility of extending to men certain rights, privileges, and benefits of law currently enjoyed by women only, the basic fallacy in its reasoning is its apparent assumption that the unadorned Equal Rights Amendment, would, if adopted and ratified, deprive women of many of these rights, privileges, and benefits.

I suggest that this need not happen at all. In *Women and the*

Law, I pointed out how it would be consistent with judicial precedent for the courts, in interpreting the Fourteenth Amendment's equal-protection clause in sex-discrimination cases, to cure the invalid inequality by extending the benefits of particular laws to the sex (male or female) that had not previously enjoyed those benefits rather than by removing them from the one that had. That analysis, I suggested, was equally applicable with respect to the Equal Rights Amendment.

This, I believe, is the spirit in which the Supreme Court, aided by the legislative history, will interpret the Equal Rights Amendment as worded in S.J. Res. 61. This, I believe, is the spirit in which the Court can and should interpret the Fourteenth Amendment's equal-protection clause in forthcoming sex-discrimination cases.

I would also stress that the Amendment as worded in S.J. Res. 61 empowers Congress and the states, within their respective jurisdictions, to enforce the new article by appropriate legislation. This, I suggest, is the ultimate corrective, the ultimate guarantee of social consensus with regard to decisions to extend one-way rules or abrogate them.

In sum, I believe that S.J. Res. 231 is based on an invalid assumption as to the probable effects of the Equal Rights Amendment as worded in S.J. Res. 61, and therefore recommend its rejection. Though I am absolutely certain that the sponsor of S.J. Res 231 is as interested as I am in advancing the status of American women in law and society, he has proposed a way that I simply cannot support. The fact of the matter is that this is an extraordinarily difficult question about which reasonable men and women do differ. My hope is that, in the course of these hearings, understanding of all of us will be advanced, and that the ultimate decision is the right one.

EQUAL RIGHTS AMENDMENT, PROTECTIVE LABOR LAWS, AND THE OVERTIME ILLUSION

Finally, I should like to turn my attention to how the Equal Rights Amendment, if adopted, could work in the area that has been the subject of greatest controversy. I am referring specifically to the Amendment's effect upon the state's protective labor laws that currently apply to women only. Parenthetically, I would point out that my analysis here also applies to the effects of the equal-protection clause if and when the Supreme Court begins to inter-pret that clause vigorously in the sex-discrimination area.

Reading the testimony presented to the Judiciary Committee's Subcommittee on Constitutional Amendments during its earlier hearings this year, and the testimony presented at prior Senate committee hearings on the proposed Amendment, I am struck by what I regard as a peculiar fact. That fact is that certain groups or organizations that, according to all reasonable expectations, should be allied on the issue of equality without regard to sex are in fact divided over the desirability of the Amendment as a way of achiev-ing that goal. I am speaking of the basic division between women's organizations, which have supported it, and organized labor, which has for the most part, opposed it.

By and large, representatives of organized labor have expressed a fear that, should the Amendment become part of our fundamen-tal law, many of the protections that have been won for women workers over years of difficult struggle would be nullified. On the other hand, some supporters of the Amendment have expressed a suspicion that labor's principal motive in opposing it is to monopo-lize for men both jobs and other supposed benefits, which I shall soon discuss. Though this suspicion is understandable if we recall longstanding collective-bargaining agreements providing substan-tial sex-based wage differentials for the same or similar jobs, it is not, in my opinion, an accurate reading of the motives of the Amendment's trade union opponents.

In *Women and the Law*, I quoted a 1964 statement by Con-gresswoman Martha Griffiths of Michigan, which not only charac-terized organized labor's basic attitude in this area, but also pointed the way to what I believe is the ultimate solution to its knotty problems. "Some people," said Congresswoman Griffiths, "have suggested to me that labor opposes 'no discrimination on account of sex' because they feel that through the years protective legislation has been built up to safeguard the health of women. Some legisla-tion was to safeguard the health of women, but it should have safeguarded the health of men, also.[8]

Basing my analysis upon the same principle, I suggested in *Women and the Law* how this could be done. Specifically, I demonstrated how, consistently with what had already been done in administrative and constitutional law decision, the equality of treatment required in this area could be achieved by *extending* protective laws to men rather than by removing them from women. The Equal Employment Opportunity Commission, I suggested, should pursue this approach in administering the anti-sex-discrimination provisions of Title VII of the 1964 Civil Rights Act. In areas that were beyond the jurisdictional reach of the EEOC, I urged reliance upon past judicial precedents such as those I have just referred to in my discussion of S.J. Res. 231, to achieve the same extension of those laws rather than their abrogation.

This analysis, I still believe, is a sound one. Not only has the Labor Department, in administering the Equal Pay Act of 1963, determined that where state law provides a minimum wage for women only, the Equal Pay Act entitles men in that state to the same minimum wage if they are covered by the federal law, but the EEOC also has taken the position that the benefits of state laws, presently applicable to women only—such as those requiring minimum wages, rest periods, seats at work—are required by Title VII to be extended to men. Even in those situations that are beyond the jurisdictional reach of Title VII and the Equal Pay Act, I suggested, the judicial extension technique employed in equal protection and other constitutional cases, could lead to the same results.

Moreover, these results can also be achieved under the proposed Equal Rights Amendment—especially if the legislative history disclosed that Congress intends this. The fears of some opponents of the Amendment that its adoption would nullify laws that currently protect women only is thus unfounded—since the equality of treatment required by the Amendment can be achieved by extending the benefits of those laws to men rather than removing them from women. Moreover, the failure of any court to do this can be corrected through the legislative process.

Thus, as I stated in an article in the *Family Law Quarterly,*

the current renewed concern with the legal status of women will in many respects result in improving the situation of men as well as women. Just as breakthroughs in the legal status of American blacks has benefitted other racial and ethnic "minorities," so the effort to provide women with equal employment opportunity can substantially improve the situation of male employees in industry and commerce.

But the problem does not stop there. Essentially, I have been discussing the fate of certain protective labor laws—minimum wages, rest periods, seats at work—about which there can be little doubt that they provide valuable protections and benefits not only worth preserving for women, but also worth extending to men.

But the major source of controversy concerns two types of state protective labor laws, now applicable to women only, about which there is much confusion as to whether they in fact represent a burden or benefit. I am referring to those state laws limiting the weights that women are permitted to lift or carry in industry, or restricting the number of hours that women may work in a day or a week.

[The testimony here describes an earlier version of the extension and restructuring remedies for weight-lifting restrictions and hours-limitation laws, which are examined in chapter 4, above.]

The path that is ultimately taken depends on many factors. But the point that I would stress is that the claim that the Equal Rights Amendment would nullify state protective laws in the hours-limitations area is unfounded. As I have explained, there are several ways in which the right not to work overtime—which after all, is at the heart of the hours-limitation laws for women only—can not only be preserved for women, but can be made equally available to men. Above all, it is important for organized labor to begin to reassess its overtime work policies. When that is done, the claim of many of us that the liberation of American women will lead to the liberation of American men as well will be understood for the truth that it is.

6

The New Mexico Equal Rights Amendment: Introduction and Overview*

In November 1972, New Mexico voters will be asked to approve or disapprove an amendment to Article II, section 18 of the state constitution, which would in express terms, prohibit discrimination based on sex. Specifically the amendment would add to the due-process and equal-protection guarantees of that section the following language: "Equality of rights under law shall not be denied on account of the sex of any person." If approved by the New Mexico electorate, the amendment will become effective on July 1, 1973.

At the same time, a proposed amendment to the United States Constitution will in all likelihood still be making its way through the ratification process. That federal constitutional amendment—if approved by three-fourths (thirty-eight) of the fifty state legislatures—would add to the United States Constitution similar language, which, in its crucial part, reads: "Equality of rights under the law shall not be denied or abridged by the United States or by any state on account of sex." As of July 19, 1972, (the 124th anniversary of the 1848 Seneca Falls Women's Rights Convention) twenty states had approved the federal amendment. It will become effective two years after its ratification by the requisite number of states.

The New Mexico amendment was approved by the state legisla-

*This chapter is a slightly revised version of an article entitled *The New Mexico Equal Rights Amendment: Introduction and Overview.* 3 NEW MEXICO L. REV. 1 (1973) by Leo Kanowitz, copyright © 1973 by the New Mexico Law Review. Reprinted with permission.

ture and thus placed on the November ballot in the early part of 1972. At that time, the federal amendment had been approved in the United States House of Representatives by the necessary two-thirds vote. But it seemed to be facing a difficult fight in the United States Senate because of the determined opposition of North Carolina's Sam Irvin, among other United States senators. Contemplating this determined opposition to the federal Equal Rights Amendment and the possible seven-year delay in its ratification, New Mexico equal rights proponents concluded that immediate action was needed in New Mexico to assure prompt rewriting of state laws that continue to make arbitrary, biased, and harmful distinctions solely on the basis of sex.

Since the approval of the state amendment by the New Mexico legislature, the federal amendment has won approval in both houses of Congress. Indeed, when the amendment finally came to a vote in the United States Senate, the forecast opposition turned out to be illusory; the amendment was approved by an overwhelming vote of eighty-four to eight. Within a month after Senate approval the legislatures of fifteen states had voted to approve the amendment. And, as noted above, by July 19, 1972, twenty states had approved the amendment, leaving only eighteen more states required before it would become part of the United States Constitution. Thus, it appears that, barring any unforeseen complications, the federal amendment will be ratified long before the seven-year limit within which it must pass or fail.

Because the federal amendment would prohibit official sex discrimination not only at the federal level but at the state level as well, the question arises whether any purpose is to be served by adopting a similar change in the New Mexico constitution. My answer, which will be explained below, is an unqualified yes. Many people, both lawyers and nonlawyers, may also ask why any amendment is needed in the light of the recent United States Supreme Court case of *Reed v. Reed*,[1] holding that a particular state's sex-based discrimination violated the Fourteenth Amendment's equal-protection clause. The answer to that quesion is found in the history of the movement for amending both federal and state constitutions so as to guarantee equal rights without regard to sex.

The widespread existence of separate rules of law for men and women solely on the basis of sex has been chronicled elsewhere.[2]

Not only have such separate rules existed at common law, but even under modern statutes they persist in many forms.

Differences in the legal treatment accorded to men and women as such have been the subject of attacks in a large number of cases decided by the highest courts of the states as well as by the United States Supreme Court itself. Most such attacks have been based on assertions that particular sex-based distinctions in the law violate individual sections of the United States and state constitutions. The fate of such attacks—which, by and large, have been unsuccessful—is detailed in chapter 5. But for purposes of clarity, I would like to summarize those failed attacks, and describe some recent developments on the constitutional law front.

Before the 1970s, the United States Supreme Court had decided a series of cases in which particular sex-discriminatory rules or practices had been challenged on constitutional grounds. Uniformly the Court held that each of the challenged sex-based disparities were constitutionally permissible. In 1872, the court decided in *Bradwell v. The State*[3] that the privileges-and-immunities clauses of the United States Constitution did not prevent the state of Illinois from denying women the right to be licensed as attorneys in that state. In 1908, in the well-known case of *Muller v. Oregon,*[4] the court held that separate labor legislation for women and men did not violate the due-process guarantee of the Fourteenth Amendment. In 1954, in *Goesart v. Cleary,*[5] the court upheld a Michigan law prohibiting women from serving as bartenders in certain establishments, unless those establishments were owned by the husbands or fathers of the women concerned. And, in 1961, in *Hoyt v. Florida,*[6] the court held that the equal-protection guarantee was not violated by a state provision under which women, without regard to their marital status or family situation, would not be required to serve on juries unless they indicated their desire to do so by registering with the clerk of the court, a privilege that was not available to men subject to jury service.

These and similar decisions at the state level caused equal rights proponents to seek a constitutional amendment that would specifically address the question of sex discrimination in the law. Since 1923, efforts have been made in Congress toward the adoption of such a constitutional amendment. Until this year, such efforts have proved unsuccessful, partly as a result of the unwillingness of cru-

cial committee chairmen to hold hearings on the proposed amendment. In 1971, however, approval of the Equal Rights Amendment
in Congress came closer than it ever had before, and success was
finally achieved in 1972.

The essential problem with the earlier challenges to sex-discriminatory laws and practices was the acceptance by the United States
Supreme Court of the principle that "sex is a reasonable basis for
classification." The court thus rationalized separate treatment for
men and women in a wide variety of situations without considering
whether the attributes of individual men and women conformed to
basic assumptions about the sexes generally. In the latter half of
the 1960s, however, a series of decisions by state courts and lower
federal courts began to cast some doubt upon the validity of that
principle in particular situations. In 1966, a three-judge federal
court in Alabama decided that the equal-protection clause of the
Fourteenth Amendment was violated by a state's absolute denial to
women of their right to serve on juries.[7] And in 1968 in *United
States ex rel. Robinson v. York*,[8] another federal court held that a
state law requiring longer prison terms for women than for men
who were convicted of the same crime also violated the equal-
protection guarantee of the Fourteenth Amendment.

During this period, not all challenges to official sex-discrimination
achieved the same result. For example, a state court ruling permitting husbands, but not wives, to sue for loss of consortium (i.e., the
right to a spouse's services, society, companionship, assistance,
and sexual relations) as a result of injury negligently inflicted upon
their spouses was held not to violate the equal protection guarantee.[9] Similarly, a three-judge federal court held that a state's maintenance of a women-only college to which men had been denied
admission because of their sex did not violate the equal-protection
guarantee—again invoking the ancient shibboleth that "sex is a
reasonable basis for classification."[10] Interestingly, in each of the
last two cases, the United States Supreme Court denied certiorari. Though this is not a disposition on the merits, the denials indicated that the Court was going to choose carefully the case or cases
in which it would give its latest thinking on sex discrimination and
the Constitutiton.

In 1971, the Court finally decided on the merits a case attacking
a particular species of sex discrimination as violating the equal-

protection clause of the United States Constitution. In that case, *Reed v. Reed*,[11] the court held that an Idaho law preferring males to females as administrators of estates did in fact violate the equal-protection clause of the Fourteenth Amendment. Significantly, however, though the court was asked in the briefs of the parties to hold that sex, like race, was a "suspect" classification, thereby requiring any state that would justify a sex-based distinction to establish the *necessity* for such distinction by "overwhelming" or "compelling" reasons,[12] the court failed to enunciate this principle. Instead, *Reed* merely held that legislation that distinguished on the basis of sex would violate the equal-protection guarantee if the distinction was arbitrary and unreasonable. Presumably, this meant that if there were *any* rational basis for the distinction, it would be up-held—which is the classic formula for testing state economic regulation against the equal-protection clause.

Though the United States Supreme Court has not categorically rejected the suggestion that, for purposes of equal-protection review, a state's sex-based classification should be "suspect" like its racial classifications,[13] a subsequent decision by the United States Supreme Court casts much doubt on the Court's willingness to adopt that standard. In *Forbush v. Wallace*, [14] a three-judge federal court had, in the face of an equal-protection challenge, upheld Alabama's requirement that married women be registered with that state's motor vehicle bureau by their married names, and the state's common law rule requiring a married woman to assume her husband's surname as her legal name. Significantly, however, the three-judge court emphasized the easy availability under Alabama law of a means to change a married woman's name to some name other than her husband's (a right that does not appear to exist for married women in many other states).[15] The United States Supreme Court affirmed without an opinion in *Forbush v. Wallace*. Whether an affirmance without opinion by the United States Supreme Court is of any greater precedential value than a denial of certiorari is questionable. Equal rights proponents can still hope that the Court may in the future be persuaded to reconsider the *Forbush*-type problem and reach a different result.

Meanwhile, the current posture of the United States Supreme Court with respect to equal-protection challenges against official sex discrimination leaves much to be desired. Though in *Reed*, the

Court for the first time struck down on equal-protection grounds a state law that discriminated between the sexes, it treated the problem as one in the economic sphere rather than in the racial sphere, as it had been urged to do. The Court's affirmance without opinion in *Williams v. McNair*[16] and its denial of certiorari in *Miskunas v. Union Carbide Corp.*[17] also suggest a go-slow attitude on its part.[18] Finally, the Court's affirmance, albeit without opinion, in *Forbush v. Wallce* raises serious questions about its willingness to recognize, insofar as sex-based legal distinctions are concerned, the right of people to be treated as individuals rather than simply as members of a group whose general attributes do not necessarily correspond to their own individual characteristics.

Despite the Supreme Court's reluctance to move in this area, other courts have been less timid about applying the "suspect classification" analysis to classification based on sex. An early case indicating a willingness to do this was the abovementioned case of *Robinson v. York*, although in that case the court did not follow the logical implications of its theoretical construct to their fullest extent. By contrast, the California Supreme Court, in the landmark case of *Sail'er Inn v. Kirby*,[19] has wholeheartedly adopted the "suspect classification" analysis for classifications based on sex, thereby invalidating that state's law prohibiting women from serving as bartenders under certain circumstances.

Since the United States Supreme Court has often followed the lead of the California Supreme Court in developing new approaches to social and legal problems of the day,[20] it is far from certain that it will never adopt the "suspect classification" rationale in the sex-discrimination area, despite its demonstrated reluctance to take that step.

The fact remains, however, that the Court, as of this writing, has not adopted that analysis, and there is no guarantee that it will do so. Even were it to do so, the suspect-classification test would not necessarily preclude classification based upon sex, since all it requires is a greater burden of justification for such a classification.[21]

For these reasons, equal rights proponents have insisted upon the need for a constitutional amendment that (except in those very rare and narrowly defined circumstances where discernible sex-based biological differences clearly justify sex distinctions in the law) would prohibit any official discrimination or distinction based upon sex. It has been suggested that even under the Equal Rights Amendment certain distinctions based upon sex, such as a state's regulation of wet nurses and sperm donors, would continue to be permissible.[22] The reason for this is that these biological differences inhere in the very nature of the sexes. But if a state attempts to distinguish between the sexes merely on the basis of statistical probability or widespread generalization, it would violate the equal rights principle.

Thus, if and when the Equal Rights Amendment becomes part of the United States Constitution, it is clear, from its legislative history, that any state or federal distinction based upon sex, which is not inextricably linked to the biological characteristics of men and women, and which does not exist in all men and all women, would be invalid. At the same time, it is clear that the amendment would permit many individual men and women to continue to receive the same legal treatment they receive now. But such treatment would be accorded them because of their individual circumstances, and not because of any assumptions about them based on their sex. Because the language of New Mexico's Equal Rights Amendment tracks that of the federal Equal Rights Amendment, it is equally clear that its interpretation would be comparable.

Why, then, is there any need for an amendment to the state consitution? For one thing, it is by no means certain that the federal Equal Rights Amendment would be ratified in the very near future—although at this writing, it seems likely that ratification will occur well within the seven-year period required under the congressional resolution sending the measure to the states. Should ratification of the federal amendment be delayed, the adoption of the New Mexico amendment would insure that, in New Mexico at least, the equal rights principle would be quickly implemented. (It is worth noting that equal rights amendments to state constitutions will be before the electorate of various other states in November 1972, including Texas and Colorado. Pennsylvania adopted a similar state amendment in 1971).[23]

There is, moreover, another important difference between the federal amendment and that proposed for New Mexico. As mentioned earlier, the federal amendment would not go into effect until two years after its ratification. This delay was designed by Congress to give the states adequate opportunity to revise their own laws so as to implement the equal rights principle enunciated in the amendment. Above all, Congress was concerned that any disparities based upon sex under state law should be corrected in the first instance by the legislative representatives of the states themselves, rather than by federal or state courts. By contrast, the New Mexico amendment, if approved by voters in November 1972, would go into effect by July 1973, a delay of approximately seven months. As this symposium demonstrates, however, the shorter delay in the effective date for the New Mexico amendment should not seriously impede the ability of the New Mexico legislature to enact implementing legislation in the forthcoming 1973 session. In addition to the materials of this symposium, a committee of New Mexico Law School students, both male and female, has prepared a comprehensive memorandum suggesting alternative ways of curing present sex-based inequalities under New Mexico law, evaluating those alternatives, and recommending one or more approaches in a variety of fields. [24]

Perhaps more important than the possibilities of earlier action under the state amendment than under the federal amendment is the symbolic significance of what many of us hope will be the positive approval of New Mexico voters this November. In contrast to the ratification process for the federal amendment, which requires action by state legislatures, the New Mexico amendment would require approval by a popular vote of ordinary New Mexican voters in an ordinary election. In some ways, this resembles the recent approval in Switzerland of women's right to vote in that country's federal elections. Though in some respects it was at best a minor accomplishment for the Swiss to approve this basic human right, it is significant that approval finally came by a popular vote of that country's male voters.

Ratification of the state Equal Rights Amendment by New Mexico voters would, therefore, be understood as an unequivocal commitment by ordinary men and women in our state to the ideal of equal treatment without regard to sex, and to the concomitant ideal that people ought to be treated in law and society as individual human beings and not merely as members of a "class" to which they might belong, but whose general characteristics may or may not conform to their individual attributes.

All signs point to a positive vote on the state Equal Rights Amendment this November. Diverse organizations such as the League of Women Voters, the Business and Professional Women's Association, the Communications Workers of America and other labor oganizations, student groups at the University of New Mexico and throughout the state, among others, have already voiced their approval and support of the state amendment.

The important point to keep in mind is that we are entering a new era in American life insofar as the legal and social status of the sexes are concerned. Older assumptions, unproven by fact or experience, concerning the general characteristics of men and women are being challenged because of the injustices they have caused to both sexes in our society. In numerous areas of contemporary life, a reevaluation of past practices and concepts is under way. Adoption of the state Equal Rights Amendment, along with the federal Equal Rights Amendment, will represent law's contribution to such a reevaluation.

7

The ERA:
The Task Ahead*

On March 22, 1972, the United States Congress adopted a joint resolution proposing the Equal Rights Amendment (ERA) to the federal Constitution and setting a seven-year limit within which the necessary thirty-eight-state legislative ratifications were to have occurred.[1] When it became clear to the ERA's supporters that those ratifications would not be forthcoming by the original deadline, they successfully persuaded Congress to extend it by an additional thirty-nine months.[2] The Amendment has still not been ratified.[3]

I want to discuss what has impeded the ratification efforts up to now, and what can be done to assure that the Amendment will be ratified within the extended period that Congress has granted. In particular, I would like to explore the following questions: (1) What have been the positive results to this point in the campaign that has brought the ERA so close to ratification despite its highly controversial implications? (2) What mistakes have been made in that campaign? (3) How can they be avoided in future efforts on behalf of ERA ratification?

---

*This chapter is a slightly revised version of an article entitled *The ERA: The Task Ahead*, 6 HASTINGS CON. L. Q. 637 (1979) by Leo Kanowitz, copyright © 1979 by the Hastings Constitutional Law Quarterly. Reprinted with permission. The article was based on a speech delivered by the author on March 20, 1979 at New Mexico State University, where he was serving from March 14 to March 31, 1979, as Distinguished Visiting Professor. The speech was given two days before the expiration of the seven-year time limit originally prescribed by Congress for the states to ratify the Equal Rights Amendment.

BACKGROUND: THE PERCEIVED NEED

In addressing these questions, one has to begin with the state of affairs that led initially to the perceived need for an Equal Rights Amendment to the federal Constitution.[4] It will come as no great revelation that on a social level in the United States, as in other countries, men and women have been assigned specific roles solely on the basis of their sex. That such an assignment has been arbitrary and bears no relationship to the abilities, desires, and hopes of individual men and women has long been evident to most people who have thought about the matter.

As long as discriminatory treatment of the sexes occurred strictly in the private, social sphere, relatively little could be done about it. I say "relatively" because governments could have acted as they have done in recent years, under the commerce clause of the federal Constitution[5] or the inherent police power of the states,[6] to prohibit such discrimination even in the private sphere. But this kind of decision requires a heightened level of commitment to the eradication of sex discrimintion. It requires new, positive acts by either the federal or state legislatures, or both, acts that can be induced only if the right combination of political circumstances and pressures converge and are felt.

By contrast, when social prejudices about the appropriate roles of the sexes are translated into government action, with the result that laws—whether in the form of statutes, or of decisions by courts or administrative agencies—accord one kind of official treatment to men and another to women, the validity of such differential treatment is immediately suspect in the light of various constitutional restraints on governmental power.[7] Those restraints flow from the two privileges and immunities clauses, which require respect for rights inhering in state and federal citizenship;[8] the due-process clauses of the Fifth[9] and Fourteenth Amendments;[10] and the equal-protection clause of the Fourteenth Amendment.[11]

That sex-discriminatory laws existed and still exist is now probably a matter of common knowledge. When the congressional joint declaration sending the ERA on its ratification road was first passed in 1972, thousands of laws in the states and at the federal level drew sharp distinctions between the sexes on the basis of widely held, but questionable, assumptions and generalizations about them. Some made the husband the head and master of the family.[12] Many required wives to assume their husbands' surnames and lose their own.[13] Others granted preferences to mothers over fathers in disputes involving the custody of minor children.[14] Still others gave husbands superior rights to·manage and control their wives' property.[15] Some required women to be sentenced to longer prison terms than men upon conviction of the same crime.[16] Others denied the right of women to serve on a jury.[17] Some provided protection to women in the work place while denying such protection to men.[18] At the federal level, only men were subject to the obligation of compulsory military service.[19] And women who contributed large sums to the Social Security system were denied benefits for their spouses and children equal to those accorded men who made the same payments.[20]

The list can be enlarged. These are only examples of how the law treated one sex less favorably than another—at times preferring the male to the female, at other times reversing its preference. It is no surprise, therefore, to learn that over the years constitutional challenges to such official discriminatory treatment had found their way to the United States Supreme Court.

I will not review the many decisions of the state courts and lower federal courts upholding sex-discriminatory laws against a variety of constitutional challenges.[21] Suffice it to say that these decisions were numerous and virtually unanimous in sustaining such differential treatment by govenment on the basis of sex. But I do want to describe four important pre-1972 cases decided by the Supreme Court in this area, all of which rejected constitutional challenges to official sex discrimination.

One is the crucial 1908 decision in *Muller v. Oregon*.[22] In that case, the Court upheld, as against a challenge under the due-process clause of the Fourteenth Amendment, a state statute prescribing maximum hours for only women workers in certain kinds of employment—a statute that had been enacted without regard to the capacities of *individual* men and women to work beyond the maximum number of hours it prescribed. The Court's justification for this result, when all its rhetoric in a lengthy opinion is reduced to its essential point, was simply that women and men *generally* have different physiques.

In *Goesaert v. Cleary*,[23] another case decided under the equal-protection clause of the Fourteenth Amendment in 1954, the Court held that equal protection was not violated by a state statute prohibiting women who were not related by blood or marriage to the bar owners from working as bartenders, though the statute did not impose similar limitations on the employment rights of males who wished to pursue that occupation.[24] In still another case, *Hoyt v. Florida*,[25] decided in 1961, the Court again rejected an equal-protection challenge to a sex-discriminatory law limiting the right of women to serve as jurors without imposing a similar limitation on the right of males to do so.[26]

The case of *Bradwell v. The State*[27]—although the earliest of this group of four decisions, having been rendered by the Court in 1872—is especially instructive. In *Bradwell*, the United States Supreme Court, rejecting challenges under the privileges and immunities clauses of the federal Constitution, upheld the right of a state to deny women, solely on the basis of their sex, the right to practice law.[28] More important than *Bradwell's* result, however, is the language employed by a concurring Justice, Mr. Justice Bradley, explaining the reasons for his vote. As he saw it:

Man is, or should be, woman's protector and defender. The natural and proper timidity and delicacy which belongs to the female sex evidently unfits it for many of the occupations of civil life. The constitution of the family organization, which is founded in the divine ordinance, as well as in the nature of things, indicates the domestic sphere as that which properly belongs to the domain and functions of womanhood. The harmony, not to say identity, of interests and views which belong, or should belong, to the family institution is repugnant to the idea of a woman adopting a distinct and independent career from that of her husband.[29]

Elsewhere in his opinion, Justice Bradley noted: "The paramount destiny and mission of woman are to fulfil the noble and benign offices of wife and mother. This is the law of the Creator. And the rules of civil society must be adapted to the general constitution of things, and cannot be based upon exceptional cases."[30] In the same case, the Illinois Supreme Court had earlier written: "That God designed the sexes to occupy different spheres of action, and that it belonged to men to make, apply and execute the laws, was regarded as an almost axiomatic truth."[31]

As charitable as one tries to be, one cannot help concluding that the attitudes expressed in these excerpts indicate a thoughtless, prejudiced, and reactionary view of women in society. If one is less charitable, one is reminded by these words of Adolph Hitler's infamous statement about the appropriate role of women in society: *Kinder, Kirche, und Kuche*—"Children, Church, and Kitchen."

For present purposes, what is important is that despite some subtle degrees of sophistication in the three later Supreme Court decisions alluded to above, at their core they expressed to some degree or another the fundamentally sexist assumptions underlying Mr. Justice Bradley's opinion in *Bradwell v. The State.* To be sure, they each relied on detailed analyses of the particular issues before the Court. But, especially in view of later developments in the Court, it is clear that the results they reached were by no means inevitable. The prevailing sexist bias of the society at large, one has to conclude, must have played a role in the results actually reached in those cases.

Equally important, these cases developed the doctrine that "sex is a reasonable basis for classification." In earlier cases under the due-process and equal-protection clauses,[32] the Court had in the realm of social and economic legislation established the principle that, to pass muster under these constitutional provisions, a law need only create a reasonable classification designed to implement a legitimate govenmental policy. Sex classification by definition thus became automatically valid.

By contrast, between the last of these four decisions[33] and the early 1970s, the Court had developed a different standard of scrutiny under the Fourteenth Amendment's equal-protection guarantee for classifications characterized by the Court as "suspect"—such as those based on race, national origin, or alienage—or for those that curbed what the Court could characterize as a "fundamental" right of one group without curbing that same right for another group that seemed to be similarly situated.[34] In cases involving suspect classification[35] or in those infringing upon fundamental rights,[36] the Court imposed a greater burden of justification on one who sought to rely on the governmentally imposed classification. It was not sufficient that the classification be rationally related to the achievement of a legitimate governmental policy, as was true generally with regard to economic and social legislation. Rather, to pass muster the classification had to be shown to be necessary for the achievement of an overwhelming or compelling state interest. In this formulation "necessary" meant absolutely necessary—that is, the test would not be satisfied if less drastic alternatives would have achieved the same ends. Similarly, what constituted a compelling or overwhelming state interest was also strictly construed. Once such a test was imposed, it became obviously much more difficult for a race-based classification, for example, to pass constitutional muster. [37]

In recent years, therefore, much of the effort of those bringing sex-discrimination cases before the United States Supreme Court has been aimed at convincing the Court to adopt for sex classifications the same heightened level of scrutiny that it now requires for racial classifications. [38] The underlying argument, of course, has been that analytically, the fundamental social, political, and legal factors are the same in both instances. [39] The Court's response to those efforts—and the reasons for that response—will be dealt with below.

It was against this background of the Supreme Court's insensitivity to the problems of sex discrimination in American law that the movement for the adoption of the Equal Rights Amendment, which began in the early 1920s, led on March 22, 1972, to congressional adoption of a joint resolution proposing the ERA to the states for ratification. [40] The text of the Equal Rights Amendment is short and concise. It provides:

SECTION 1. Equality of rights under the law shall not be denied or abridged by the United States or by any State on account of sex.

SECTION 2. The Congress shall have the power to enforce, by appropriate legislation, the provisions of this article.

SECTION 3. This amendment shall take effect two years after the date of ratification. [41]

Despite the relative conciseness of the ERA's language, it has not been without its interpretive problems. One view of the amendment's basic effect is that it would at least require the courts to treat sex-based classifications as "suspect" in the same manner that it has treated classifications based upon race, national origin, and alienage. [42] Another is that the amendment would absolutely prohibit any classification based upon sex, except in those extremely rare instances when the matter being legislated about involves a trait present in all members of one sex, but not in any members of the other sex.[43] The classic examples of permissible sex-based classifications under such an interpretation are those stemming from a state law that would regulate wet nurses or sperm donors and whose reach would be limited, respectively, to women in one case and to men in the other. Except for such rare cases, however, the amendment would prohibit any differential treatment based on sex. Although large numbers of individual men and women might continue to be accorded differential treatment under law following ERA ratification, such differential treatment would be the result of their individual differences, and not because of their sex or gender.

IMPRESSIONS OF ERA DANGERS BY SOME OPPONENTS

Aside from the uncertainty as to the standard of justification that the Amendment would impose upon sex-based classifications, other perceived consequences of the amendment have led to considerable opposition to its passage. For example, from the time the ERA was first making its way through the congressional process that led to the joint resolution sending it to the states for ratification, it was clear that a crucial and highly emotional issue engendered by the proposal was whether women would, as a result of the amendment, be subject to the same duty of compulsory military service that had previously been the lot of male members of our society in times of international crisis. ERA opponents claimed that women would be subject to the draft. ERA proponents were somewhat divided in their position on this issue, some claiming that they would be, others that they would not.

My own position, maintained throughout the entire period, has been that the clear impact of the amendment would require women to be subjected to the same burdens as men vis-à-vis their government, and that they would be subject to the draft whenever one was instituted, just as they would be entitled to the same benefits flowing from military service as male members of the armed services. [44] This does not mean, of course, that women would be drafted in the same numbers as men. The armed services could continue to impose minimal physical requirements for various kinds of military occupations. That fact, plus the general differences in the male and female physiques, produced in part by social conditioning, and, perhaps, genetic factors, suggest that, were a draft reinstituted and were it sex-neutral in its operation, many more men than women would find themselves in the armed services on a compulsory basis.

Opposition to the potential draftability of women undoubtedly reflects a concern that it could lead to the sending of women to foreign battlefields where they would face all the horrors of combat. My response to this—the only one that, in my opinion, makes sense in the context of the ERA debate—is that having our youth torn apart by enemy shrapnel is equally horrendous whether the victims are male or female; that our relative equanimity in the face of this prospect periodically faced by the young male members of our society, and our consternation at the thought of this happening to female members of our society, is unfair, irrational, and reveals the fundamental sexist bias of the society at large in the basic realm of a life-and-death issue.[45] Whether we should ever have a draft at all, I suggested, is an entirely distinct question from whether, if we do have a draft, women and men may be treated unequally.

That position will, in my opinion, utlimately prevail. Given enough time to overcome the emotional biases triggered by the possibility of drafting American women into the armed forces, especially in time of war, most Americans will come to understand the need to do this if the promise of our nation's greatness is to be fulfilled. Still I do not doubt that the complexity of this issue coupled with its emotionality has caused many people to oppose the ERA who might otherwise have supported it wholeheartedly.

A second emotionally charged issue stemming from the ERA is whether it would result in depriving wives of the right to the financial support from their husbands that they appear to enjoy under existing legal doctrine, both during the ongoing marriage and, in the form of alimony, when marriages are dissolved by divorce or a comparable proceeding. The answers to these fears are clear, though once again they require explanation. In the ongoing marriage, the wife's right to support is more theoretical than real, most courts refusing to fix the amount and frequency of support because of the administrative problems doing so would create, so long as the bare minima of existence are being maintained.[46] As for postmarital support, even without the ERA, the proposed Uniform

Marriage and Divorce Act,[47] versions of which have already been adopted by many states,[48] requires the issue to be determined on a sex-neutral basis, the judicial inquiry being limited to ascertaining the financial needs and abilities of the parties to the marriage.[49] The United States Supreme Court reached a similar conclusion when it invalidated on equal-protection grounds a state law permitting alimony awards to wives but not to husbands.[50] That such an approach is more equitable than the traditional one should be self-evident. This too is, in my view, a conclusion that will be ultimately reached by most people who think about the problem. Nevertheless, this issue also has proved to be a stumbling block to garnering universal and total support for the ERA.

Still another fundamental concern that has engendered some opposition to the ERA is the fear that, following its adoption, the exisiting preferences for mothers over fathers in disputes over the custody of minor children will be abrogated.[51] Again, I cannot refute this analysis of the ERA opponents as to the amendment's probable effect. Where they are wrong, however, is in the premise upon which they base their further conclusion that this effect provides a proper reason for opposing the ERA. It simply assumes that, all other things being equal, it is right, just, fair, and proper to prefer mothers over fathers at all times in custody disputes solely on the basis of their sex.[52] A moment's reflection will reveal the illogic of that position. That fathers are capable of maintaining, and should be encouraged to maintain, meaningful relationships with their children is a self-evident proposition. Social science research suggests, moreover, that this would have a profoundly ameliorative effect upon such problems in American society as crime and delinquency, let alone confusions about sexuality. Once again, developments under existing constitutional provisions suggest that the courts, as well as lawyers and their clients, are becoming increasingly aware of these factors;[53] the presumption favoring mothers as custodians of children of tender years has recently been discarded in many states.[54] But, like the other issues mentioned earlier, this one too has engendered much emotional anti-ERA sentiment.

An issue that has plagued the ERA campaign from the beginning has been its potential effect upon state protective laws that have previously applied to women workers only. This caused initial op-

position to the amendment from leaders of organized labor. They
believed that the hard-won gains for women workers in many states,
such as weight-lifting restrictions,[55] minimum-wage guarantees,[56]
and maximum-hours provisions,[57] would all be lost as a result of
the amendment. My own position, I must admit, was at one time
lukewarm on the amendment precisely because of my concerns
about its potential effects in this area.[58] Only after my own research convinced me that the application of these laws to women
only was the result of historical accident, and that the way was
open to achieve sex equality in this realm by extending the benefits
of such laws to both sexes without sacrificing those hard-won social
gains, did I wholeheartedly and enthusiastically support the amendment.[59] At the same time, there is no doubt that apprehensions
about the possible effects of the ERA upon women-only state protective labor laws have turned many a potential ERA supporter
into an opponent. Again, with enough time to explore this complex
issue in the course of the national debate, many, if not most, of
those opponents will undoubtedly be persuaded to change their
minds.

Finally, a substantive objection to the ERA, which did not arise
until the amendment came up for consideration before various
state legislatures. has been based on Section 2, which provides that
"The Congress shall have the power to enforce, by appropriate
legislation, the provisions of this article." Though similar language
appears in other constitutional amendments, most notably the crucial Fourteenth, ERA opponents soon began to raise the alarm that
it would permit the federal government to interfere with state
control of areas that have historically been regarded as exclusively
of state concern. These areas include marriage and family laws,
abortion, child-parent and husband-wife relationships. The specter
of the giant, impersonal, and remote Washington bureaucracy making decisions that vitally affect such questions in Arizona, Nevada,
Georgia, and South Carolina has inevitably aroused additional opposition from certain sections of those states' populations.

But here, too, the spuriousness of this anti-ERA argument can
be seen if one but casts a glance at the already enormous power of
the national Congress to legislate in almost unlimited fashion in
almost unlimited areas, as a result of the Supreme Court's expan-
sive interpretations of the commerce clause,[60] among other con-

stitutional provisions.[61] That Congress has not legislated about marriage and divorce, husband and wife, and children and parent relationships, does not, in my opinion, result from an absence of congressional power to do so. Rather, it reflects two fundamental political facts. One is that Congress has much else to occupy its attention. The other is that members of the House of Representatives and United States Senate are elected by voters of separate states; they are, therefore, ultimately responsible, 'politically speaking, to the wishes and desires of their constituents within the states. Section 2 of the ERA, therefore, would not confer any powers on Congress that it does not already enjoy. Nevertheless, once again, this perception of a possible ERA effect has contributed to some opposition to the amendment.

These, then, are the bases for some of the principal substantive objections to the amendment. Whether the objections are based on major or minor considerations. there are, as I have tried to demonstrate, principled, logical, and dispositive answers that can be and often have been brought to bear by the amendment's supporters. Those answers, unfortunately, have not always been communicated, partly because many ERA opponents have refused "to be confused by the facts." Others, though willing to listen, have often found it hard to understand because of the complexities and legal technicalities that are unavoidably involved in those answers.

Despite such difficulties, public opinion polls demonstrate that most Americans support ERA ratification.[62] Among these supporters are undoubtedly many who understand the issues in all their complexity and who have made considered decisions that the costs of not ratifying the amendment far outweigh the benefits that might flow from its ratification. At the same time, there are probably many who, as counterparts to ERA opponents, intuitively feel that a constitutional amendment guaranteeing equality of the sexes under law is desirable, while not necessarily perceiving all its complexities and technicalities, or even making the effort to do so.

TACTICAL ERRORS BY SOME ERA PROPONENTS

Notwithstanding the overwhelming support for the ERA, however, it was not ratified within the original seven-year period. Why? For one thing, because of the concerns mentioned earlier,

unfounded as they might be, much of the opposition to the amendment has been as determined as the support for it. For another,
the amending process was deliberately made difficult by the framers
of the federal Constitution. Not only must the joint resolution
sending the amemdment on its ratification road be adopted by the
extraordinary majority of two-thirds of each house of Congress, but
it has to be ratified by three-fourths of the state legislatures, i.e.,
thirty-eight of the fifty.[63] The result is that a determined, well-
organized opposition can effectively block a proposed amendment.
And in the case of the ERA, the opposition has been decidedly
determined and well-organized.

Not coincidentally, refusal to ratify has occurred chiefly in the
states of the old Confederacy, and in the states where the Mormon
Church, a principal foe of the amendment, has been extremely
influential.[64] For many, the ERA has been merely part of a larger
battle between "conservatives" and "liberals."

Here I must allude to some overall tactical errors of certain
sections—at times the most visible and vocal sections—of the wom-
en's rights movement that also contributed to the failure to achieve
the ERA's ratification within the original seven years. At one stage
of, but to some extent throughout, the campaign for the amendment, many of its supporters conveyed the strong impression—at
times unwittingly, at other times deliberately—that they regard
women who work in the home and who do not hold jobs in the
world outside as being somehow less worthy human beings than
those who do hold such jobs. To the extent that this view has been
associated with support for the ERA, it has inevitably engendered
opposition from women who sincerely and honestly believe that
they can fulfill themselves in the roles of wife and mother—though
they might have welcomed the views of the vast majority of ERA
proponents that they should have a choice in such matters, and
that they should not be forced into such roles by laws and governmental actions. But, as I have suggested, that view held by a
majority of ERA supporters has often not been nearly as visible or
discernible as the view of a minority of other ERA supporters,
which, to employ the vernacular, simply turned many people off.

Another error committed by some elements in the women's
rights movement has been to allow the impression to take hold that
adoption of the ERA will, somehow, legitimize homosexual rela-

tionships under American law and in American society. I hesitate to speak for others, but I suspect that many of the people who originally testified on behalf of the ERA before various congressional committees—in my case before both the United States Senate Judiciary Committee[65] and the United States House Judiciary Committee[66]—share my belief that it is high time that state and federal governments take their feet off the necks of people whose sexual preferences differ from those of the majority. But, for a very simple reason, we did not suggest to the members of Congress before whom we appeared that this goal was to be achieved by adoption of the ERA. That reason was our perception that it was going to be an enormously difficult task to persuade legislators and citizens alike simply to examine their longstanding prejudices about fixed roles for men and women in law and society. To add to it the burden of persuading them to revise their attitudes about what many perceived to be sexual deviationism, in the context of a campaign for the ERA, would simply make that task much more difficult, if not impossible.

Moreover, there were promising developments with respect to the rights of homosexuals under other existing provisions of the federal Constitution.[67] Therefore, as I understood it—and I assume the others shared my views—to introduce the homosexuality issue into the ERA campaign was simply to load that campaign with an issue that, though admittedly related, was sufficiently tangential and emotionally charged to require its separation from the question of equal treatment of the sexes under the law. But the impression created by the words and actions of many ERA proponents that the ERA will achieve so-called gay liberation has inevitably hardened the opposition of those who are already inclined to oppose the ERA, and has turned many a potential supporter of the amendment into an opponent.

Still another tactical shortcoming has been that, despite the recognition by most thoughtful members of the women's rights movement that both men and women have been victims of a social and legal system that arbitrarily assigns roles on the basis of sex, some women have conveyed the impression that the fundamental issue involves a struggle by women *against* men. Thus, many men, potential allies in this struggle for fundamental human rights, have been deterred from lending their support by what they perceive as the ERA's threat to their own self-interest as a result of the context within which some pro-ERA activists have waged the campaign for the amendment.

Finally, the abortion issue, though related to the question of women's rights in a very direct sense, has never really been involved in either the text or the potential impact of the ERA. Nevertheless, many opponents of an unlimited right to abortion—an issue that is perceived one way if attention is focused upon the right of a woman to control her own body, but another way if the rights of a fetus or the value to be assigned to the potentiality of life of the fetus is one's central concern—have associated the abortion question with the ERA. Because of their strong antiabortion stand, often based on deeply felt religious and moral conviction, their ability to judge the ERA on its merits has been greatly impaired.

These were in my view, some of the major factors that kept the ERA from being ratified within the first seven years. They were by no means the only ones. For example, the extraordinary three-fifths majority vote of its legislators required by Illinois to ratify a federal constitutional amendment[68]—a requirement that is not without its own constitutional problems—has undoubtedly been another contributing factor, especially if Illinois's strategic importance and the likely effect its ratification might have had on other undecided states is considered. The opponents' concentration of their efforts in the most promising states—considered from their viewpoint—also played a part. So did the organizational effectiveness of the anti-ERA leadership. Finally, there is the effect of the news media, which have often delighted in featuring the antics of some fringe elements of the women's rights movement because this made good copy, while often ignoring the positions which were thoughtful, sophisticated, and cogent, of the vast majority of participants in that movement.

ACHIEVEMENTS TO DATE

Having examined some of the more important reasons why the ERA has not yet been ratified, I would now like to discuss the positive results produced by the pro-ERA campaign to date. For one thing, the thirty-five state ratifications garnered so far will of course be crucial if the remaining three ratifications are obtained within the next thirty-nine months. For another, the pro-ERA efforts during these past seven years have undoubtedly contributed to the changed jurisprudence of the United States Supreme Court on the subject of sex discrimination and the existing provisions of the United States Constitution. Nor was the Court the only insitution in American life to develop a new understanding of the sex-role issue during these last seven years. The Congress, the state legislatures, the state courts, and, above all, the American people, now entertain views about the roles of men and women in our society that are fundamentally different from, and decidely more progressive than, the views they had when the campaign to ratify the amendment was first launched.

At the Supreme Court level, when the start of the ratification process became imminent, the case of *Reed v. Reed*[69] was decided. It invalidated, as a violation of the Fourteenth Amendment's equal-protection guarantee, an Idaho statute that preferred women over similarly situated men for appointment as administrators of dead persons' estates. Though purporting to apply the "any-rational-basis" test that had prevailed in past sex-discrimination cases, the Court, both in its result and in some of its language, left the strong impression that it was applying a more stringent standard in judging this sex-based classification than any it had previously applied.

That the Court had in fact done this in *Reed* soon became apparent in another decision, *Frontiero v. Richardson*,[70] invalidating, under the equal-protection aspect of the Fifth Amendment's due-process clause, federal statutes providing greater benefits to male members of the armed services than to female members. In *Frontiero*, four members of the Court expressly adopted the suspect-classification analysis for classifications based upon sex.[71] This test, you will recall, imposes a much more burdensome and difficult standard of justification upon one who seeks to sustain the classification than does the any-rational-basis test for equal-protection purposes that is applied to ordinary economic and social legislation. Had the views of these four members of the Court become the majority view, sex classifications would now be treated in the same manner as classifications based upon race, national origin, and alienage. They could be supported only by a showing that they are necessary to achieve an overwhelming or compelling governmental interest. But four members of the Court do not a majority make.

The result in *Frontiero* was reached only because it was concurred in by another member of the Court, Justice Stewart, in a short, cryptic opinion, which did not embrace the suspect characterization of sex-based classifications.[72]

Finally, in *Craig v. Boren*,[73] a Court majority endorsed a level of scrutiny of sex-based classifications that falls somewhere between the any-rational-basis test that had previously prevailed in this area and the suspect classification, heightened scrutiny of the compelling governmental interest test.[74] *Craig* also established that discrimination directed against males because of their sex or gender is just as constitutionally vulnerable as that directed against females if the new test is not satisfied.[75]

Along with these decisions, the Court, in several other cases, held that if the purpose of a law-imposed classification was to grant a preference to women in order to correct the present effects of past discrimination, such a preference, or benign discrimination, is constitutionally permissible. The leading case for this proposition is *Kahn v. Shevin*,[76] upholding a Florida tax exemption for widows, though no similar exemption was provided for widowers in that state. In that case, two members of the Court suggest that men, unlike women, have not been the victims of past sex discrimination.[77] That view, I suggest, is shortsighted. It fails to appreciate that whether one talks of the male's unique obligation of compulsory military service, his primary duty for spousal and child support, or his lack of the same kinds of protective labor legislation that have traditionally been enjoyed by women, he has paid an awesome price for other advantages he has presumably enjoyed over women in our society.

Significantly, the "benign discrimination" that the Court permitted on behalf of women in the face of due-process and equal-protection challenges under the Fifth and Fourteenth Amendments has not been allowed when the issue confronting the Court was whether a state medical school could constitutionally prefer black people over white people solely on the basis of race in its admissions policies, absent a record of any prior racial discrimination by that school.[78] Were the ERA to become part of the Constitution, moreover, the "benign" sex discrimination allowed in such cases as *Kahn v. Shevin*[79] and *Califano v. Webster*[80] would, in my opinion, be impermissible, since its prohibition against unequal treatment on the basis of sex is absolute.[81] That the ERA is perceived as having this effect is no doubt cause for the opposition to the amendment from some Americans who believe that the law's remaining preferences for women should be preserved.

Despite the Court's uneven record in the sex-discrimination area during the past seven years, caused chiefly by its benign-discrimination doctrine, it has dramatically improved its performance over what it was at the start of the period. In cases in which women or men can be shown to be subject to differential treatment by the law, such treatment can now be sustained only if it satisfies the heightened level of scrutiny prescribed by *Craig v. Boren*.[82] In the Court's words in that case: "To withstand constitutional challenge . . . classifications by gender must serve *important* governmental objectives and must be *substantially* related to achievement of those objectives."[83] While this burden of justification is not as great as I and other equal-rights advocates would like, being less onerous than the one applied in race-discrimination cases and much less than would be required by the ERA, it nevertheless represents a significant step forward from the "any-rational-basis" test that had prevailed at the beginning of the ratification campaign. This new standard will have the practical effect of invalidating numerous sex-discriminatory laws and official practices that would have passed constitutional muster under the earlier doctrine.

That this progress by the Court—as incomplete as it has been— was prompted in large part by the pro-ERA campaign appears self-evident. To be sure, other developments in the campaign for sex equality, aside from the pro-ERA efforts, also contributed to the changed perceptions by members of the Court. Indeed, various members of the Court have candidly acknowledged the fact that we are living in a new day insofar as society's views on sex roles are concerned.[84] And Justice Powell, while drawing a negative inference from the fact, also has admitted that the campaign to ratify the ERA is a factor to be considered in deciding whether to give the existing constitutional provisions a more important role in sex-discrimination cases.[85] While his conclusion has been that the Court should tread carefully in this area because the American people will be making the fundamental political decision about sex equality under the Constitution when they either ratify or fail to ratify the ERA,[86] it is clear that other members of the Court understand that the pro-ERA drive has been made necessary by the Court's prior grudging application of existing constitutional provisions to the problems of sex discrimination and the law. Their new rulings in sex-discrimination cases have been heading in the direction, although falling far short of the goal, of making the ERA a constitutional redundancy—a development I had looked forward to when testifying in support of the ERA in Congress.[87]

In speaking of the effect of the pro-ERA campaign upon the Supreme Court, one must recognize that this effect followed another—namely, the one upon the understanding of the American people themselves. Only after Americans were persuaded of the rightness of equal treatment without regard to sex as a social principle did their convictions filter down (or up) to members of the Court.

Although I cannot document this, my life's experience has convinced me that people learn best under stress. One can cajole and try to pesuade in calm, dispassionate tones with limited results. But the same arguments made in the context of a hard-fought *contest* over a social or political issue seem to be perceived with greater intensity by those to whom they are directed. As mentioned earlier,[88] more than the ERA campaign has been occurring in recent years to heighten people's consciousness about sex roles in American society. But the ERA has been a central theme around which other efforts have often been mobilized.

Nor has the changed jurisprudence of the United States Supreme Court in applying existing constitutional provisions to sex-discrimination cases been the only positive effect of the national ERA campaign. Equal rights provisions, many tracking the language of the proposed federal ERA, are now contained in the constitutions of at least sixteen states.[89] Though some antedated the ERA ratification campaign, most were adopted after the campaign was started, and were undoubtedly inspired by it. Having personally participated in the successful efforts to adopt an equal rights amendment to the New Mexico Constitution,[90] I can attest to the close links between the national campaign and the one directed toward achieving a state equal rights constitutional guarantee.

What is more, during the entire period of the ERA campaign, important gains for the principle of sex-based equality were made through new laws enacted by Congress and the state legislatures. To be sure, the 1963 Equal Pay Act,[91] Title VII of the 1964 Civil

Rights Act,[92] and the amendment of Executive Order 11246 by Order 11375,[93] all of which outlawed various forms of sex discrimination in employment, preceded the ratification phase of the ERA campaign. Still, they coincided with the heightened efforts to shepherd the ERA through Congress that occurred during those years. Since the ratification phase of the ERA campaign began, moreover, new legislation such as Title IX of the Education Amendments of 1972,[94] the Equal Credit Opportunity Act,[95] and many other legislative attacks on sex-discriminatory laws and practices, have been enacted.

THE YEARS AHEAD

To this point, we have been examining developments of the past. The question now is what does the future hold for the principle of sex equality under American law? Specifically, what is the likely future course of the United States Supreme Court decisions in this field, and what are the prospects for ratification of the ERA within the next thirty-nine months?

In my opinion, certain members of the Court may conclude that the temporary setback suffered by the ERA signifies the American people's rejection of the principle of equality of the sexes under the law. Such a conclusion, I suggest, would be mistaken. It would fail to take into account the evidence of the public polls referred to above.[96] What is more important, it would ignore the feelings of large numbers of proequality advocates who have been persuaded by ERA opponents that a new constitutional provision is unnecessary because the Court has already embarked upon a vigorous application of existing constitutional provisions to sex-discrimination issues. Their opposition has therefore been based upon their assumption—nurtured by many anti-ERA leaders—that the ERA is unnecessary because the Court can—indeed must—guarantee sex equality under the equal-protection clause of the Fourteenth Amendment and the due-process clause of the Fifth Amendment, among other existing constitutional provisions. And, of course, with the additional thirty-nine months allotted by Congress for the ratification process to go forward, the amendment cannot be said to have been rejected by the American people.[97]

In 1970, testifying in support of the ERA before the United

States Senate Judiciary Committee. I stated that, "even after the adoption of the Equal Rights Amendment, the crucial factor will continue to be the responsiveness of the judiciary to the social impulse toward equal treatment without regard to sex."[98] I continue to believe that. The need for intensive political activity seeking equal treatment without regard to sex will be as crucial in the years ahead as it has been in the past. Such activity will obviously occur on many fronts. But what better rallying point to guarantee that such activity will be sustained than the continued efforts on behalf on the ERA.

Above all, it is crucial that such activity be intensified by those who understand the fundamental issue as being one of ending discrimination against *women and men* solely because of their sex. They should make sure that the American public understands the issue in these terms, rather than as one involving a battle of the sexes. At the same time, they should take care not to becloud the remaining months of the ERA campaign with issues—no matter how meritorious they might be in their own right—that are extraneous to the ERA's fundamental aims and that unnecessarily deter potential allies from joining in the campaign.

If this is done, we can look forward with some confidence to the creation of a truly sex-neutral society in our country that will inspire the rest of the world; a society in which the original promise of America's greatness will have come much closer to fulfillment; a society in which, because of the demonstrated relationship between rigid sex-role stratification and the tendency toward human aggression,[99] family relations will be improved, crime and delinquency diminished, and violent solutions to disputes between nations less likely to be sought.

8

The Equal Rights Movement: Shortcomings and Future Prospects

In an earlier chapter, I examined what I believed had gone right, and what had gone wrong, in the campaign to ratify the Equal Rights Amendment. I now offer some further reflections about aspects of the feminist movement of recent years that have been particularly thought-provoking. Though it is probably unnecessary, it should be stressed that my perspective is that of a person who has applauded most of the efforts and activities of that movement, and has in numerous ways participated in it himself, while sometimes finding himself disappointed, if not chagrined, by certain of its occasional manifestations.

To speak of "the" feminist movement is probably misleading. In the last fifteen years, numerous groups, reflecting diverse political and ideological tendencies, have claimed with varying degrees of justification to be in the vanguard of feminism. Not only are representatives of the major political parties—the Democratic and Republican—represented in these groups, so are many others: socialists, communists, and other varieties of Marxists. Some participants in "the" feminist movement are avowedly homosexual in their own behavior, and often identify the establishment of homosexual rights, and especially the rights of Lesbians, to be the movement's most important goal. Some female participants are decidedly antimale in their orientation.

The great diversity of views represented in the feminist movement suggests that not every action undertaken in the name of feminism represents the will of all the movement's participants, or even of a majority of them. As a result, some of the activities of "the movement" described and criticized below often may be the work of only a small segment of that movement. At other times, howev-

er, those activities are either engaged in or supported by many of
the movement's adherents.

THE BOYCOTT OF THE STATES THAT FAILED
TO RATIFY THE ERA

As described elsewhere in this volume, for the proposed Equal
Rights Amendment to become part of the federal Constitution, it
must be ratified by July 1982 by three-fourths (that is, thirty-eight)
of the fifty state legislatures. To date, only thirty-five states have
ratified the amendment, and among these, several have since purported to rescind those ratifications, an act of doubtful constitutional validity.

The failure of fifteen state legislatures to ratify the ERA thus far
has not been the result of a lack of effort on the part of the amendment's supporters. In each of those states, the ratification issue has
come up repeatedly before the respective state legislatures, following the holding of hearings before appropriate committees at which
the amendment's supporters and opponents were given an opportunity to express their views. Traditional lobbying outside the formal hearings on the question has also been conducted by those
who support or oppose ratification by the respective states. While
in some instances the votes not to ratify were close, the fact remains that no state legislature has voted to ratify the amendment
since January 1977, when the Indiana legislature, after a hard-
fought campaign, did so.

Undaunted, ERA proponents have vowed to persevere in their
efforts to achieve ERA ratification. Aside from continued lobbying
and testifying at legislative hearings on the question, they have
adopted a variety of other tactics. These include seeking the electoral defeat of state representatives and senators who, by their
earlier votes, evinced hostility to the amendment, and their re-
placement through the electoral process by representatives whose
campaign promises suggest that they would support the amendment when it again comes before the legislature. They also sought
to enlist the aid of former President Carter and his administration
to exert influence upon various state legislative bodies to persuade
them to support the amendment.

One technique employed by ERA supporters, and specifically

by the National Organization for Women (NOW), has evoked much controversy and some litigation. NOW has practiced, and urged other groups to practice, an economic boycott of those states that have failed to ratify the amendment, as a means of pressuring them to do so. The principal manifestations of that boycott have involved the decisions of various organizations of scholars, professionals, and others, either to refuse to schedule conferences and conventions in nonratifying states, or to cancel previous commitments to do so. Many organizations, such as the American Political Science Association and the AFL-CIO have participated in the boycott, while some, such as the American Psychiatric Association, have decided, after much internal debate, to honor previous commitments to hold conventions in states that have not ratified the amendment.

The thinking of the boycott organizers appears to be based on the longstanding practice of the organized labor movement to launch consumer boycotts against the products of manufacturers with whom labor organizations have disputes, as a means of exerting additional economic pressure on those employers to settle the disputes on the terms desired by the labor oganizations. If a nonratifying state, such as Louisiana, Missouri, or Arizona, is made to feel the economic pressure of nonscheduled or cancelled conferences or of reduced tourism in the state, the argument runs, those states' legislators will soon be led to vote for ERA ratification, not necessarily because they now understand the amendment's merits, but to remove the economic pressure.

Shortly after the economic boycott started, the attorney general of Missouri, one of the boycotted nonratifying states, sued the National Organization for Women, claiming that the boycott violated the federal antitrust laws that prohibit conspiracies in restraint of trade. This suit proved unsuccessful, the United States District Court in Missouri[1] and the Eighth Circuit Court of Appeals,[2] in decisions left undisturbed by the United States Supreme Court,[3] holding that the NOW boycott represented a form of protected political activity that was exempted from coverage under the antitrust laws.

That the boycott is lawful does not, however, mean that it is wise. In fact, this technique may ultimately return to haunt proponents of sex equality in the law in ways that are yet unforeseen and unimagined.

To the extent that the economic boycott finds its inspiration in the labor boycott, important differences between the two techniques should be emphasized. In a labor boycott, members of the public who sympathize with the demands of the striking union will withhold their purchases of products that are produced by the employer with whom the labor organization has a dispute. It is not likely, however, that other members of the public who oppose the strikers' position or demands will express their views by increasing their purchases of the struck product. By contrast, in an economic boycott based on ideological grounds and aimed at pressuring a state legislature to ratify the ERA, there is always a real possibility that those holding an opposite ideological position could resort to the same technique to produce a political result that they desire.

An experience of the San Francisco Board of Supervisors illustrates how the economic boycott as a means of inducing political action, once it is unleashed, can be used to further any ideological cause. Because of that body's expression of support for the United Farm Workers in their labor struggles with the agricultural growers of California, the American Farm Bureau, consisting of growers from California and other states, which had reserved 6,000 San Francisco hotel rooms and was slated to spend more than $5 million in San Francisco, abruptly cancelled its scheduled convention in that city. That anti-ERA groups have not organized a retaliatory economic boycott of states that have ratified the ERA is probably due in large part to the great doubt as to whether a state's efforts at rescinding its earlier ratifications has any efficacy in law.

The traditional labor boycott and the economic boycott of nonratifying states are distinguishable for still another basic reason. The labor boycott is normally tied to a strike at the premises of the employer whose products are being boycotted. The boycott is organized only as an additional form of economic pressure, in addition to that already exerted by the strike itself, upon the employer with whom the dispute exists. If the boycott succeeds, the demand for that employer's products will decrease. This will cause economic harm to be suffered not only by that employer, but also by that employer's employees. The resultant economic harm to those employees is, however, neither unforeseen nor extraordinary. In many ways, it resembles the economic harm that they inflict upon themselves when they engage in a strike and deprive themselves of their regular earnings. The harm to the employees from the strike and from the boycott are voluntarily incurred, indeed encouraged, because it is the inevitable result of their efforts to impose severe economic harm on their employer to "bring him to his senses." When consumers withhold purchases of products manufactured or produced by the employer with whom a group of employees or a labor organization has a labor dispute, it is because those employees or that organization have requested that kind of "assistance" knowing that it will harm them as well.

This is not the case with the economic boycott of nonratifying states. To be sure, if an organization such as NOW or the American Historical Association or the Society of American Law Teachers decides, only because the state has not ratified the ERA, not to hold its annual convention in Arizona or Louisiana or Missouri, great harm may be caused the state's economy. Proprietors of hotels, transportation companies, entertainment industries, restaurants, and other enterprises that cater to the convention or tourist trade will suffer, as will their employees and the families of their employees. But unlike the labor organization and its members who have asked others to engage in a boycott, these groups have not as a rule made such a request. Many of the adversely affected owners and employees of the industries injured by the economic boycott are, moreover, likely to be ERA supporters, including some who have made that support known to their elected representatives. It is also probable that in many cases, their support of the amendment, as is true of much of the support and the opposition to it nationwide,[4] is not based on a profound knowledge of the amendment's import and effects; it is the kind of support that in the political arena is often characterized as "soft."

In the light of such considerations, it would not be surprising if the economic boycott of nonratifying states, indiscriminately harming pro- and anti-ERA residents of those states—and especially when requests for such boycotts have not emanated from anyone within those states—might have hardened existing opposition to the amendment and turned some "soft" supporters into opponents. How much more effective it would have been had the groups supporting the ERA proceeded with their original plans to hold conventions in the nonratifying states, and taken advantage of their temporary presence there to engage in the available forms of local political activity and publicity aimed at convincing the local populations to persuade their legislators to ratify the amendment.

Boycotting the nonratifying states is, in my view, an ill-conceived and counterproductive tactic. Energies and funds expended in organizing such a boycott are much better spent in efforts at positive rather than negative persuasion. Americans are not likely to change their opinions on matters of political and ideological importance as a result of coercion or pressure. Such tactics are more likely to engender opposition where none existed before, and to stiffen any opposition that was there already.

THE ANTIPORNOGRAPHY CAMPAIGN

At various times in the last decade, some groups of women have engaged in what can only be described as vigilante tactics aimed at destroying the presses that print "pornographic" matter or at harassing theater owners who display allegedly pornographic films or present "obscene" shows.[5] The purported justifications for such actions have been diverse, but they usually encompass the following arguments: Pornography is sexist. It exploits women. It provokes male sexual aggression against the female. It degrades and humiliates women. It creates an atmosphere in which men believe they are justified in violating women's personalities and bodies.

The argument that exposure to pornography provokes males into antifemale sexual aggression has been largely refuted by the report of the United States President's Commission on Obscenity and Pornography of September 1970. Following extensive studies of the subject by groups of behavioral scientists, twelve of the eighteen members of the commission supported the basic recommendation that "federal, state and local legislation prohibiting the sale, exhibition and distribution of sexual materials to consenting adults should be repealed."[6] The commission's majority report also concluded, in its section on the effects of explicit sexual material, that, "in general, established patterns of sexual behavior were found to be very stable and not altered substantially by exposure to erotica. When sexual activity occurred following the viewing or reading of these materials, it constituted a temporary activation of individual's preexisting patterns of sexual behavior."[7] In addition, "Exposure to erotic stimuli appears to have little or no effect on already established attitudinal commitments regarding either sexuality or sexual morality."[8] On pornography's effects upon criminal and delinquent behavior, the commission concluded that "empirical research designed to clarify the question has found no evidence to date that exposure to explicit sexual materials plays a significant role in the causation of delinquent or criminal behavior among youth or adults. The Commission cannot conclude that exposure to erotic materials is a factor in the causation of sex crime or sex delinquency."[9]

That much of what is classifiable as "pornography" or "obscenity" (a difficult legal concept that has troubled members of the United States Supreme Court from the time of the *Roth* decision)[10] exploits women and tends to degrade and humiliate them is much more demonstrable. While many films, books, and other expressions of art and ideas might properly be described as "erotic"—simply displaying graphically intimate sexual behavior, without members of one sex dominating or displaying aggression toward the other—many depict the female, not as the equal sexual partner of the male, but rather as the male's sexual victim. Such displays concededly promote or reinforce the notion that the female's primary function in life is to serve the male in every sphere, including the sexual.

The message contained in this kind of "pornography" is clearly objectionable to anyone who believes in the principle of sex equality. But so are other messages frequently found in plays, movies, novels, works of nonfiction, and the like. One may object to any of these works because they depict poor people, blacks, millionaires, business executives, foreigners, Southerners, Jews, Italians, hockey players, Hollywood producers, or others in an unfavorable light. Numerous appropriate ways exist, however, for those objections to be registered. If advance notice of their contents is obtained, one can simply withhold one's patronage from those that are objectionable; i.e., not buy the book, or attend the film or play. Such advance notice can often be ensured by film and book critics who inform others of these materials' contents and of their own reactions to them.

But violent efforts to prevent the publication of objectionable matter, on the ground that it degrades or humiliates women, threaten a fundamental value in American life that is as important, if not more so, to proponents of equal rights without regard to sex—or even of women's rights alone—as it is to the rest of the American population. That value, freedom of expression, is guaranteed against governmental enforcement by state and federal constitutions. It is, moreover, an indispensable prerequisite to the achievement of a society and a world in which injustices based on the arbitrary assignment of sex roles will have been eliminated.

Participants in the sex-equality movement during the last two decades know that the thinking of many Americans on this subject has undergone a remarkable transformation. Whereas the notion of equality between the sexes is today widely, though not universally, accepted, proponents of such a notion in public fora or even in private conversations, were likely, as recently as fifteen years ago, to encounter vehement hostility from most men and many women.

Levels of outrage and resentment are difficult to compare. We do not know whether the offense taken by sex-equality opponents at the talk, or writing, about sex equality is always as intense as that taken by others at the antifemale message of much pornography. But surely, some antiequality advocates have been profoundly disturbed by books, articles, movies, television programs, and magazines that promote a view of the sexes and of their relationship that is opposed to their own. To admit the legitimacy of "vigilante" tactics by those who are affronted by antifemale pornography would, it seems clear, make it extremely difficult, if not impossible, to oppose similar tactics by those who reject with equal vehemence the idea of sex equality and who see in such an idea a threat to the very foundations of their existence.

If such violent reactions to the notion of sex equality are difficult for some to imagine—now that the benefits of the positive consciousness-raising impact of recent women's movement's activities have been realized—the point can be more readily demonstrated if one contemplates the still strong reactions of many Americans to efforts to establish the rights of homosexuals not to be discriminated against because of their sexual preferences. As suggested earlier, part of the diversity that characterizes the modern women's movement lies in the fact that a significant, and vocal, element of that movement has placed the rights of homosexuals, and more particularly of Lesbians, at the head of its agenda. While such an assigned priority, or even the appropriateness of a pro-Lesbian plank for the women's movement at all, can be debated, a reasona-

ble argument can be made that the strong antihomosexual sentiment in American society represents merely a specific reflection of
the idea of sex-role allocation, i.e., that women and men are expectd
to conform not only to different standards in their economic, famil-
ial, and social activities, but also in their sexual behavior.

Be that as it may, the fact remains that many Americans do
react strongly, and at times violently, to the notion of homosexual
rights. In the face of such a reality, it is as important for the
women's movement as for other groups in American society to
preserve and protect the right of all people to express ideas in
books, articles, films, and other media, no matter how offensive
those ideas may be to some people.

Freedom of expression in American society is a value to be
cherished and guarded. The correctness of our views will ultimately
be determined by how well they withstand competition from opposing ideas. They will never prevail simply because contrary ideas
are suppressed. Any illusions that they have prevailed under such
circumstances will be necesarily shortlived. What is more important is that, once we admit the legitimacy of suppressing others'
ideas because they disturb us—or even outrage us—we have necessarily conceded the legitimacy of their suppressing our own ideas
for the same reasons.

It should be stressed that in referring to "vigilante" tactics, I
have intended to distinguish between legitimate and nonlegitimate
activity. Protests against pornography, whether those protests are
by individuals, groups, or organizations—or by picketing, leafleting,
or demonstrating—are clearly examples of legitimate tactics. In
one form or another, they represent the exercise of freedom of
expression, which is guaranteed to protestors, as to others, by the
federal and state constitutions. The right of some to publish pornography is not diminished by recognition of the right of others
peacefully to protest, through their own speech, against such pornography or to urge others to withhold their patronage from the
purveyors of antifemale pornography. Entirely distinguishable,
however, are activities that go beyond mere forms of speech and
constitute harassment, violence, disruption, trespass—in short, what
I have referred to as "vigilante" tactics. Such tactics are not protected by any constitutional guarantees and are, as I have attempted
to demonstrate, antithetical to the values of freedom of expression.

Fortunately, the "vigilante" tactics of some elements of the women's movement have been confined to a few people and isolated instances. At the same time, because of their dramatic impact, they have received an inordinate amount of media coverage. All of us who cherish the fundamental goals of the women's movement must take heed that such tactics not be seized upon by its opponents as reflecting upon the movement as a whole, and as justification for employing similar tactics against efforts to express the ideas of the movement themselves.

THE FUTURE

As of this writing in mid-December 1980, the United States is preparing to change presidential administrations. Within a month, Jimmy Carter will have left the White House and Ronald Reagan will be the fortieth president of the United States. For the first time in twenty-five years, most United States senators will be members of the Republican party. In the House of Representatives, Republicans, while still a minority, will be close to the Democrats in the number of seats they hold, and can probably count on enough conservative Democrats to vote with them on issues of broad social policy to enable them to prevail in such areas.

What will this drastic change in the national political lineup mean for the future of the sex-equality movement? Will the gains of recent years be lost or strengthened? Will the ERA be ratified? Will new legislative initiatives in the area of equal rights be undertaken? And will the involvement of men in the sex-equality movement become less or more important than it has been in the past?

An overriding fact that must be taken into account in any assessment of future legislative and judicial trends is that the 1980 platform of the Republican party and the campaign statements of Ronald Reagan himself both opposed ratification of the ERA. In the case of the Republican platform, this represented a significant departure from that party's ERA position of prior years.

The electoral defeat of Jimmy Carter and Ronald Reagan's victory were obviously the result of many factors: a declining American economy, general frustration at America's inability to effect the release of the United States hostages in Teheran, the political activities of the self-styled Moral Majority, the debilitating effect of the Edward Kennedy challenge for the Democratic party nomination, and widespread yearnings among many American voters for new directions and initiatives in governmental policies.

At the same time, the conduct of certain sections of the American women's movement also undoubtedly contributed to the 1980 election results. When Carter was challenged by Kennedy for the Democratic nomination, for example, much of the organized women's movement threw its support to Kennedy. This occurred, despite Carter's outstanding record of appointing more women federal judges than all previous presidents combined, of appointing a record number of women to other high-level governmental positions, including three cabinet members, and of actively supporting the Equal Rights Amendment and new federal legislation aimed at ending sex discrimination in American law and society.

The claim by some women's movement leaders that Carter did not exert sufficient pressure on state legislatures to ratify the ERA misconceives, in my view, the appropriate relationship between the federal and state governments and, more particularly, between the United States president and members of state legislatures. If they ponder the possibility of President Reagan "pressuring" state legislators to ratify an antiabortion amendment—should such an amendment be proposed by Congress or by a constitutional convention during a Reagan administration—they would soon realize how inappropriate such a role is for a United States president.

Even after Carter won the Democratic party nomination—and although leading feminist political groups continued to voice their opposition to Reagan because of his anti-ERA stand—many still withheld their active support from Carter. While the failure to support Carter may merely have reflected the diversity of the women's movement, whose adherents included supporters of Edward Kennedy, John Anderson, and even Reagan, the fact remains that, when confronted with a real choice between an anti-ERA candidate and one whose record on equal rights, while concededly not perfect, had been outstanding, many of the influential and vocal members of the organized women's movement equivocated.

The significance for the equal-rights movement of a Ronald Reagan presidency and of the massive Republican gains in the 1980 elections is admittedly difficult to predict. For those who are optimistically inclined, Reagan's campaign statements that both his and the

Republican party's opposition to the ERA are not to be equated with opposition to the idea of equal rights for women might be taken at face value. Conceivably, therefore, new legislative initiatives aimed at improving the status of women in American law and society may very well emanate from the Reagan administration in the coming years.

The presence of only one woman—the United States representative to the United Nations—among the top Reagan cabinet, or cabinet-level appointees, does not bode particularly well for such a prospect, however. Moreover, if the sex-equality movement is understood as being aimed at ending sex discrimination, and not simply discrimination against women, the importance of ERA ratification becomes readily apparent. While, as indicated earlier, it would be inappropriate, in my opinion, for an American president to "pressure" state legislators to ratify the amendment, this does not mean that the negative pronouncements of Reagan and the Republican platform on the amendment will not have their effects. If nothing else, they establish a climate of opinion—quite different from the one prevailing under Carter—that stamps anti-ERA sentiment with political and social acceptability. Whatever the difficulties faced before the 1980 Republican victories in the efforts to obtain the ratification of the amendment by three additional states, these will be greatly compounded after those victories. With a Republican Senate majority and a Republican-conservative-Democrat House majority, congressional extension of the ratification deadline beyond the July 1982 date to which a Congress controlled by the Democratic Party had already extended the original ratification deadline, is highly unlikely. In sum, while proratification efforts will undoubtedly continue, prospects for ERA ratification have been greatly diminished by the recent turn of political events in the United States.

Despite such a forecast, other recent developments, and those that may soon occur in Supreme Court sex-discrimination cases, present a distinct possibility of significant, positive breakthroughs under existing constitutional provisions and enacted legislation. The 1980 decision of the Court in *Wengler v. Druggists Mutual Ins. Co.*,[11] invalidating on equal-protection grounds a state law that denied a widower benefits on his wife's work-related death unless he was either mentally or physically incapacitated or could prove dependence on his wife's earnings, but granted a widow death benefits without proof of dependence, is a case in point. By holding that the statute in question discriminated against both men and women, the Court moved significantly closer to recognizing the dual aspect of laws that purport to discriminate "benignly" and an ultimate repudiation of that doctrine, along the lines urged earlier in these pages.

Other cases now pending before the Court may also drastically affect the existing sex-discrimination jurisprudence of the Court. In *Minnick v. California Department of Corrections*,[12] the Court will be confronted with a decision of the California Court of Appeal upholding a preferential hiring policy favoring women and minorities in filling prison guards' positions. Aside from the opportunity it offers the Court of reexamining the "benign"-discrimination doctrine as it applies to the area of sex discrimination, *Minnick* also raises the question of whether a state may constitutionally grant preferences to a group, not because they had been the victims of past discrimination, but because of the "needs" of the groups they are to serve on their jobs. Similarly, *Michael M. v. Superior Court of Sonoma County*,[13] raises another equal-protection challenge to a sex-discriminatory rule of law. In *Michael M.*, a four-to-three majority of the California Supreme Court upheld that state's "statutory rape" law, under which only females can be victims and only males can be guilty of the crime. The United States Supreme Court's resolution of this question may tell us much about the future direction of court decisions affecting sex roles in American law and society.

Perhaps the most significant decision in this realm that the Court will decide in its present term is *Goldberg v. Rostker*.[14] In *Goldberg*, lower federal courts had invalidated the federal system of draft registration as a violation of the equal-protection component of Fifth Amendment due process because only males, and not females, were subject to it. Given the level of emotionalism surrounding the question of women and the draft, and its logical corollary, women in combat, and the fact that this has been the most troublesome issue surrounding the ERA debate from its inception, *Goldberg* may prove to be the Court's most important sex-discrimination case in its entire history. A determination by the Court that the male-only draft registration law violates the federal Constitution would undermine a principal argument of anti-ERA forces in American society, while paradoxically making ERA ratification, though still desirable, less crucial than it has heretofore been. By contrast, if the Court were to uphold the male-only draft, the position of ERA opponents would arguably be strengthened. Such a decision could also signal a drastic retreat from the Court's progressive sex-discrimination cases of recent years. Should that indeed be the import of such a decision, the need for ERA ratification would be heightened, rather than lessened.

The power of a United States president to nominate persons to fill vacancies on the United States Supreme Court, lower federal courts, and numerous federal agencies (such as the Equal Employment Opportunity Commission and the National Labor Relations Board) will undoubtedly be used by President Reagan in the same way it has been used by previous presidents. An effort to fill such positions with persons whose ideological convictions are compatible with the president's and those of the party in power will be made. Given the previous expressions of that ideology by Reagan and his party, the chances are great that equal rights efforts will face a difficult battle once the nominating and appointing powers have been exercised.

In the light of such prospects, it should be increasingly clear to all believers in the principle of equal treatment without regard to sex that the political success of the sex-equality movement requires the maximum participation of all Americans—men as well as women. Only if the greatest number of women and men are actively involved in seeking an end to the American legal system's arbitrary assignment of sex roles will the political authorities who now appear to be in the ascendant be persuaded to continue the progressive developments of the past fifteen years, and to improve upon those developments.

The overwhelming majority of participants in the women's movement have understood the common plight of women and men as victims of legal and social discrimination based on sex. Some participants in that movement have indicated, however, that they are either oblivious to the past and present victimization of men on the basis of sex, or if they are aware of such victimization, that they regard it as insignificant in comparison to the many and grievous complaints of women at the unjust treatment by the law and by society in general. The latter attitude, I have attempted to demonstrate, unnecessarily weakens the sex-equality movement. When those attitudes are reexamined and the movement's adherents effectively communicate to all Americans their understanding of the common plight of both sexes in American society and law, the political strength needed to overcome the temporary reverses of the 1980 elections will have been achieved.

Appendix

Can a State Rescind its Equal Rights Amendment Ratification: Who Decides and How*

On March 22, 1972, by a vote of 84 to 8,[1] the United States Senate adopted a joint resolution proposing the addition of the Equal Rights Amendment (ERA) to the United States Constitution.[2] This resolution was previously adopted by the House of Representatives by a vote of 354 to 24 on October 12, 1971.[3] Pursuant to the joint resolution's language, the proposed amendment must be ratified by at least three-fourths (thirty-eight) of the fifty state legislatures within seven years of the resolution's passage (i.e., by March 22, 1979) to become part of the Constitution.[4] If fewer than thirty-eight state legislatures have ratified by that date, the proponents of the ERA, should they wish to continue their efforts to add such an amendment to the Constitution, would have to start anew.

As of this writing, thirty-five states have ratified the ERA.[5] It would thus appear that only three more state legislative ratifications are needed by March 1979 to complete the ratification process and for the Amendment to become the twenty-seventh of the United States Constitution. A problem has arisen, however, with three of those state ratifications. Tennessee, Nebraska, and Idaho, having first ratified the Amendment, have since purported to rescind their earlier ratifications.[6] In addition, because of efforts exerted by the Amendment's opponents, further rescissions could occur by March 22, 1979.[7] As a result of these developments, to

*This appendix is a slightly revised version of an article entitled *Can a State Rescind Its Equal Rights Amendment Ratification: Who Decides and How?* 28 HASTINGS L. J. 979 (1977) by Leo Kanowitz and Marilyn Klinger. Copyright © 1977 by Hastings College of the Law. Reprinted with permission.

achieve the requisite thirty-eight state ratifications, the final count may have to include one or more states that first ratified and subsequently attempted to rescind their ratifications.

The above problem raises two initial questions. First, which branch of the federal government is to decide whether those rescinded ratifications should be included in the final count—the United States Supreme Court or the United States Congress? Second, how should the substantive issue be resolved on the merits?

It is possible that, when March 22, 1979, arrives, the questions posed herein will have been mooted by events. Conceivably, in view of the strong support evinced for the ERA by President Carter (and increased efforts by ERA supporters),[8] more than thirty-eight unrescinded state legislative ratifications will have occurred by then, obviating the need to include any rescinded ratifications in the count.[9] On the other hand, the ERA may encounter hard times in the next few years. Voter rejection of proposed state equal rights amendments to the New York and New Jersey constitutions in November 1975[10] suggests that new state legislative ratifications of ERA may be difficult to attain. As a result of such setbacks and widespread apprehensions, unfounded as they might be, that the proposed Amendment portends a disruption of familiar life patterns, the nation may have to confront the problem suggested above: whether states that have withdrawn their earlier ratifications are to be counted as having ratified the Amendment when the final tally is made.

Our conclusions are as follows: (1) the United States Supreme Court, rather than Congress, is the branch of government to decide the question of rescindability, as this is a justiciable issue and not a political question; (2) a state, once having ratified the ERA, may not rescind, and any purported rescission by a state is of no legal effect; (3) even if the Court should decide that the issue is nonjusticiable, that is, one to be decided by Congress rather than the Court, Congress should count all state ratifications of the ERA without regard to subsequent efforts to rescind.

ARTICLE V OF THE CONSTITUTION

The amending process of the federal Constitution is set forth in article V.[11] The article provides for two alternative methods of initiating proposed amendments and two alternative methods for ratifying them. An amendment can be, and all twenty-six existing amendments have been, initiated upon adoption of a joint resolution by a two-thirds vote of each house of Congress. The second method, which has never been employed, authorizes Congress, upon application from two-thirds of the state legislatures, to convoke a national convention for proposing amendments.[12] If an amendment is ultimately proposed, either by joint resolution or convention, such amendment

shall be valid to all Intents and Purposes, as Part of [the] Constitution, when ratified by the Legislatures of three fourths of the several States, or by Conventions in three fourths thereof, as the one or the other Mode of Ratification may be proposed by the Congress. . . .[13]

In other words, Congress proposes the ratification method[14] and upon ratification by three-fourths of the states—either by legislative decree or by convention—the amendment becomes a part of the Constitution.

JUSTICIABILITY VS. POLITICAL QUESTION

Marbury v. Madison: The Classic Theory of Judicial Review

In 1803, Chief Justice John Marshall wrote the decision in *Marbury v. Madison*[15] in which he declared: "[I]t is emphatically the province and duty of the judicial department to say what the law is. . . . The judicial power of the United States is extended to all cases arising under the constitution."[16] In the light of this unequivocal statement of principle, it would seem that any case or controversy arising under article V of the Constitution is subject to judicial review, i.e., justiciable. Indeed, from 1798 to 1939 the Supreme Court agreed.

Prior to 1939

Before 1939, the United States Supreme Court consistently held that issues relating to the amendment of the federal Constitution were clearly justiciable. Five of the justices who joined in the opinion of the Court in *Hollingsworth v. Virginia*,[17] holding that presidential approval was not required in the constitutional amending process, had been involved directly in the conception and birth of the Constitution.[18] These five justices presumed without discussion that article V issues were subject to judicial review.

The nineteenth-century courts were not faced with the present question. But in the early 1920s four cases decided by the Supreme Court dealt specifically with article V. In *Hawke v. Smith*[19] the Court invalidated an Ohio constitutional provision requiring submittal of proposed United States constitutional amendments to popular referendum because it did not accord with the term "legislatures" in article V. The Court stressed:

> [R]atification by a State of a constitutional amendment is not an act of legislation within the proper sense of the word.
>   [T]he power to ratify a proposed amendment to the Federal Constitution has its source in the Federal Constitution.[20]

The validity of the procedures used to exercise this power was a question arising under the Constitution. Hence, judicial review was based on article III, section 2.[21]

In the *National Prohibition Cases* in 1920,[22] the Court interpreted the language of article V, "two-thirds of both Houses," to mean two-thirds of the members present and voting of a quorum. *Dillon v. Gloss*,[23] decided the following year, held that a congressionally imposed seven-year limit within which the states could ratify an amendment was reasonable and "that the fair inference or implication from Article V is that the ratification *must* be within some reasonable time after the proposal."[24] In 1922, the Court in *Leser v. Garnett*[25] judged the ratifications of the Nineteenth Amendment by Missouri, Tennessee, and West Virginia effective, although state constitutional and procedural provisions allegedly rendered the ratifications inoperative.[26] In addition, in *United States v. Sprague*,[27] the Court held that the choice between ratification by state legislature or by convention was within the discretion of Congress, rejecting the argument that ratification by convention was constitutionally required because the Eighteenth Amendment dealt with "powers over individuals."[28] That the Court unhesitatingly decided the issues presented by these cases suggests that the justiciability of questions arising from the amending process was, in the Court's view, a self-evident truth.[29] In 1939, however, the Supreme Court decided a case that seemed to change all that had preceded it.

Coleman v. Miller: Dictum or Law?

Coleman v. Miller,[30] or more precisely, language in that case, raises the principal obstacle to any conclusion that the United States Supreme Court, rather than Congress, is the ultimate arbiter of the effectiveness of purported state withdrawals of earlier ERA ratifications.

The issue of *Coleman v. Miller* arose from the absence of a deadline date for ratification of the proposed Child Labor Amendment[31] submitted by Congress in 1924. In 1925 the Kansas legislature rejected the proposed amendment and so certified to the United States secretary of state. Twelve years later the Kansas Senate, with the aid of a tie-breaking vote from the state's lieutenant governor, voted to ratify that same previously rejected amendment. The Kansas House of Representatives followed suit.

Almost immediately thereafter a suit was brought in the Supreme Court of Kansas by members of the Kansas Senate challenging the Kansas legislature's action on grounds that, inter alia, the proposed amendment had lost its vitality because of the previous rejections by Kansas and other states and the undue length of time the amendment had awaited ratification. The state's supreme court upheld the ratification,[32] and certiorari was granted by the United States Supreme Court.[33]

The Court initially discussed the previous congressional treatment of ratifications following rejections and also withdrawals of previous ratifications of constitutional amendments, noting that Congress had determined that neither rejections nor withdrawals have any effect.[34] The Court then concluded:

[T]he question of the efficacy of ratifications by state legislatures, *in the light of previous rejection or attempted withdrawal*, should be regarded as a political question pertaining to the political departments, with the ultimate authority in the Congress . . . .[35]

It is important to note that the Court in *Coleman* was presented only with the justiciability of the Kansas legislature's attempt at ratification following an earlier rejection of the Child Labor Amendment.[36] Its language regarding the justiciability of cases involving *rescission* of ratification went beyond the immediate issue presented to it. Nevertheless *Coleman v. Miller* was the first (and only) decision to announce that purported state withdrawals of earlier ratifications and state ratifications of earlier rejected amendments presented nonjusticiable political questions, though dictum in the 1849 case of *Luther v. Borden* [37] had hinted that this might be the case. [38]

In *Coleman,* the Court stated two reasons for finding the ratification-rescission question a political one. First, Congress had previously made the determination as to the effectiveness of subsequent action. Second, the Court saw no constitutional or statutory basis for judicial interference. [39] The first reason seems to be a classic example of mistaking the familiar for the necessary. [40] The second reason is also questionable, since, as Professor Orfield has observed, "there were no stronger constitutional or statutory bases for the decisions rendered" [41] in *Dillon v. Gloss, Leser v. Garnett,* or any of the numerous other cases arising under article V.

Moreover, an examination of the vote in *Coleman* reveals that four concurring justices insisted, inter alia, that article V matters were political and were therefore never justiciable. [42] Three justices would have limited nonjusticiability to the narrow facts of the case: ratification by a state when the same amendment had been earlier rejected by that state. [43] Two dissenters regarded the article V issues raised in *Coleman* as susceptible to judicial determination, since *Dillon v. Gloss* had adjudicated similar issues without hesitation. [44] *Coleman v. Miller* can therefore be viewed, in spite of its far-ranging dictum, as leaving open the question whether the purported rescission of a state's earlier ratification of a constitutional amendment is a justiciable matter.

A showing that *Coleman's* treatment of purported withdrawals of state ratifications of constitutional amendments is dictum has no impact if it is determined that its finding of nonjusticiability as to rejection-ratification issues logically compels a finding of nonjusticiability as to ratification-rescission issues. Indeed, this poses a considerable problem. The *Coleman* Court's conclusion that the effect of a previous rejection of a subsequent ratification is nonjusticiable was based on a historical survey showing that either Congress or its delegatee, the secretary of state, [45] had always made the determination whether enough states had ratified a proposed amendment to make it law. The *Coleman* Court apparently felt that determining the effect of a prior rejection on a state's ratification was part of the process of counting up the number of states ratifying an amendment. If this is true, the effect of a purported withdrawal of ratification would also seem part of the same process.

There is a way to overcome this hurdle. We have said that the *Coleman* Court's statement that the effect of a purported withdrawal of a ratification by a state is dictum. It is also possible to view as dictum the Court's statement on the justiciability of the direct problem presented to them—the effect of a rejection on a subsequent ratification.

This view derives from the second holding of *Coleman v. Miller:* that Congress has the power to declare a proposed amendment no longer viable and to refuse recognition of its ratification if too much time has passed since the amendment was originally proposed. In *Coleman,* there was clearly great doubt as to whether the Child Labor Amendment was still viable after thirteen years. In fact, two dissenting justices [46] insisted that the amendment was indeed no longer viable. Thus it may have been unnecessary for the Court to determine the effect of a prior rejection on a state's ratification since in fact the question might have been moot in light of the nonviability of the Child Labor Amendment. Therefore, even the language in *Coleman* pertaining to the nonjusticiability of the rejection-ratification issue can be considered dictum not necessary to the disposition of the case. [47]

When a rejection-ratification issue relating to an amendment that is *clearly* still viable is presented to the Supreme Court, then the Court will be free to determine the question directly, unfettered by any direct and inevitable holding of the *Coleman v. Miller* decision. If Congress continues its practice of requiring ratification within seven years, [48] the Court will be presented *only* with ratification issues relating to viable amendments, as is the case in the present ERA controversy.

Baker v. Carr

The contours of the political question doctrine have taken on new dimensions in recent Supreme Court decisions, most notably in the landmark case of *Baker v. Carr.* [49]

In *Baker v. Carr*, plaintiffs, state voters, asserted that their state legislature was apportioned in a manner violating the Fourteenth Amendment's equal-protection guarantee. Attacks on malapportion-

ment had been mounted before 1962, both on the basis of the
equal-protection clause and on the basis of the "republican form of
government" guarantee of article IV, section 4. These attacks had
been uniformly rejected on the ground that legislative apportionment was a question involving the allocation of political power and
was not justiciable in the courts.

The Court in *Baker v. Carr,* however, decided for the first time
that the equal-protection claim presented by malapportionment
should indeed be justiciable,[50] and while *Baker v. Carr* is generally regarded as a landmark equal-protection case, it is important
for present purposes because of the majority opinion's survey of
past Supreme Court decisions on the justiciability-political question issue,[51] followed by a succinct restatement of the present state
of the law on this question:

Prominent on the surface of any case held to involve a political question is
found a textually demonstrable constitutional commitment of the issue to
a coordinate political department; or a lack of judicially discoverable and
manageable standards for resolving it; or the impossibility of deciding
without an initial policy determination of a kind clearly for nonjudicial
discretion; or the impossibility of a court's undertaking independent resolution without expressing lack of respect due coordinate branches of government; or an unusual need for unquestioning adherence to a political
decision already made; or the potentiality of embarrassment from multifarious pronouncements by various departments on one question.[52]

The Court then observed:

Unless one of [the above] formulations is inextricable from the case at bar,
there should be no dismissal for nonjusticiability on the ground of a
political question's presence. The doctrine of which we treat is one of
"political questions," not one of "political cases."[53]

Applying this new test to the equal-protection challenge to the
malapportioned state legislature in *Baker* itself, the Court concluded
that the case could be decided on the merits.[54]

A careful reading of the *Baker* tests for determining the presence
or absence of a political question suggests that they are by no
means free of ambiguity. These guidelines leave much room for the
exercise of judicial discretion in their application to specific factual
situations. Their production of the *Baker* result on the merits is

probably best explained by the practical need for the Court to act in the malapportionment situation, since, for a variety of reasons, most notably a revulsion from the idea of committing political suicide, no other branch of government was likely to act under the circumstances.

Powell v. McCormack

If the Court took the bold step that it did in *Baker v. Carr* because, in the absence of judicial action, no other body could or would do anything to remedy the inequities in state legislative apportionment, the Court's resolution of the political question—justiciability dispute in *Powell v. McCormack*[55] cannot be explained on such pragmatic grounds. In that case, Adam Clayton Powell, a member of the United States House of Representatives, was denied his seat in the House[56] by over a two-thirds vote of his colleagues. Powell had been accused of engaging in misconduct both related and unrelated to his governmental duties as representative and committee chairman. In the appeal by Powell and voters of his congressional district following suit seeking reinstatement of Powell to his House seat, the respondents, members and custodians of the House of Representatives, contended, inter alia, that the decision to exclude Powell was supported by the expulsion power in article I, section 5[57] of the federal Constitution. That power, respondents argued, allowed the House to expel a member for reasons set forth by that body. Respondents also maintained that the issue was not justiciable because it involved a political question.

The Court, in holding that Powell was improperly excluded from his membership in the House and requiring that he be permitted to take his rightful place in that body, concluded that the case did not involve a political question but that, on the contrary, it presented a justiciable issue.[58] Specifically, the Court's extended examination of relevant historical materials.[59] revealed that congressional power, under article I. section 5, to judge the qualifications of its members was "at most a 'textually demonstrable commitment' to Congress to judge *only* the qualifications expressly set forth in the Constitution,"[60] those requirements of age, citizenship, and residence contained in article I, section 2.[61] As a result, concluded the Court, the House was without the power to exclude a member-elect who met the Constitution's requirements.[62]

The *Powell* decision is especially significant in that it reflects an awareness on the part of the Court that the American "system of government requires that federal courts on occasion interpret the Constitution in a manner at variance with the construction given the document by another branch."[63] In the Court's view:

Such a determination falls within the traditional role accorded courts to interpret the law and does not involve a "lack of the respect due [a] coordinate [branch] of government," nor does it involve an "initial policy determination of a kind clearly for nonjudicial discretion."[64]

The Present Mood of the Court: Justice Powell, an Illustration

The opinion in *Powell* not only recognized the essential role of the Court as the ultimate interpreter of the meaning of constitutional language, it also signaled the Court's reassertion of its supremacy within its own sphere and of its right to exercise its constitutional prerogatives, especially in relation to Congress.

Powell v. McCormack, moreover, appears to be a sound application of *Baker's* constitutional test for justiciability. At the same time, it evokes a mood of judicial activism,[65] a willingness to reach out to resolve social issues that other branches of government ignored.[66] Although in *Baker* the Court asserted that "[t]he non-justiciability of a political question is primarily a function of the separation of powers,"[67] derived directly from the Constitution, there is so much room for discretionary manipulation of the *Baker* tests that one cannot help suspecting that a finding by the Court of the presence of a political question, like its determination of such related questions as standing, ripeness, or mootness, may often reflect attitudes of members of the Court on the appropriate role of the federal judiciary in the American political system rather than the application of the *Baker* tests to new factual situations.

Except for a few of its holdover members, the present Supreme Court, which may confront the question of the justiciability of ERA ratification withdrawals, clearly harbors different judicial philosophies from the activist Warren Court.[68] The growing influence of Justice Powell, one of the newer members of the Court, on recent standing issues reflects the Court's increasing tendency to embrace the virtues of judicial self-restraint over the activism of the Warren era. To be sure, in one sense standing implicates different concerns than those raised by the political-question doctrine.[69] Yet the Court has noted that they are both aspects of the fundamental problem of justiciability.[70]

That is why Justice Powell's views, first expressed in a concurring opinion in *United States v. Richardson*[71] and later adopted as the prevailing view of the Court in *Warth v. Seldin*,[72] reveal much about the Court's present mood with respect to its relationship with Congress when collisions between them are in the offing.

Richardson was a mandamus action by a federal taxpayer to compel the secretary of the treasury to publish an accounting of the receipts and expenditures of the Central Intelligence Agency and to enjoin any further publication of a consolidated statement that did not reflect its receipts and expenditures. The taxpayer asserted standing to bring the action based on the allegation that Congress had violated article I, section 9, clause 7[73] of the Constitution.

The majority opinion, delivered by Chief Justice Burger, held the taxpayer had failed to bring himself within the scope of the standing requirements of *Flast v. Cohen.*[74] The taxpayer's challenge was not addressed to the taxing or spending power, but to the statutes regulating the CIA's accounting and reporting procedures; there was, consequently, no "logical nexus" between his status as "taxpayer" and the Congress's alleged failure to require more detailed reports of the CIA's expenditures.[75] The Court also rejected the respondent's assertion that he was aggrieved by the CIA's failure to account because he did not satisfactorily "show that he *has sustained or is immediately in danger of sustaining a direct injury* as the result of that action."[76]

Mr. Justice Powell concurred in the *Richardson* result, while rejecting, because of its own illogic,[77] the Court's adherence to the "logical-nexus" test for taxpayer standing developed in *Flast v. Cohen.* That illogic had been underscored in *Flast* itself both by Justice Harlan,[78] a leading proponent of judicial self-restraint, and by Justice Douglas,[79] the activist nonpareil.

What makes Justice Powell's concurrence in *Richardson* significant for present purposes is his express rationale for agreeing with the result. According to Justice Powell:

Relaxation of standing requirements is directly related to the expansion of judicial power. . . . [A]llowing unrestricted taxpayer or citizen standing would significantly alter the allocation of power at the national level, with a shift away from a democratic form of government. . . . [R]epeated and essentially head-on confrontations between the life-tenured branch and the representative branches of government will not, in the long run, be beneficial to either. The public confidence essential to the former and the vitality critical to the latter may well erode if we do not exercise self-restraint in the utilization of our power to negative the actions of the other branches.[80]

Furthermore, Justice Powell emphasized that the Court was the "insulated judicial branch"[81] of the federal government. Allowing unrestricted taxpayer or citizen standing, he stated, "underestimates the ability of the representative branches of the Federal Government to respond to the citizen pressure that has been responsible in large measure for the concurrent drift toward expanded standing."[82] Justice Powell concluded that the Court "should limit the expansion of federal taxpayer and citizen standing in the absence of specific statutory authorization to an outer boundary drawn by the *results* in *Flast* and *Baker v. Carr.*"[83] Taxpayer and citizen suits, he stressed, were attempts "to employ a federal court as a forum in which to air . . . generalized grievances about the conduct of government or the allocation of power in the Federal System."[84] The Court, he asserted, should affirm "traditional prudential barriers" to disallow such use of the federal judiciary.

By 1975, the philosophical perspective of Justice Powell, revealed in his *Richardson* concurrence, had become the perspective of a Court majority, as expressed in the *Warth v. Seldin*[85] opinion written by Justice Powell himself. In *Warth,* various petitioners had sought declaratory and injunctive relief and damages against a town and members of its zoning, planning, and town boards, claiming that the town's zoning ordinance excluded persons of low and moderate income from living in the town, thereby violating petitioners' constitutional and statutory rights.[86]

The opinion examined the relationships of the different petitioners to the allegations set forth and then tested those relationships against standing principles, concluding, to the dismay of the dissent,[87] that none of the petitioners had sustained a claim to standing.

Justice Powell for the majority emphasized that standing requirements stem not only from constitutional dictates, but also from "prudential" considerations, thereby reiterating his views in the *Richardson* concurrence.[88] Powell insisted that in both its constitutional and prudential dimensions, standing "is founded in concern about the proper—and properly limited—role of the Courts in a democratic society."[89]

The acquiescence by a majority of the Burger court in *Warth v. Seldin* to the notion that the standing doctrine is based as much, if not more, upon nonconstitutional "prudential" considerations as upon the dictates of the constitutional separation-of-powers doctrine discloses a mood of the Court in 1976 that is markedly different from what it was at the time it rendered its opinions in *Baker v. Carr* (1962), *Flast v. Cohen* (1968), and *Powell v. McCormack* (1969). The Court's willingness to respect congressional authority as evidenced by Powell's language in *Richardson*[90] and *Warth*[91] is diametrically opposed to the aggressive assertion of judicial prerogatives in the political question arena in *Baker* and *Powell*.[92]

As a result of these developments, it is not unlikely that the Court, as currently constituted, may be less willing than in the past to resolve the present ERA justiciability issue in a manner that precludes Congress from making a determination allegedly committed to it by the Constitution.

On the other hand, despite such current philosophical tendencies on the Court, the *Baker v. Carr* test remains its most authoritative doctrinal definition of a nonjusticiable political question. As will be demonstrated subsequently, applying that political-question test to the ERA rescindability issue points almost ineluctably to a conclusion of justiciability.

The *Baker v. Carr* Test

Some phases of the *Baker* test can be disposed of as being clearly inapplicable to the question at hand. For example, the "potentiality of embarrassment from multifarious pronouncements by various departments on one question"[93] relates to the foreign-relations activities of the United States government[94] and is therefore irrelevant to the present issue. The same observation can be made with respect to "an unusual need for unquestioning adherence to a political decision already made,"[95] especially when, in the case of ERA ratification, *whether* a political decision has been made is precisely the point in question.

By contrast, other aspects of the *Baker* test are much more germane to the justiciability of the effect of a purported withdrawal by any state of its ERA ratification. One such aspect is "the impossibility of a court's undertaking independent resolution without expressing lack of the respect due coordinate branches of government."[96] The validity of a state's rescission attempt hinges on the meaning of the constitutional language "when ratified." It would seem that the Court's interpretation of this language is no more indicative of a lack of the respect due a coordinate branch of the federal government than are the frequently encountered invalidations of congressional legislation on grounds that the legislation exceeds constitutional authority.[97]

Nor does a decision by the Court whether a state may rescind its prior ratification of a pending constitutional amendment require "an initial policy determination of a kind clearly for nonjudicial discretion."[98] The only policy determination involved in this issue is that laid out by the framers of the Constitution, whose intentions have always been examined when the Court interprets constitutional language.

Another facet of the *Baker* test is "a lack of judicially discoverable and manageable standards" for resolving the issue.[99] But the Court would be able, through the process of interpreting constitutional language, to explicate the meaning of article V. The Court has always found such a standard manageable.[100]

Perhaps the most troublesome aspect of the *Baker* test is the "textually demonstrable constitutional commitment of the issue to a coordinate political department."[101] The existence and scope of such a commitment are matters to be resolved by the Court.[102] In *Powell v. McCormack*, the Court, while examining the "scope of any 'textual commitment' under Art. I, § 5,"[103] explored the historical background of the passage in question to determine the framers' intent. In the case of article V, there is sparse discussion in the Constitutional Convention debates; much of the recorded deliberation deals with Congress's role in proposing constitutional amendments rather than with their ratification.[104] After brief and sporadic debate on an amending article proposed by Edmund Randolph,[105] James Madison proposed an amending article virtually identical to the present article V, and following another day of debate, it and the entire Constitution were approved and signed.[106]

Thus, the Constitutional Convention debates shed little light upon the framers' intent regarding the phrase "when ratified."

Militating against a finding that the Constitution makes a textual commitment of amendment controversies to Congress are the indications that the framers were unwilling to leave the entire amending process within the exclusive control of Congress.[107] Article V requires amendments to be ratified by three-fourths of the states, and provides for an alternative means of amendment initiation through a convention on the application of two-thirds of the states.[108]

Chief Justice Warren, in *Powell*, explained that to determine whether there was a textual commitment, the Court must first discover if the Constitution has granted any power to Congress through the article and must then determine whether the exercise of that power is susceptible of judicial supervision.[109] In the light of the *Powell* decision, it is difficult to conclude that the effectiveness of state ratifications should be left to congressional determination. Arguably, such a conclusion might derive from the facts that one of the two ways of amendment initiation is through the federal legislative process and that, regardless of how an amendment is initiated, Congress determines its mode of ratification—by state legislature or by convention. The language of article V clearly limits Congress's powers, however, to: (1) proposing amendments, (2) calling a convention for proposing amendments when enough states so request, and (3) proposing the mode of ratification. There simply is no mention of congressional authority to interfere with the ratification process once the mode of ratification is chosen.

The present situation is remarkably similar to that of *Powell v. McCormack*, in which Congress's power with regard to *expulsion* of a member was limited to the specific qualifications of age and residency and therefore did not extend a right to *exclude* a member for alleged misconduct. In other words, the Court interpreted the phrase, "Each House shall be the Judge of the . . . Qualifications of its own Members"[110] to be limited to those standing qualifications set out in article I, section 2, clause 2;[111] that is, only congressional judgment as to the standing qualifications was held to be a textually demonstrable commitment to Congress.

The textually demonstrable commitment in the constitutional amendment process is similarly limited to proposing amendments, calling a convention should two-thirds of the states so request, and specifying one of the two modes of ratifying. At most, one can infer additional congressional power to propose only incidental regulations to carry out that commitment. Nor is this proposed application of the textual commitment phase of the *Baker* test incompatible with the result in *Coleman v. Miller*.[112] If the dictum in that case is disregarded, as it should be, it is clear that *Coleman* decided only that, when a constitutional amendment may no longer be viable, the Court could not prevent the question of the validity of a ratification after a prior rejection from coming before the political departments.[113]

Such an interpretation is an entirely different proposition from reading into article V's language a textually demonstrable commitment to Congress to decide the effect to be given to a state's withdrawal of its earlier ratification of a federal constitutional amendment. For, as one commentator has observed, while

the duty imposed on Congress by Article V implies certain powers incident to fulfilling that duty . . . .The Constitution commits numerous powers to the political branches without committing absolute and unreviewable discretion in the exercise of those powers.

RESCISSION EFFICACY IF JUSTICIABLE

Whether a state, having first ratified a proposed constitutional amendment, can rescind that ratification, is not entirely an undecided question in American constitutional law. With respect to three present amendments to the federal Constitution—the Fourteenth,[115] Fifteenth,[116] and Nineteenth[117]—either Congress itself or the secretary of state, in promulgating the amendments,[118] included within the requisite number of ratifying states one or more states that had first ratified and then purported to rescind.[119] In other words, in each instance efforts to rescind were regarded as void and without effect.

The apparent rationale for this action by Congress and the secretary of state is that the language of article V confers upon the state legislatures (or state ratifying conventions) only the authority to ratify[120] a proposed federal constitutional amendment.[121] Once that function is exercised, the state legislature (or state convention) has exhausted all of its article V power, so that nothing it purports to do thereafter in connection with the pending constitutional amendment is of any force or effect. In 1887, Judge Jameson expressed it this way:

The power of a State legislature to participate in amending the Federal Constitution exists only by virtue of a special grant in the Constitution. . .
   So, when the State legislature has done the act or thing which the power contemplated and authorized—when the power [to ratify] has been exercised—it, *ipso facto*, ceases to exist . . . .[122]

Of course, neither Congress nor the secretary of state is bound by principles of stare decisis, that is, they are not bound by their own precedents. Nor, a fortiori, is the United States Supreme Court bound by executive or legislative interpretations of constitutional language. Nevertheless, it is submitted that past dispositions by Congress and the secretary of state were sound, both as a matter of policy and of logic, and should be followed by the United States Supreme Court when and if it is faced with the substantive question of the efficacy of a purported rescission of a state's ERA ratification.[123]

   To support the above conclusion, there is first, the very language of article V itself. In *United States v. Sprague*,[124] specifically referring to article V, the Court said:

The Constitution was written to·be understood by the voters; its words and phrases were used in their normal and ordinary as distinguished from technical meaning; where the intention is clear there is no room for construction and no excuse for interpolation or addition.[125]

With those words in mind, it should be stressed that article V provides that proposed amendments become part of the Constitution "when ratified by the Legislatures of three-fourths of the several States, or by Conventions in three-fourths thereof . . . ." The crucial word in this formulation is "ratified."[126] As the Supreme Court has explained, "ratification by a State of a constitutional amendment is . . . the expression of assent . . . of the State to a proposed amendment to the constitution."[127]

   Although the term "ratified" has also been used to indicate the final result of amendment approval, that is, the attainment of approval or ratification by three-fourths of the states, its article V

meaning is: the individual acts of ratification by each state signify-
ing its approval and assent to the proposed amendment. That the
framers intended this meaning appears from their intentions with
respect to the initial ratifications by state conventions of the original
Constitution. Replying to a letter from Alexander Hamilton, James
Madison observed:

[A] reservation of a right to withdraw, if [the Bill of Rights] be not decided
on under the form of the Constitution within a certain time, is a *conditional* ratification . . . . In short, any *condition* whatever must vitiate the
ratification. . . . The idea of reserving a right to withdraw was started at
Richmond, and considered as a conditional ratification which was abandoned as worse than a rejection.[128]

Moreover, in the light of the Court's characterization of the Constitution as "an instrument drawn with such meticulous care and by men
who so well understood how to make language fit their thought,"[129]
the fact that article V includes no language expressly authorizing
rescission of a once-ratified amendment points strongly toward the
conclusion that rescissions were not within the framers' intent.

A second rationale supporting nonrescindability of state ratifications of constitutional amendments stems from the practical difficulty of amending the Constitution. That amending the Constitution
should be a more difficult task than amending or passing ordinary
legislation is almost a self-evident proposition.[130] A constitution is
a basic charter for a people, designed to provide their fundamental
governmental doctrine for a substantial period of time, if not indef-
initely. By contrast, legislative acts are designed to deal with specific social or economic needs as perceived at specific times. Still,
constitutions should not be made so difficult to amend that they
become virtually impossible to alter[131] when, in the light of fundamentally changed perceptions of a society's basic needs, such
amendments appear necessary to massive numbers of the people in
the society governed by that constitution. The danger to be avoided
is, as Professor Orfield has observed, that the "amending process
may be made so difficult as to prevent the adoption of amendments
which are unquestionably sound."[132]

In a two-hundred-year period, the United States Constitution
has been amended a mere seventeen times (counting the Bill of
Rights as a single amendment). During the same period, there

have been over five thousand amendments proposed to Congress.[133] This low success ratio suggests that amending the federal Constitution is already an enormously difficult undertaking. In addition, the efforts to secure passage of a joint congressional resolution proposing the ERA spanned a fifty-year period, from 1923 to 1972.[134] Against this background, it is arguable that the ERA has had sufficiently difficult hurdles to overcome in the *normal* course of the ratification process. To confront it with an additional, perhaps insurmountable, hurdle (the possibility that states which first ratified it will be able to rescind that ratification before three-fourths of the states have signified their ratification of the Amendment or before the time limit for ratification has expired) is to make amending the Constitution qualitatively much more difficult than the framers had contemplated.

This leads to still another, more political reason supporting the view that ratification rescissions should not be accorded any effect: the practical exigencies of the process iself. Recognition of a power of the states to rescind their ratifications would, it is submitted, create an enormous potential for tactical abuse. ERA proponents, state legislators, and members of Congress were, in view of congressional precedent,[135] justified in presuming that once a state ratified the amendment, no more attention need be paid to it. Recognizing that article V does not require unanimity of endorsement, proponents have tended to select the most promising states within which to concentrate their finite resources of funds, energy, and influence in order to achieve their goal. Permitting a state to withdraw its ratification could upset the entire tactical and strategic approach of the Amendment's proponents in a way not contemplated when it was first submitted to the states by Congress.

Against these considerations, there is the superficially attractive argument in favor of allowing a state legislature to reverse its ratification decision[136] (in either direction) on a proposed constitutional amendment when it decides that its earlier action was a mistake. But in view of historical precedent, the intentions of the framers, and the difficulty entailed in amending the federal Constitution, the unfettered right of a state legislature to change its decision, once it has ratified an amendment, hardly seems justifiable.

Moreover, legislative mistakes in judgment with regard to adopted constitutional amendments are not irrevocable. One need only refer to our nation's experience with the "noble experiment."[137] The American people, having first been persuaded of the desirability of adding the Eighteenth Amendment, prohibiting the "manufacture, sale, or transportation of intoxicating liquors within, the importation thereof into, or the exportation thereof from the United States and all territory subject to the jurisdiction thereof for beverage purposes" were subsequently persuaded to amend the federal Constitution once more by adding the Twenty-First Amendment, repealing the Eighteenth. What must be stressed, however, is that in order to undo what they came to perceive as the mistake of prohibition, Americans had to submit to the same laborious process they confronted when the Eighteenth Amendment was originally introduced and ratified. There was no resort to the "shortcut" of rescinding individual state ratifications prior to its total ratification by the necessary three-fourths of the state legislatures.

We do not wish to be understood as suggesting that the American people will regret the addition of the ERA to the federal Constitution.[138] Despite the gloomy prophesies by some ERA opponents of its supposed negative effects, we believe that the Amendment will cure widespread injustices resulting from unwarranted assumptions about the differences between men and women. The addition of that Amendment to the federal Constitution will not, in our opinion, be a mistake.[139] The point is that, even if it is concluded after some years of experience with the ERA that its adoption was a mistake, recourse in the form of repeal will be available.[140]

RESCISSION EFFICACY IF NOT JUSTICIABLE

As indicated earlier, [141] purported rescissions by some states of their earlier ratifications of the Fourteenth, Fifteenth, and Nineteenth Amendments were regarded as nullities by Congress, on the theory that a state's ratification exhausts its entire power with respect to the amendment ratified.[142] This theory, as we have explained, is sound for many reasons.[143] Should the Court decide, however, that the issue is nonjusticiable, can one be certain that Congress will accord "rescinded"ratifications of the ERA the same treatment accorded rescissions of earlier amendments?

That Congress would not be required to accord the same treatment to ERA ratification rescissions as it has historically accorded recissions of earlier amendments flows from the fact that Congress, not being a court, is not bound by principles of stare decisis. Nevertheless, were it not for some congressional activity in the late 1960s and early 1970s there would be no reason to think that Congress would treat the ratification process surrounding the ERA any differently than it has treated that process with respect to the Fourteenth, Fifteenth, and Nineteenth Amendments.

The slight uncertainty as to how Congress might treat rescissions of ERA ratifications[144] stems from Congress's efforts, initiated in 1967[145] and pursued until 1973,[146] to prescribe procedures for the *convention method* of proposing amendments and their ratification.[147] Passed in the Senate by a vote of eighty-four to nothing in 1971,[148] the bill[149] was reintroduced as S. 1272 in the 93rd Congress on March 19, 1973, by Senators Ervin and Brock.[150] It again passed the Senate on July 9, 1973, was sent to the House the next day, but never emerged from the House Judiciary Committee.

The bill has been called "a thoroughly misconceived piece of legislation."[151] For present purposes, it is important to note that its section 13(a) provided:

Any State may rescind its ratification of a proposed amendment by the same processes by which it ratified the proposed amendment, except that no State may rescind when there are existing valid ratifications of such amendment by three-fourths of the States.[152]

Even recognizing the elasticity of the "necessary and proper" clause[153] of article I, section 8, there is serious doubt about Congress's power to proscribe detailed state procedures under article V's authorization to propose one of the modes of ratification, i.e., by state convention or by state legislatures.

In this connection, it is important to distinguish Congress's powers with respect to the calling of a constitutional convention pursuant to article V and its authority to prescribe state legislative procedures for ratifying proposed amendments. Thus, Professor Bonfield has stated that Congress does have the implied power under

its authority to call a convention . . . to fix the time and place of meeting, the number of delegates, the manner and date of their election, their qualifications, the basis of apportioning delegates, the basis for voting in convention, the vote required in convention to propose an amendment to the states, and the financing and staffing of the convention.[154]

By contrast, congressional power to regulate legislative rules of procedure in ratifying amendments has been seriously questioned by Professor Orfield. In his view:

The constitutionality of congressional regulation would seem exceedingly doubtful. The states cannot be coerced into adopting an amendment. . . . Congress has done its work when it proposes [the amendment and the mode of ratification], and the matter of adoption is for the states.[155]

But even if it is determined that Congress can prescribe detailed state legislative procedures for ratifying convention-proposed amendments, what significance attaches to the fact that the Ervin bill passed the Senate so overwhelmingly? Does this apparent congressional endorsement of the states' freedom to rescind prior ratifications of amendments *proposed by the convention method* reveal probable congressional sentiment with respect to rescissions of proposed amendments such as the ERA, initiated not by a constitutional convention, but by a vote of well over two-thirds of the members of both houses of Congress?

A negative answer is warranted by the fact that ratification of congressionally proposed amendments implicates political and social considerations entirely different from those involved when amendments are proposed by a convention of the states convened, ultimately, as a result of their own initiative. A constitutional convention represents an extraordinary, extralegislative institution, one that, in many respects, shatters the traditional tripartite division of the federal government and becomes in effect a fourth branch.[156] Though Congress may ultimately become involved in the process, pursuant to its authority under article V to propose a "mode" of ratification, Congress's involvement in a convention-sponsored amendment is limited. Essentially, the impetus of the amendment comes from outside Congress itself. Under these circumstances, it is not unreasonable for Congress to assume an attitude toward the states that in effect tells them, "You may change your decisions about ratifying *your own* proposed amendment all you want, at least until we have received valid and unrescinded ratifications of such amendment from three-fourths of the states."

By contrast, when confronted with a congressionally sponsored amendment, of which the ERA is an example and which is by definition Congress's own creature, there is no reason to conclude that either the House or the Senate ever intended to abandon the traditional approach to ratification rescissions that had been followed in adopting the Fourteenth, Fifteenth, and Nineteenth Amendments.[157]

Therefore, should the Court hold the issue nonjusticiable and thus one for congressional evaluation and determination, Congress probably will follow two hundred years of practice and decide that rescissions are inefficacious with regard to the ERA.

CONCLUSION

Whether a state's purported rescission of an earlier ratification of the proposed ERA is effective is a justiciable nonpolitical question to be determined ultimately by the United States Supreme Court. Moreover, the Court, in examining the merits of that question, should hold that a purported rescission by a state that had previously ratified the Amendment is null and void, since by ratifying the Amendment a state exhausts all its powers under article V. Finally, if, because of the broad discretion it retains under the *Baker V. Carr* test for determining the presence of a political question as well as its present marked inclination to exercise restraint in its dealings with Congress, the Court decides that the effect of the purported rescissions by the ratifying legislatures is for Congress to determine, Congress should adhere to its past practice of counting only the earlier ratifications and ignore any subsequent efforts at rescission.

Postscript

While this book was in press, a number of developments with important implications for the future of the American sex-equality movement were taking place in the courts and the political arena. For one thing, between early March and late June 1981, the United States Supreme Court decided several sex-discrimination cases, two of which have a profound bearing on the subjects treated in this book.

The first of those two important decisions was in the case of *Michael M. v. Superior Court of Sonoma County.*[1] In *Michael M.*, the Court upheld the California law under which a male commits the felony of statutory rape if he has sexual relations with a female below the age of eighteen who is not his wife, although a female who engages in sexual intercourse with a male below the age of eighteen to whom she is not married cannot be guilty of that crime.

Accepting the justification for the statute offered by the State (that the legislature had sought to prevent illegitimate teen-age pregnancies), a four-member plurality of the Court decided that "[b]ecause virtually all of the significant harmful and inescapably identifiable consequences of teenage pregnancy fall on the young female, a legislature acts well within its authority when it elects to punish only the participant who, by nature, suffers few of the consequences of his conduct."[2] In effect, although not in its language, the plurality opinion adopts the view that even though the words of the challenged statute make a distinction on the basis of sex, the distinction is one that is really based upon function. In the words of Justice Rehnquist, the author of the plurality opinion: "[T]his Court has consistently upheld statutes where the gender classification is not invidious, but rather realistically reflects the fact that the sexes are not similarly situated in certain circumstances."[3] Concurring in the judgment, Justice Blackmun filed a separate opinion in which he stated, without detailed analysis, that the gender classification in *Michael M.* satisfied the constitutional test for alleged sex discrimination that the Court had previously enunciated in *Craig v. Boren*[4]—while chiding members of the plurality for what he characterized as an inconsistency in their treatment of the social problem of teenage pregnancies in this context and (in another case decided on the same day) in the context of a state law requiring notice to a minor's parents before she would be permitted to receive an abortion.[5]

Four members of the Court dissented in *Michael M.* One of the two dissenting opinions, written by Justice Brennan, was joined in by Justices White and Marshall. In that dissent, Justice Brennan stressed that, even if the State's claim that the statute's purpose was to prevent teen-age pregnancies was accepted, the State had still not met its burden of showing that, because it "punishes only males, and not females, it more effectively deters minors from having sexual intercourse."[6] In Justice Brennan's view, the fact that thirty-seven other states had sex-neutral statutory-rape laws undermined the State's claim that a sex-neutral law would be less effective than a gender-based statute in deterring sexual activity. That twice as many people would be subject to prosecution under a sex-neutral statutory-rape law also suggested that such a law would be patently more effective than the California law in question. For these reasons, concluded Justice Brennan, the state had not met its burden of proving that the statutory classification was substantially related to the achievement of its asserted goal, that is, it had failed to satisfy the second prong of the *Craig v. Boren* test. As for Justice Stevens, he too dissented, primarily because he saw the statute as aimed at protecting young females against pregnancy, and in his view, "a total exemption for the members of the more endangered class [is] utterly irrational."[7]

More important, perhaps, than the specific result in *Michael M.* is some of the language and rationale of Justice Rehnquist's plurality opinion. Significantly, this opinion speaks of *Califano v. Webster*,[8] *Schlesinger v. Ballard*,[9] and *Kahn v. Shevin*[10] as cases in which "the gender classification [was] not invidious, but rather realistically reflect[ed] the fact that the sexes are not similarly situated in certain circumstances."[11] This may be an indication that, at least for this group of four judges, the benign-discrimination rationale of *Kahn, Webster,* and *Ballard* may be subject to revision. While the results in those cases would not be any the less objectionable to sex-equality proponents under the apparent new rationale of dissimilarly situated sexes than it was under the benign-discrimination rationale, it nevertheless signals further discomfort with the idea of benign discrimination in the gender context.

Regardless of what it implies for the ultimate fate of the benign-discrimination doctrine, the plurality opinion is significant for the extraordinary deference it appears to accord a State's present assertion of its original reason for the enactment of a statute. It would appear that in the majority's view, a State's asserted reason for the enactment of a statute may be rejected *only* "if it could not have been a goal of the legislation."[12] Moreover, in the opinion of the *Michael M.* plurality, the validity of a State's asserted reason for having enacted a statute is not undermined by the fact that it may have been accompanied by other reasons that were invalid, or indeed unconstitutional. In Justice Rehnquist's words:

Even if the preservation of female chastity were one of the motives of the statute, and even if that motive be impermissible . . . "it is a familiar practice of constitutional law that this court will not strike down an otherwise constitutional statute on the basis of an alleged illicit motive."[13]

Carried to its extreme, the language of the plurality opinion in *Michael M.* conjures up disturbing possibilities with respect to future equal-protection challenges to gender-based classifications. Conceivably, a state could successfully defend such a classification by advancing what can only be regarded as its current speculation about the statute's original purpose. Only if what is asserted as the statute's original purpose could not possibly have been its goal will it necessarily be rejected. In addition, although the record might be clear that the legislature had specific invalid goals in mind when it originally enacted the statute, the classification may still be constitutional so long as any valid goal, no matter how minimal, may have also been in the minds of the legislators. For the plurality opinion does not tell us anything about the necessary quantum relationship between improper and proper goals for validating the sex-based classification. If quantification is possible here, would a gender classification, 98 percent of whose motivation stemmed from improper goals and only 2 percent from permissible goals, be valid? If it could be shown that the California legislature, in enacting the statutory-rape law at issue in *Michael M.*, had overwhelmingly intended to preserve female chastity as its primary goal, would it be sufficient, in order to validate the classification, to show that, merely as a slight afterthought, the legislature had also concluded that the statute might also assist in curbing teenage pregnancy?

When to such considerations are added the linking of cases like *Kahn* and *Webster*, in which many differences in the stituations of individual men and women were present (whereas all women and all men are alike with respect to the potential ability to become or not become pregnant), equal-rights proponents may have much to be troubled by in the *Michael M.* plurality opinion. At the least, it can be read as signaling a growing disenchantment among four members of the Court with the recent decisional thrust toward formal equality of the sexes under existing constitutional provisions. It also seems to indicate that, although these four members may not be prepared to lead a wholesale retreat from the point the Court had previously reached, they are ready to halt any further forward movement on the sex-equality front.

The second important sex-discrimination decision, which dealt with the constitutional status of the male-only draft-registration law, was handed down by the U.S. Supreme Court on June 25, 1981. In *Rostker v. Goldberg*,[14] by a vote of 6 to 3, the Court, reversing a three-judge federal district court, held that the draft-registration law did not violate the equal-protection guarantee that is implied, with respect to the federal government, in the Due Process Clause of the Fifth Amendment.

Because of the reasons the Court advances for the result it reaches in *Goldberg*, the significance of the decision for future constitutional attacks on sex discriminatory laws and official practices is difficult to assess. On the one hand, Justice Rehnquist's majority opinion in *Goldberg* expressly rejects the Government's request that the Court apply, because of the deference due to Congress's regulation of military matters, only the rational-basis test that had long prevailed in the sex-discrimination-equal-protection arena.

Instead, the Court purports to apply the *Craig v. Boren* test, which requires that, to satisfy the equal protection standard, a gender classification must be substantially related to an important governmental objective. On the other hand, while applying the *Craig* test to the male-only draft registration law, the *Goldberg* decision holds that an extraordinary amount of deference must be accorded to congressional judgments concerning the nation's military affairs. With that principle in mind, the *Goldberg* majority determines that Congress did not violate the *Craig* test, first, because "[n]o one [can] deny that . . . the Government's interest in raising and supporting armies is an 'important governmental interest' ";[15] and second, because the means chosen by the government substantially serves this important governmental interest. For the latter proposition, the majority relies heavily on the ineligibility of women for combat duty—a federal-law disqualification which, like the exclusion of women naval personnel from sea duty and combat in *Schlesinger v. Ballard*,[16] was not challenged by any of the parties in *Goldberg*. Because of the combat restrictions on women, states the *Goldberg* majority, men and women "are simply not similarly situated for purposes of a draft or registration for a draft."[17] As a result, the gender classification in the male-only draft-registration requirement "is not invidious, but rather realistically reflects the fact that the sexes are not similarly situated."[18]

The principal ground for the two dissenting opinions in *Goldberg* filed by Justices White and Marshall, both of which were joined in by Justice Brennan, was that the record revealed that, if a draft were ever reinstituted, as many as one-third of the total number of military personnel would be needed for exclusively noncombat tasks, and that, even after voluntary enlistments were taken into consideration, at least 80,000 such positions would still have to be filled with draftees. Since the ineligibility of women for combat would not disable them from filling this large number of positions in the armed services in the event of a draft, their exclusion from the draft-registration requirement did not substantially serve an important governmental interest—or, to put it differently, males and females were not dissimilarly situated, in the view of the dissenters, at least with respect to such exclusively noncombat military positions.

Two observations should be made about the *Goldberg* decision.

The first is that, if the majority's reasoning in that case is applied by the Court in the same manner to other sex-discrimination challenges in the future, many of the sex-equality legal victories of recent years will surely be cancelled. For it is the dissenters in *Goldberg* who, in this author's opinion, are faithful to the *Craig v. Boren* standard in stating that it would invalidate the male-only draft-registration requirement.

There is reason to believe, however, that the *Goldberg* majority's reasoning will not be followed in other types of sex-discrimination challenges that are likely to come before the Court in the near future. In *Goldberg,* the Court repeatedly stresses that it must show extraordinary deference to Congress's judgments about the nation's military affairs. While the majority insists that it is not abdicating its responsibility to make sure that Congress acts constitutionally in this area (an insistence that is viewed with some skepticism by Justices Marshall and Brennan), it still emphasizes that "perhaps in no other area has the Court accorded Congress greater deference."[19]

An analogy can be drawn from another area of constitutional litigation. In *California v. LaRue,*[20] the Court held in 1972 that, although live nude dancing might be a form of expression that is ordinarily protected by the First Amendment, the states could regulate, indeed suppress, such dancing in places in which liquor is served, pursuant to their authority to regulate liquor traffic granted by the Twenty-First Amendment. That did not mean, however, that the Court had abandoned the ordinary standards of first-amendment litigation in areas outside those involving liquor traffic subject to state regulation.[21] By the same token, it is reasonable to assume that *Goldberg's* loose application of the *Craig v. Boren* test, against the background of special deference to congressional authority over national defense and military affairs, does not necessarily spell a wholesale retreat from the *Craig v. Boren* standard, but is to be understood as being limited to the kind of case *Goldberg* represents.

The most disappointing aspect of *Goldberg* is its strong intimation that a male-only draft, and a male-only combat requirement, would both be constitutional in the opinion of a majority of the present justices. *Goldberg's* holding is, of course, limited to the male-only draft-registration requirement. As Justice Marshall notes in his dissent:

In this case we are not called upon to decide whether either men or women can be drafted at all, whether they must be drafted in equal numbers, in what order they should be drafted, or once inducted, how they are to be trained for their respective functions. In addition, this case does not involve a challenge to the statutes or policies that prohibit female members of the Armed Forces from serving in combat.[22]

The *Goldberg* plaintiffs, who had challenged the male-only registration requirement, did not concede the constitutional validity of these restrictions on women in combat, but took the position that their validity was irrelevant, for purposes of the case.[23] Still, the majority's heavy reliance on women's combat restrictions in holding that men and women were not similarly situated and that the male-only registration requirement was therefore constitutional suggests that, although the validity of those combat restrictions for women was not an issue, that validity was decided *sub silentio* by the use the majority made of those restrictions in arriving at its result. In addition, Justice White, in dissent, stated: "I assume what has not been challenged in this case—that excluding women from combat positions does not offend the Constitution."[24] Even Justice Marshall, despite his careful insistence on excluding the combat-exclusion and the other above-mentioned issues from the case, elsewhere in his opinion, commenting on the Senate Report accompanying the law creating the male-only draft-registration requirement, states that the

Report's speculation that a statute authorizing differential induction of male and female draftees would be vulnerable to constitutional challenge is unfounded. The unchallenged restrictions on the assignment of women to combat, the need to preserve military flexibility, and the other factors discussed in the Senate Report provide more than ample grounds for concluding that the discriminatory means employed by such a statute would be substantially related to the achievement of important governmental objectives.[25]

All members of the Court have thus implied in one way or another that, in their view, a male-only draft and a male-only combat requirement would be constitutional while recognizing that those issues were not actually before the Court in *Goldberg*. Such a result would be consistent with the Court's deference to Congress on military affairs, which is the foundation of the actual result in *Goldberg;* and once again, would not necessarily portend a major retreat from the basic *Craig v. Boren* standard.

But the Court's validation of a male-only draft and combat obligation, if and when it occurs, would in other ways contradict the ideological thrust of the Court's recent sex-discrimination decisions. Both the holding and the language of *Goldberg* imply that women are not full and equal members of the social polity. In Justice Marshall's words, *Goldberg* placed the Court's imprimatur "on one of the most potent remaining public expressions of 'ancient canards about the proper role of women . . . [and categorically excluded] women from a fundamental civic obligation.' "[26]

While it is important to understand the adverse effects upon women of the *Goldberg* decision, the negative impact upon men of *Goldberg's* actual result and of its implications for any potential draft and combat responsibility should not be overlooked. To the extent that the burdens and dangers of involuntary military service and combat may be imposed upon males alone, with the Court's approval, law-endorsed antimale discrimination is present in the most fundamental life-and-death realms. All the more reason for men to increase their participation in the movement for ERA ratification and in other activities aimed at ending arbitrary sex-role assignments in American law and society.

Finally, in early July 1981, President Reagan nominated Sandra Day O'Connor, a judge in the Arizona State Court of Appeals, to be the first woman Justice of the United States Supreme Court. As of this writing, congressional hearings on the nomination have not been held, and the appointment has therefore not yet been confirmed. Despite strong objections to the nomination from the so-called Moral Majority and other right-wing political groups, the prospects for confirmation appear bright. Barring any unforeseen complications, Sandra Day O'Connor should be the first woman member of the United States Supreme Court by the time this book is published.

If the appointment is approved as expected, Judge O'Connor will fill the highest federal government position ever held by a woman. At first glance, President Reagan's naming of Judge O'Connor to the Court would appear to contradict the forebodings about his administration's future actions on sex-discrimination issues expressed in Chapter 8. The fact remains, however, that, as of this date, out of the 450 highest positions in the administration, only 45 have been filled by women, a much lower percentage than that achieved under the Carter administration. There is also a risk, as former U.S. Court of Appeals Judge Shirley Hufstedler has noted, of "a token woman on the Supreme Court to avoid addressing women's issues."

On the other hand, Justice O'Connor, as she will be known when the appointment is confirmed, is likely to bring perspectives to the problems of sex discrimination and the law that are greatly needed on the Court at this time. It is true that she is reputed not to be of an innovative and adventurous disposition when it comes to legal theories. Still, her respect for legal precedent in the law, her ability to follow the logic of a legal principle no matter where it may take her, and her apparent lack of dogmatism about sex roles could well lead her to consider more fully the situation of both sexes in future constitutional challenges to sex-discrimination laws and official practices. Despite her reputed deferential attitude toward legislative judgment, for example, it is quite possible that her approach to a male-only draft or male-only combat-liability might be considerably different from the expressed or implied approaches of the Court's present members. Time will tell.

Whatever Justice O'Connor's response to sex-discrimination cases and controversies may be, her appointment is still an event to be applauded by all Americans who understand the need to end sex discrimination against both men and women in American society. If nothing else, the symbolism of this long-awaited sexual desegregation of the Court will inevitably promote a general awareness that no realm of American life should remain the exclusive preserve of either sex. As indicated in the preceding pages, males as well as females have a major stake in promoting such an awareness.

NOTES

Chapter 1. Introduction

1. Gorer, *Man Has No "Killer" Instinct*, NEW YORK TIMES MAGAZINE, November 27, 1966, at 107.

2. See chapters 3 and 4 *infra*.

Chapter 3. Benign Sex Discrimination

1. 438 U.S. 265 (1978).

2. The Supreme Court in its most recent decision involving benign discrimination, Fullilove v. Klutznick, 48 U.S.L.W. 4979 (1980), failed to shed new light on the question. In *Fullilove*, a group of white contractors challenged the Mitchell Amendment to the Public Works Employment Act of 1977 under the equal-protection aspect of the Fifth Amendment. The Mitchell Amendment requires 10 percent of each federal grant for any local public works project to "be expended for minority business enterprises"—generally enterprises "at least 50 per centum of which [are] owned by minority group members." 42 U.S.C. § 6705(f)(2) (Supp. II 1978). The Act defines "minority group members" as United States citizens "who are Negroes, Spanish-speaking, Orientals, Indians, Eskimos and Aleuts." *Id.* While a plurality of the Court upheld the constitutional validity of the Minority Business Enterprise program, 48 U.S.L.W. at 4991, the Court failed to reach a majority consensus as to the proper standard for judicial review in benign-discrimination cases. Chief Justice Burger, announcing the judgment of the Court, joined by Justices White and Powell, refrained from adopting any of the analyses articulated in cases such as *Bakke*, stating only that the Minority Business Enterprise "provision would survive judicial review under either 'test' articulated in the several *Bakke* opinions." *Id.* Concurring in the opinion, Justice Powell found that because Congress was given the unique constitutional role of implementing the post–Civil War amendments, it need only choose a "reasonably necessary means to effectuate its purpose." *Id.* at 4997–98. Justice Marshall, joined by Justices Brennan and Blackmun, concurred in the judgment reiterating the intermediate standard of review they set forth in *Bakke*. *Id.* at 4998–99. Finally, Justice Stewart, joined by Justice Rehnquist, dissented on the grounds that the equal-protection standard absolutely prohibits invidious discrimination by government. *Id.* at 4999.

3. Califano v. Webster, 430 U.S. 313 (1977); Schlesinger v. Ballard, 419 U.S. 498 (1975); Kahn v. Shevin, 416 U.S. 351 (1974). *See also* Muller v. Oregon, 208 U.S. 412 (1908), for earlier approval and application of the benign-discrimination

principle in the context of a due-process, rather than an equal-protection, challenge to a statute that prohibited overtime work (no more than ten hours a day) for women, but not for men.

4. Orr v. Orr, 440 U.S. 268 (1979); Califano v. Goldfarb, 430 U.S. 199 (1977); Weinberger v. Wiesenfeld, 420 U.S. 636 (1975). *Cf.* Personnel Adm'r of Mass. v. Feeney, 442 U.S. 256 (1979) (absolute preference for veterans for civil service jobs held constitutional). See text accompanying notes 115–21 *infra* for a discussion of the promale benign-discrimination implication in the dissenting opinion of Justices Marshall and Brennan in *Feeney.*.

5. The proposed Equal Rights Amendment provides: "Section 1. Equality of rights under the law shall not be denied or abridged by the United States or by any State on account of sex.

"Section 2. The Congress shall have the power to enforce, by appropriate legislation, the provisions of this article.

"Section 3. The Amendment shall take effect two years after the date of ratification." Congress adopted the joint resolution proposing the Equal Rights Amendment to the federal Constitution on March 22, 1972, and set a seven-year limit within which the necessary thirty-eight-state legislative ratifications were to have occurred. *See* S.J. Res. 8, 92d Cong., 2d Sess. (1972); H.R.J. Res. 208, 92d Cong., 2d Sess., 86 Stat. 1523 (1972). By the middle of 1978, only thirty-five states had ratified the amendment, and among those, several had purported to rescind their earlier ratifications. *See Appendix, infra.* When it became apparent that the necessary thirty-eight ratifications would not be forthcoming by the original deadline, Congress, in 1978, extended the deadline by an additional thirty-nine months until July 1982. *See* Note, *The Amending Process: Extending the Ratification Deadline of the Proposed Equal Rights Amendment,* 10 RUT. -CAM. L.J. 91, 94 n.11 (1978). Why the Equal Rights Amendment failed to achieve ratification within the original seven-year period that Congress had prescribed, and the difficulties that ratification efforts are likely to encounter during the extended period, are examined in Chapter 7, *infra.* The possibility that the ERA may not be ratified suggests the desirability of a closer look at whether some of the intended aims of the ERA, see note 6 *infra,* such as the elimination of the benign-sex-discrimination doctrine, can be achieved within the existing constitutional framework.

6. [W]hile classification by *race* would be 'suspect,' it is not totally prohibited. And where the courts determine that the purpose of the differentiation is to *benefit* members of the minority race, rather than to impose a status of inferiority, they are likely to find there are 'compelling reasons' for the *special* treatment. *Such an approach would not be permissible under the Equal Rights Amendment."* Brown, Emerson, Falk & Freedman, *The Equal Rights Amendment: A Constitutional Basis for Equal Rights for Women.* 80 YALE L.J. 871, 904 (1971) (emphasis added).

7. 443 U.S. 76 (1979). The Court, however, found the circumstances to be inappropriate for judicial restructuring in the *Westcott* case itself. See notes 19–31, Chapter 4, and accompanying text *infra.*

8. 404 U.S. 71 (1971).

9. "The Equal Protection Clause . . . [denies] to States the power to legislate that different treatment be accorded to persons placed by a statute into different classes on the basis of criteria wholly unrelated to the objective of that statute." *Id.* at 75–76.

10. The major pre-*Reed* sex-classification cases were Hoyt v. Florida, 368 U.S. 57 (1961) (equal protection is not violated by a statute permitting women to serve on juries only if they volunteer, but requiring men to serve unless they have a recognized excuse); Goesaert v. Cleary, 335 U.S. 464 (1948) (equal protection is not violated by a state statute limiting the right of women to work as bartenders to the wives and daughters of the bar owners); Muller v. Oregon, 208 U.S. 412 (1908) (a maximum-hours law for women, but not for men, does not violate the Fourteenth Amendment's due-process guarantee). For criticism of the Court's decisions in these cases, see L. KANOWITZ, WOMEN AND THE LAW: THE UNFINISHED REVOLUTION, *passim*, University of New Mexico Press, Albuquerque (1969) [hereinafter cited as KANOWITZ, WOMEN AND THE LAW.].

11. 429 U.S. 190 (1976).

12. OKLA. STAT. tit. 37, §§ 241, 245 (1958 & Supp. 1976), prohibited the sale of 3.2 percent beer to males under the age of 21 and to females under the age of 18.

13. 429 U.S. at 197. This more demanding test is to be applied under either the Fourteenth Amendment's equal-protection clause or the equal-protection aspect of the Fifth Amendment. *Cf.* Bolling v. Sharpe, 347 U.S. 497 (1954) (applying Fifth Amendment due-process to prohibit racial segregation in District of Columbia schools where equal-protection clause would apply against states.)

14. 429 U.S. at 197 (emphasis added).

15. *See* Craig v. Boren, 429 U.S. 190, 218 (1976) (Rehnquist, J., dissenting). *Cf.* Stanton v. Stanton, 421 U.S. 7, 17 (1975) (*"under any test—compelling state interest, or rational basis, or something in between*—§ 15–2–1, in the context of child support, does not survive an equal protection attack") (emphasis added).

16. *See generally Developments in the Law—Equal Protection*, 82 HARV. L. REV. 1065 (1969).

17. *See, e.g.*, Loving v. Virginia, 388 U.S. 1 (1967).

18. *See, e.g.*, Korematsu v. United States, 323 U.S. 214 (1944).

19. Graham v. Richardson, 403 U.S. 365 (1971). *But see* Foley v. Connelie, 435 U.S. 291 (1978), which applied a "rational-relationship" test to uphold New York's exclusion of aliens from appointment as state troopers.

20. 411 U.S. 677 (1973).

21. *Id.* at 686.

22. *Id.* at 686–87. A holding substantially similar to the *Frontiero* plurality opinion had been rendered two years earlier, under the equal-protection clauses of the Fourteenth Amendment and the California Constitution, *inter alia*, by the California Supreme Court in Sail'er Inn v. Kirby, 5 Cal. 3d 1, 485 P.2d 529, 95 Cal. Rptr. 329 (1971). The California court cited essentially the same reasons as the *Frontiero* plurality did two years later for holding sex to be a suspect classification. *Sail'er Inn* is marred by its confused conclusion that "sexual classifications are properly treated as suspect, particularly when those classifications are made with respect to a fundamental interest such as employment." 5 Cal. 3d at 20, 485 P.2d at 541, 95 Cal. Rptr. at 341. Classifications are either suspect or they are not. That a classification is made with respect to a fundamental interest may be an alternative reason for triggering the overwhelming-interest test, see text accompanying note 16 *supra*, but it should not have any bearing on whether the classification is suspect.

23. Under 37 U.S.C. § 403 (1976), a member of the uniformed services with dependents was entitled to an increased "basic allowance for quarters" and, under 10 U.S.C. § 1076 (1976), a member's dependents were provided comprehensive

medical and dental care. A serviceman could claim his wife as a "dependent" without regard to whether she was in fact dependent upon him for any part of her support. 37 U.S.C. § 401(1) (1976); 10 U.S.C. § 1072(2)(A) (1976). A servicewoman could not claim her husband as a "dependent" under these programs unless he was in fact dependent upon her for over one-half of his support. 37 U.S.C. § 401 (repealed by Act of July 3, 1973, Pub. L. No. 93–64, § 103(2), 87 Stat. 147; 10 U.S.C. § 1072(2)(C) (1976)).

24. 416 U.S. 351(1974).

25. *Cf.* Muller v. Oregon, 208 U.S. 412 (1908) (earlier decision addressing application of benign-discrimination principle in the context of a due-process challenge). *Muller* is discussed at note 3 *supra*.

26. DeFunis v. Odegaard, 416 U.S. 312, 336 (1974) (Douglas, J., dissenting) ("[t]here is no constitutional right for any race to be preferred").

27. "There can be no doubt, therefore, that Florida's differing treatment of widows and widowers 'rest[s] upon some ground of difference having a fair and substantial relation to the object of the legislation' " 416 U.S. at 355 (quoting Reed v. Reed, 404 U.S. 71, 76 (1971) (brackets by the Court). But see text accompanying notes 14–15 *supra*, suggesting that similar language in Craig v. Boren, 429 U.S. 190 (1976), later was construed as creating an "intermediate" test.

28. 416 U.S. at 353 (emphasis added). Since Justice Douglas did not identify "the" woman and "the" man to whom he referred, he obviously was talking about the average woman and the average man, thus overlooking the extent to which individual men and women do not conform to his model.

29. 419 U.S. 498 (1975).

30. *Id.* at 508–9.

31. *Id.* at 508.

32. Three years later, a federal district court held that the exclusion of women from sea duty violated the equal-protection aspect of Fifth Amendment due process. Owens v. Brown, 455 F. Supp. 291 (D.D.C. 1978). It is arguable that, rather than being a case decided on benign-discrimination grounds, *Ballard* merely held that no violation of the equal-protection principle had occurred because of "the demonstrable fact that male and female line officers in the Navy are *not* similarly situated with respect to opportunities for professional service." 419 U.S. at 508. At the same time, much of the language in *Ballard* is consistent with the benign-discrimination rationale.

33. 430 U.S. 313 (1977).

34. Social Security Act, 64 Stat. 506 § 215 (1950) (current version at 42 U.S.C. § 415 (1976 & Supp. II 1978)).

35. 420 U.S. 636 (1975).

36. *Id.* at 648.

37. *Id.*.

38. *Id.* at 652.

39. *Id.* at 651–52: That the classification was seen by the majority in *Wiesenfeld* as "entirely irrational" rendered it violative of equal protection even under the traditional "any-rational-basis" test.

40. Benefits also were extended to the surviving spouses of deceased covered female employees. See discussion of "dual aspect" laws at notes 165–73 and accompanying text *infra*. As to the propriety of extending the benefits of a statute, rather than invalidating it, to cure a constitutional defect caused by the underinclusiveness of its coverage, see text accompanying note 4, chapter 4 *infra*.

41. 420 U.S. at 648 (emphasis added). This observation demonstrates the majority's willingness to permit one large group of women to be deliberately discriminated against by the government if its purpose is to "benignly" discriminate in favor of another large group of women. See text accompanying notes 161–65 *infra*.

42. 430 U.S. 199 (1977).

43. 42 U.S.C. § 402(f)(1)(D)(1976) (repealed by Pub. L. 95–216, § 334(d)(1), 91 Stat. 1527 (1977)). The Social Security Act gave survivors' benefits based on earnings of a deceased husband to his widow regardless of dependency, but § 402(f)(1)(D) required dependency by the widower upon his deceased wife to entitle him to such benefits.

44. 430 U.S. at 214–16.

45. Califano v. Goldfarb, 430 U.S. 199 (1977); Weinberger v. Wiesenfeld, 420 U.S. 636 (1975). Although both involved classifications created by Congress, there is no reason to believe that the same standards would not apply if such classifications were created by state legislatures or local governments, or even by state and federal courts exercising their common law powers.

46. 440 U.S. 268 (1979).

47. ALA. CODE tit. 30, §§ 30–2–51 to –53 (1975).

48. On remand, the Alabama Court of Civil Appeal validated the alimony statutes by extending their benefits to needy husbands as well as wives. Orr v. Orr, 374 So. 2d 895 (Ala. Civ. App. 1979), *cert. denied*, 100 S.Ct. 993 (1980).

49. 440 U.S. at 280 (quoting Orr v. Orr, 351 So. 2d 904, 905 (Ala. Civ. App. 1977)).

50. 440 U.S. at 280 (emphasis added).

51. Such inquiries had been expressly or impliedly made in all previous sex-based benign-discrimination cases. *See generally id.* at 290–91, 296–97 (Rehnquist, J., dissenting).

52. *Id.* at 281.

53. *Id.* at 281–82 (emphasis added).

54. *Id.* at 281 (emphasis by the Court omitted; emphasis added).

55. (See text accompanying note 50 *supra*.

56. See text accompanying note 53 *supra*.

57. Justice Blackmun's insistence in his *Orr* concurrence that the Court's language concerning discrimination "'in the sphere' of the relevant preference statute . . . does not imply that society-wide discrimination is always irrelevant," and "that the language in no way cuts back" on *Kahn* appears in context to be a valiant, but futile, attempt to deny the obvious. 440 U.S. at 284.

58. *See* Kahn v. Shevin, 416 U.S. 351, 360–62 (1974) (White, J., dissenting).

59. *See* Craig v. Boren, 429 U.S. 190, 202–14 (1976) (Stevens, J., concurring). See text accompanying notes 75–78 *infra*.

60. Orr v. Orr, 440 U.S. 268, 278–82 (1977).

61. 416 U.S. at 360 (Brennan, J., dissenting).

62. *Id.* at 358–59.

63. *Id.* at 359.

64. *Id.* at 359–60 (emphasis added).

65. 429 U.S. 190 (1976).

66. Justice Blackmun concurred in Justice Brennan's opinion in *Craig* except as to part II-D thereof, which is not relevant here.

67. 429 U.S. at 197.

68. *Id.* at 219 (Rehnquist, J., dissenting).
69. See text accompanying notes 75–78 *infra*.
70. 429 U.S. 190 (1976).
71. See notes 79–80 & accompanying text *infra*.
72. 416 U.S. at 361 (White, J., dissenting).
73. *Id.* at 361–62.
74. *Id.* (emphasis added).
75. 429 U.S. 190, 212 (1976) (Stevens, J., concurring).
76. *Id.* (emphasis added).
77. *Id.* at 212 n.3.
78. *Id.* at 212 n.1.
79. *Id.* at 197. This same implication that *sex classifications*, not merely discrimination against females, should be regarded as "suspect," thus triggering the overwhelming-state-interest test, appears in Justice Brennan's plurality opinion in Frontiero v. Richardson, 411 U.S. 677 (1973).
80. 429 U.S. at 218–19 (Rehnquist, J., dissenting).
81. Whether a lower age of majority for females discriminates against males *rather than against females* is problematical; because of the classification's dual aspect it does both. See notes 138–73 & accompanying text *infra*.
82. See notes 61–69 & accompanying text *supra*.
83. Craig v. Boren, 429 U.S. at 212 n.1. See text accompanying note 78 *supra*.
84. 411 U.S. 677 (1973).
85. See notes 17–19 *supra*.
86. 411 U.S. at 686. Alienage, however, does not appear to be an immutable characteristic since aliens can, by naturalization, become American citizens. The change, however, cannot be effected instantaneously and, in some instances, cannot be effected at all.
87. *Id.* at 686–87.
88. In Personnel Adm'r of Mass. v. Feeney, 442 U.S. 256 (1979), the Court equated "invidious" gender bias with "intentional" or purposive gender bias. *Id.* at 276–81. In Parham v. Hughes, 441 U.S. 347 (1979), a Georgia statute that precluded a father who has not legitimated a child from suing for the child's wrongful death was held to be noninvidious because it did "not reflect any overbroad generalizations about men as a class, but rather the reality that in Georgia only a father can by unilateral action legitimate an illegitimate child." *Id.* at 356. *See also* Califano v. Goldfarb, 430 U.S. 199 (Stevens, J., concurring): "I . . . agree . . . that a classification which treats certain aged widows more favorably than their male counterparts is not 'invidious.' Such a classification does not imply that males are inferior to females . . . does not condemn a large class on the basis of the misconduct of an unrepresentative few . . . and does not add to the burdens of an already disadvantaged discrete minority." *Id.* at 218. Justice Stewart, concurring in Craig v. Boren, 429 U.S. 190 (1976), equates "invidiousness" with "total irrationality." *Id.* at 215.
89. 411 U.S. at 686–87. It should be noted that certain statutes, such as those based on age, have never been regarded as suspect although they share some of the same characteristics. There are undoubtedly many seventeen-year-old young men and women who have the maturity, wisdom, and self-discipline to enter into binding contracts. There are also undoubtedly many people over eighteen who are not competent to enter into such contracts. Yet in those states that set eighteen as the uniform age of majority, the latter will be allowed to enter into such

contracts, while the former will not. The effect is even more pronounced in states that have retained a twenty-one-year age-of-majority rule. Thus, an entire class of seventeen year olds will be relegated to "inferior legal status without regard to the actual capabilities of its individual members." Frontiero v. Richardson, 411 U.S. 677, 686–87 (1973). Similar classifications are made at the other end of the age spectrum. Massachusetts Bd. of Retirement v. Murgia, 427 U.S. 307 (1976). In the case of discrimination against the young, it can be argued that the status is not immutable (although it is far from clear that *both* immutability and invidiousness are required to render a status suspect), because the young person may live long enough to attain the age of majority. But not all young persons will live that long. Even for those who do, it is questionable whether the mutability requirement (in order to be *deprived* of suspect status) is satisfied by events or occurrences over which a person has no control, such as the passage of time. As for those discriminated against because of old age, there is no mutability other than by death; neither by an act of their own will nor by the passage of time will they become younger.

90. Mathews v. Lucas, 427 U.S. 495, 506 (1976).

91. Military Selective Service Act, 50 U.S.C. app. §§ 451–73 (1976).

92. *See* KANOWITZ, WOMEN AND THE LAW, *supra* note 10, at 69–75.

93. *Id.*

94. *Id.* at 111–31, 178–92. See text accompanying notes 25–37, chapter 4 *infra.*

95. *See* KANOWITZ, WOMEN AND THE LAW, *supra* note 10, at 3.

96. *Id.*

97. In Kahn v. Shevin, 416 U.S. 351 (1974), the Court nowhere limits its inquiry to previous *legal* discrimination against women before approving the benign discrimination at issue here. On the contrary, it is primarily the employment discrimination faced by women, essentially in the private sector of the economy, that in the Court's view appears to justify the preferential treatment granted by Florida in the form of a widows-only property-tax exemption. See text accompanying note 28 *supra.* Although considerable doubt has been cast by *Orr* on the relevance of past *societal* discrimination against women as a justification for a benign discrimination in their favor, see text accompanying notes 54, 57 *supra,* societal discrimination against one sex is still relevant to determining the propriety of a benign discrimination in favor of the other sex.

98. See notes 99–100 & accompanying text *infra.*

99. 435 U.S. 702 (1978).

100. *Id.* at 710 n.17 (emphasis added).

101. See notes 51–55, chapter 4, & accompanying text *infra.*

102. Califano v. Goldfarb, 430 U.S. 199, 207 (1977).

103. Kahn v. Shevin, 416 U.S. 351, 360 (1974)(Brennan, J., dissenting).

104. 419 U.S. 498 (1975).

105. See notes 29–32 & accompanying text *supra.*

106. In other words, it was a dual-aspect law. See text accompanying notes 138–74 *infra.*

107. These were antimale discriminations *within the sphere* of the purported benign discrimination favoring women. Male naval officers also were prey to all the other antimale social discrimination discussed in reference to *Kahn.* It should be noted that the requirement in *Orr* of a showing that the beneficiary of the benign discrimination has been the object of past discrimination *within that sphere*

goes only to the justification for the benign discrimination. That requirement should not prevent males from showing a generalized past discrimination against them as a reason for rejecting a benign discrimination for females. Nor should it prevent females from showing a generalized discrimination against them as a reason for resisting a benign discrimination favoring males. See text accompanying notes 116–20 *infra* for a discussion of the promale benign-discrimination implications of the veterans-preference laws in Personnel Adm'r of Mass v. Feeney, 442 U.S. 256, 281 (1979)(Marshall, J., dissenting).

108. 430 U.S. 313 (1977).

109. See note 107 *supra*.

110. See text accompanying note 41 *supra*.

111. See text accompanying note 42 *supra*.

112. 442 U.S. 256 (1979).

113. *Id.* at 270.

114. 426 U.S. 229 (1976). In *Washington* the Court distinguished the requirements for proving an unconstitutional discrimination and a discrimination that violates Title VII of the 1964 Civil Rights Act. Under Title VII, although an employer's rule is stated in sex-neutral or race-neutral terms, a prima facie case of discrimination will be made out if it is shown that the rule has a markedly disproportionate effect on one sex or one race. See Griggs v. Duke Power Co., 401 U.S. ·24 (1971). By contrast, under *Washington*, the fact that a neutrally phrased rule or statute has a disparate impact upon one race (or, as in *Feeney*, upon one sex) will not even establish a prima facie case of unconstitutional discrimination. To prove that a governmental entity has discriminated against a class in violation of the federal constitution, it is necessary to prove a governmental *purpose* to discriminate by means of the disputed rule or statute.

115. 442 U.S. at 280–81.

116. *Id.* at 281.

117. *Id.* at 285.

118. *Id.* at 286–88.

119. In exploring whether the goals of the statute were "important," Justice Marshall appears to have applied an intermediate test. *Id.* at 286. But in insisting that the implementation of those goals be by a least-drastic-alternative classification, Justice Marshall appears to apply the overwhelming interest test. *Id.* at 287–88.

120. *Id.* at 286–88.

121. Although the Marshall-Brennan dissent in *Feeney* recognized that the past discrimination against women is a reason for not allowing the absolute veterans' preference in that case, *id.* at 281, their willingness to accept a lesser promale compensatory discrimination suggests that they have not accorded as much weight to the fact of prior antifemale discrimination as it deserves.

122. Kahn v. Shevin, 416 U.S. 351, 357–60 (1974)(Brennan, J., dissenting).

123. See notes 58–81 & accompanying text *supra*.

124. 411 U.S. 677 (1973).

125. *Id.* at 689 n.22 (citations omitted).

126. *Cf.* Personnel Adm'r of Mass. v. Feeney, 442 U.S. 256, 282 (1979) (Marshall, J., dissenting) ("[t]hat a legislature seeks to advantage one group does not, as a matter of logic or common sense, exclude the possibility that it also intends to disadvantage another").

127. 411 U.S. at 689 n.22.

128. *Id.* See text accompanying note 125 *supra.*

129. *See* Gaston County v. United States, 395 U.S. 285, 296–97 (1969). *Cf.* KANOWITZ, WOMEN AND THE LAW, *supra* note 10 at 199 ("[i]n one area of legal regulation after another, they will find women continuing to be treated either differently from men or less favorably, and judges and legislators continuing to emphasize distinctions between the sexes which, though they are the results of prior unequal treatment, are often presented as justifications for such unequal treatment in the future").

130. United States v. Carolene Prods., 304 U.S. 144, 152–53 n.4 (1938).

131. For a consideration of different meanings of "invidious," see note 88 *supra.*

132. U.S. CONST. amend. XIX.

133. Registration of men for military service recently was instituted by Congress. H.R.J. Res. 521, 96th Cong., 2d Sess. (1980). A three-judge federal district court in Pennsylvania declared the registration statute unconstitutional as a violation of the guarantee of equal protection of law because of its failure to include women. With grant of a hearing by the Supreme Court probable, Juntice Brennan stayed the execution of the lower court order that had declared the statute unconstitutional. *N.Y. Times,* July 20, 1980, at 1, col. 6.

134. Califano v. Goldfarb, 430 U.S. 199, 222 (1977) (Stevens, J., concurring).

135. The powerlessness of males, despite their apparent control of the levers of political and economic power, is not unlike the powerlessness of females, who represent approximately 53 percent of the United States population.

136. 429 U.S. 190 (1976).

137. *See* note 130 & accompanying text *supra.*

138. *See also* Orr v. Orr, 440 U.S. 268 (1979), wherein the Court once again applied a heightened level of scrutiny to strike down what was perceived as an antimale discrimination in statutes that permitted females, but not males, to receive alimony.

139. ILL. ANN. STAT. ch. 3, § 1331 (Smith-Hurd 1961). Such sex-based disparities in the age of majority may now be illegal in light of Craig v. Boren, 429 U.S. 190 (1976), and Stanton v. Stanton, 421 U.S. 7 (1975).

140. In the words of former United States Senator Sam Ervin: "Legally speaking [the lower age of majority] made a woman an adult 3 years before a man. It gave her the right 3 years earlier to manage her own affairs, to make contracts to dispose of her property, and even to bring lawsuits, while it left the man under a disability. He couldn't bring a lawsuit without a legal guardian or aid of a friend. He couldn't make a contract. And he couldn't dispose of property." *Hearings on S.J. Res. 61 and S.J. Res. 231 Before the Senate Comm. on the Judiciary,* 91st Cong., 2d Sess. 182 (1970) (statement of Sam Ervin).

141. 30 Ill. 2d 225, 195 N.E.2d 638 (1964).

142. 198 U.S. 45 (1905).

143. 208 U.S. 412 (1908).

144. *Id.* at 421.

145. *Id.* at 422.

146. *See Hearings on S.J. Res. 61 and S.J. Res. 231 Before the Senate Comm. on the Judiciary,* 91st Cong., 2d Sess. 173 (1970) (statement of Leo Kanowitz).

147. Many women who worked outside the home undoubtedly were expected then, as they often are not, to bear the major family responsibility for myriad tasks within the home as well.

148. Both men and women are burdened by an hours-limitations law that

applies to both sexes by being denied the right to earn extra compensation through overtime work. But this is a shared burden. It is also offset by other social and legal institutions, such as minimum-wage laws and effective union representation, both of which are designed to insure that workers earn an adequate living without having to rely on overtime work. By contrast, the woman-only overtime-limitations laws, in addition to conferring special benefits on women, also burden them with *special* disadvantages.

149. While overtime work properly might be regarded as a social evil to be discouraged by absolute statutory prohibitions or statutory requirements for extraordinary compensation, *see* KANOWITZ, WOMEN AND THE LAW *supra* note 10, at 124–25, allowing men to work overtime inevitably reduced pressures on unions and other institutions to secure wage rates that would, of themselves, have been adequate. Because women worked in the same economic environment as men, they bore the brunt of a lower wage than they otherwise would have received had no overtime work been allowable to either sex, but were deprived of the right, available to men, to make up for lower wages by means of overtime work and the extra income it generated.

150. 430 U.S. 313 (1977).

151. The existence of equal employment opportunity legislation, such as Title VII of the 1964 Civil Rights Act, as amended, and state counterparts, of course would prevent an employer from discriminating on grounds of sex. Under Title VII, pension schemes favoring women over men have been invalidated. *See, e.g.,* Rosen v. Public Serv. Elec. & Gas Co., 477 F.2d 90 (3d Cir. 1973). *Cf.* Equal Employment Opportunity Commission Sex Discrimination Guidelines, 29 C.F.R. 1604.9(f) (1979) ("[i]t shall be an unlawful employment practice for an employer to have a pension or retirement plan which establishes different optional or compulsory retirement ages based on sex, or which differentiates in benefits on the basis of sex").

152. 419 U.S. 498 (1975).

153. 471 F.2d 287 (9th Cir. 1972), *cert. denied,* 412 U.S. 931 (1973).

154. *See also* Califano v. Goldfarb, 430 U.S. 199 (1977); Weinberger v. Wiesenfeld, 420 U.S. 636 (1975). In both cases, the Court perceived the special Social Security benefits for widows, and their denial to widowers, as a discrimination against the covered female employee in that her contributions to the Social Security system produced less protection for her family in the event of her death than was acquired by a male covered employee for his family. Dissenting in *Goldfarb,* Justice Rehnquist disputed this analysis, saying that one could on that basis have argued in *Kahn* that "the real discrimination was between the deceased spouses of the respective widow and widower, who had doubtless by their contributions to the family or marital community helped make possible the acquisition of the property which was now being disparately taxed." 430 U.S. at 239 (Rehnquist, J., dissenting). Although Justice Rehnquist scoffs at the possible use of such an argument in the *Kahn* situation, his hostility toward it once again reflects an inadequate understanding of the dual aspect of all laws that purport to discriminate benignly in favor of one sex.

155. See notes 146–49 & accompanying text *supra.*

156. Here, too, it is useful, for purposes of devising appropiate remedies, to regard the law, because of its dual aspect, as effectively comprising two separate laws. In *Kahn,* the Florida legislature can be seen as having enacted one law that stated, in effect, that widows shall be given tax preference over widowers and

another law that stated, in effect, that the tax law shall prefer husbands over wives in assuring the economic well-being of their surviving spouses.

157. 44 Ill. 2d 15, 253 N.E.2d 373 (1969).

158. In *Duley*, the surviving husband of a covered woman employee who had been fatally injured in the course of her employment was limited by the state's Workmen's Compensation Act, ILL. REV. STAT. ch. 48, § 138.7(f) (1963), to receiving a $500 burial expense and was precluded from bringing a common law tort action against the employer for his wife's death. Had the survivor been the wife of a covered male employee killed under such circumstances, she would have been entitled to substantial death benefits under the Act.

159. 44 Ill. 2d at 19, 253 N.E.2d at 375.

160. *See, e.g.*, CAL. LAB. CODE. § 3501(a) (West 1971), *invalidated in* Arp v. Workers' Comp. Appeals Bd., 19 Cal. 3d 395, 563 P.2d 849, 138 Cal. Rptr. 293 (1977).

161. 420 U.S. 636 (1975).

162. 430 U.S. 199 (1977).

163. *Id.* at 211.

164. *Id.* at 223 (Stevens, J., concurring).

165. *Id.* at 222.

166. *But see* Arp v. Workers' Comp. Appeals Bd., 19 Cal. 3d 395, 563 P.2d 849, 138 Cal. Rptr. 293 (1977), which rejected the claim of a benign purpose in a sex-discriminatory feature of the state's Workers' Compensation Act and noted, among other reasons for invalidating the statute on federal constitutional grounds, that it was "potentially disadvantage[ous to] large numbers of the very sex it purports to aid." *Id.* at 407, 563 P.2d at 855, 138 Cal. Rptr. at 300. In light of such considerations, once the majority in *Wiesenfeld* and the four-member plurality in *Goldfarb* had determined that the discrimination in question was directed against covered women employees, they ought not to have examined the statute to see whether it was "benign" toward surviving wives of covered male employees. Precedent for not inquiring as to a sex-based classification's benign purpose, even where the Court assumes such a purpose might be revealed by the inquiry, has been established in Orr v. Orr, 440 U.S. 268 (1979).

167. 440 U.S. 268 (1979).

168. *Id.* at 282.

169. *Id.* at 283. Justice Stevens had made a similar observation in his *Goldfarb* concurrence two years earlier. "The [wives] who benefit from the disparate treatment are those who were . . .nondependent on their husbands." Califano v. Goldfarb, 430 U.S. at 221 (Stevens, J., concurring).

170. Justice Stevens's position, in his concurrence in *Goldfarb*, although raising other problems, does not suffer from this defect. Although he too failed to grasp the "dual-aspect" character of the discrimination at issue in *Goldfarb*, he nevertheless would have held that the statute did not discriminate against covered women employees because of the noncontractual nature of the right to Social Security benefits. 430 U.S. at 217. He saw the issue, therefore, as going to whether widowers had been unconstitutionally discriminated against and concluded that they had been. In holding that the classification favoring widows did not reflect a benign purpose, Justice Stevens, unlike the four-member plurality who, for the reasons discussed at note 166 *supra*, should not even have tried to determine this question, did not place himself in their contradictory position.

171. 440 U.S. at 283.

172. *See* KANOWITZ, WOMEN AND THE LAW, *supra* note 10, at 4: "Not only do legal norms tend to mirror the social norms that govern male-female relationships; they also exert a profoound influence upon the development and change of those social norms. Rules of law that treat of the sexes *per se* inevitably produce far-reaching effects upon social, psychological and economic aspects of male-female reltionships beyond the limited confines of legislative chambers and courtrooms,"

173. See text accompanying note 171 *supra*. *See also* United Jewish Organizations v. Carey, 430 U.S. 144, 173–74 (1977) (Brennan, J., concurring).

174. The adverse effects for women of a women-only minimum wage or overtime pay law are qualitively different from the adverse effects upon minorities of general minimum-wage laws that are alleged to arise by some economists of the Chicago School, primarily Professor Milton Friedman. For example, the adverse effects upon women of a women-only minimum-wage law are caused by the law's dual aspect. Employers need a work force. If they have a choice, other things being equal, they will hire males rather than females because of the women-only minimum wage requirement. By contrast, in the case of a sex-neutral minimum wage, the basic problem of employers is whether to hire people who, because of inadequate training or lack of skills, may not produce enough to justify payment of the minimum wage. Presumably, if employers could pay less, they would hire such people—or so the argument runs—who would be overwhelmingly black or members of other minorities. Employer reluctance to hire women because of a women-only minimum wage is not based on any notions that the prescribed wage is higher than their work should yield. Rather, it is based on the assumption that the employer will receive as good or better work from male employees, but at a lower wage.

175. See notes 91–103 & accompanying text *supra*.

Chapter 4. Remedying Sex Discrimination

1. 411 U.S. 677 (1973). See notes 20–23, chapter 3, & accompanying text.

2. 411 U.S. at 690–91 & n.25.

3. Weinberger v. Wiesenfeld, 420 U.S. 636 (1975). See notes 35–41, chapter 3, & accompanying text.

4. Califano v. Goldfarb, 430 U.S. 199 (1977). See notes 42–43, chapter 3, & accompanying text.

5. Justice Stevens, concurring in the judgment, estimated that the decision would cost the government $750,000,000 per year. 430 U.S. at 219–20.

6. 80 U.S. (13 Wall.) 270 (1872).

7. *Id.* at 286.

8. 54 N.J. 194, 254 A.2d 525 (1969).

9. *Id.* at 202, 254 A.2d at 530.

10. 440 U.S. 268 (1979). See notes 46–57, chapter 3, & accompanying text.

11. 421 U.S. 7 (1975). See note 15, chapter 3.

12. See text accompanying notes 140–41, chapter 3, for a discussion of the benefit-burden dual aspect of sex-discriminatory laws.

13. 42 U.S.C. §§ 2000e to 2000e-17 (1976 & Supp. II 1978).

14. *See also* Craig v. Boren, 429 U.S. 190 (1976), invalidating as an equal-protection violation Oklahoma's prohibition of sales of 3.2 percent beer to eighteen-to twenty-year-old males, but not to females in that same age bracket. The case arose in the federal court in the first instance, and there was thus no state court to

which it could be remanded. By reversing the federal district court, which had upheld the prohibition of the sale to eighteen- to twenty-year-old males, the Supreme Court in effect granted the right to purchase 3.2 percent beer to males rather than take it away from females. Significantly, the Court stated that the "Oklahoma *Legislature* is free to *redefine* any cutoff age for the purchase and sale of 3.2 percent beer that it may choose, provided that the *redefinition* operates in a gender-neutral fashion."*Id.* at 210 n.24 (emphasis added).

15. Califano v. Webster, 430 U.S. 313, 314 (1977).

16. Califano v. Westcott, 443 U.S. 76 (1979). See notes 19–31 & accompanying text *infra. See also* Califano v. Goldfarb, 430 U.S. 199 (1977).

17. See notes 48–51 & accompanying text *infra* for a discussion of why extension is appropriate, notwithstanding the economic burdens it might impose on employers.

18. *See, e.g.*, State v. Fairfield Communities Land Co., 260 Ark. 277, 538 S.W.2d 698, *cert. denied*, 429 U.S. 1004 (1976); Arp. v. Workers' Comp. Appeals Bd., 19 Cal. 3d 395, 563 P.2d 849, 138 Cal. Rptr. 293 (1977).

19. *See, e.g.*, Homemakers Inc. v. Division of Indus. Welfare, 509 F.2d 20 (9th Cir. 1974), *cert. denied*, 423 U.S. 1063 (1976).

20. 443 U.S. 76 (1979).

21. Restructuring, as used in this chapter, is primarily a shorthand expression for invalidation of the detrimental aspects of a sex-discriminatory law, coupled with extension to the previously nonbenefited sex of the law's beneficial aspects.

22. 443 U.S. at 79–80. Although the parties had not argued that nullification of the program was the proper remedial choice, Justice Powell, in a dissent joined by Chief Justice Burger and Justices Stewart and Rehnquist, decried "the extension of benefits [that] Congress wished to prevent." *Id.* at 95 (Powell, J., dissenting). Justice Powell would have preferred an injunction prohibiting further payment under the program, which would "conserve the funds appropriated until Congress determines which group, if any, it does want to assist."*Id.* at 96.

23. *Id.* at 90–91.

24. *Id.* at 89–90.

25. *Id.* at 91.

26. *Id.* at 92–93.

27. *Id.* at 92.

28. *Id.*

29. *Id.*

30. *Id.*

31. *Id.*

32. *Id.* at 93.

33. 208 U.S. 412 (1908).

34. Rosenfeld v. Southern Pac. Co., 444 F.2d 1219 (9th Cir. 1971). But see text accompanying notes 59–62 *infra*, which argues that only those aspects of the law that had deprived women of equal job opportunities with men were struck down by *Rosenfeld*.

35. State v. Fairfield Communities Land Co., 260 Ark. 277, 538 S.W.2d 698, *cert. denied*, 42i U.S. 1004 (1976).

36. Homemakers Inc. v. Division of Indus. Welfare, 509 F.2d 20 (9th Cir. 1974), *cert. denied*, 423 U.S. 1063 (1976).

37. Ridinger v. General Motors Corp., 325 F. Supp. 1089 (S.D. Ohio 1971), *rev'd on other grounds*, 474 F.2d 949 (6th Cir. 1972).

38. *Id.*

39. 318 F. Supp. 1368 (E.D. Ark. 1970).

40. Hays v. Potlatch Forests, Inc., 465 F.2d 1081 (8th Cir. 1972).

41. *See id.* at 1083–84.

42. 260 Ark. 277, 538 S.W.2d 698, *cert. denied,* 429 U.S. 1004 (1976).

43. *See id.* at 278, 538 S.W.2d at 699.

44. See text accompanying notes 141–44, chapter 3.

45. *See, e.g.,* ARK. STAT. ANN. § 81–601 (1976), *held preempted by Civil Rights Act in* State v. Fairfield Communities Land Co., 260 Ark. 277, 538 S.W.2d 698 (1976); CAL. LAB. CODE §§ 1251–53 (West 1971) (repealed by Cal. Stat. 1976, ch. 1177, § 1, at 5274).

46. 243 U.S. 426 (1917).

47. By 1917 too many men had grown to depend on the availability of overtime work. In the absence of an understanding about their dual aspect, the extension of such laws to men would have burdened them with the inability to work overtime hours along with benefiting them by permitting them to refuse to work overtime. See text following note 50 *infra.*

48. The result in Potlatch Forests, Inc. v. Hays, 318 F. Supp. 1368 (E.D. Ark. 1970), *aff'd,* 465 F.2d 1081 (8th Cir. 1972), for the same reasons, also would appear to make more sense than the decision of the Ninth Circuit in Homemakers Inc. v. Division of Indus. Welfare, 509 F.2d 20 (9th Cir. 1974), *cert. denied,* 423 U.S. 1064 (1976), which refused to extend to men a state overtime-wages-and-hours law applicable to women only, because it would "usurp the legislative power vested excusively in the state." Significantly, that extension to men was subsequently effected by action of the California Legislature, CAL. LAB. CODE § 1173 (West Supp. 1980), and the California Industrial Welfare Commission Work Order No. 1-80, 8 CAL. ADMIN. CODE § 11180 (1979). The same timidity is reflected in the decision of the California Supreme Court in Arp v. Workers' Comp. Appeals Bd., 19 Cal. 3d 395, 563 P.2d 849, 138 Cal. Rptr. 293 (1977), which invalidated a workers' compensation provision giving surviving widows of covered male employees greater death benefits than was granted to surviving widowers of covered female employees who lost their lives in the course of employment. Rather than extend these benefits to the surviving spouses of female employees, however, the California court simply invalidated the provision, and left to the legislature the task of restructuring death benefits under the statute.

49. See text accompanying note 31 *supra.*

50. If an hours-limitation law is simply invalidated because it applies to women only, women will lose the benefit of the law's truly protective aspects, i.e., they can thereafter be forced to work overtime like men.

51. See text following note 53 *infra.*

52. H.R. 1784, 94th Cong., 1st Sess. (1979). *See* AFL-CIO News, October 27, 1979, at 1, col. 1.

53. Weeks v. Southern Bell Tel. & Tel. Co., 408 F.2d 228, 233 (5th Cir. 1969) (quoting Rule 69 promulgated pursuant to GA. CODE ANN. § 54–122(d) (1974)).

54. 444 F.2d 1219 (9th Cir. 1971).

55. CAL. LAB. CODE §§ 1250–52 (West 1971) (repealed by Stats. 1976, ch. 1177, § 1).

56. CAL. LAB. CODE §§ 1350–52.5 (West 1971) (amended by Stats. 1971, ch. 457, § 1).

57. 444 F.2d at 1227.

58. *Id.*

59. See text following note 141, chapter 3.

60. See notes 142–49 & accompanying text, chapter 3.

61. See text accompanying notes 18–20 *supra*.

62. See note 53 & accompanying text *supra*.

63. CAL. LAB. CODE § 1182 (West Supp. 1980) was amended in 1972 to apply to "employees" rather than to "women and minors" only. *See* Work Order No. 1–80 of California Industrial Welfare Commission, 8 CAL. ADMIN. CODE § 11180 (1979).

64. See note 52 & accompanying text *supra*.

65. See note 21 *supra*.

66. For a variety of reasons, it would be inappropriate for a court to extend the *burden* of a statute to a group upon which it had not been originally cast by the legislature. As a result, for the obligation of compulsory military service to survive constitutional challenge, it must be made sex-neutral not by a court, but by Congress itself. The unwillingness of the United States Supreme Court, in resolving equal-protection challenges, to cast a burden upon a group that had not originally been burdened by a legislature, can be seen in Police Department of Chicago v. Mosley, 408 U.S. 92 (1972).

67. United States v. Reiser, 532 F.2d 673 (9th Cir. 1976); United States v. Camara, 451 F.2d 1122 (5th Cir. 1971); United States v. Dorris, 319 F. Supp. 1308 (N.D. Ga. 1970); United States v. Cook, 311 F. Supp. 618 (W.D. Pa. 1970).

68. In what appears to be the latest case challenging the draft on constitutional grounds before the *Craig* test was announced, the Court of Appeals for the Ninth Circuit upheld the male-only draft in a one-paragraph opinion by simply asserting a "rational basis" for the gender classification. United States v. Reiser, 532 F.2d 673 (9th Cir. 1976). Applying a suspect-classification analysis, the district court had held the male-only draft unconstitutional. United States v. Reiser, 394 F. Supp. 1060 (D. Mont. 1975).

69. On June 25, 1981, while this volume was in press, the U.S. Supreme Court held that a male-only draft-registration requirement does not violate the Due Process Clause of the Fifth Amendment. Rostker v. Goldberg, 49 LW 4798 (1981). This decision is discussed in the Postscript, *infra.*

70. See notes 11 – 15, chapter 3, & accompanying text.

71. In urging the abrogation of the benign-discrimination doctrine in the gender-bias area, I do not intend to cast any doubt on the validity of laws like the Equal Pay Act of 1963, 29 U.S.C. § 206(d)(1) (1976), and Title VII of the 1964 Civil Rights Act (as amended). 42 U.S.C. §§ 2000e to 2000e-17 (1976 & Supp. II 1978). To be sure, those laws were enacted primarily to assist female victims of past discrimination in the employment sphere. At first glance, therefore, they would appear to violate the principle negatively implied by Washington v. Davis, 426 U.S. 229 (1976), and Personnel Adm'r of Mass. v. Feeney, 442 U.S. 256 (1979), namely, that a law, although phrased in sex-neutral terms, is unconstitutionally discriminatory if it was *intended* to benefit one sex more than another and in fact had that effect. But the Equal Pay Act and Title VII, despite their apparent intention primarily to benefit women victims of past discrimination, do in fact benefit both sexes. Indeed, in numerous cases male victims of employment discrimination have prevailed in the Equal Pay Act or Title VII claims. *See, e.g.,* Diaz v. Pan Am. World Airways, 442 F.2d 385 (5th Cir. 1971). Despite their primary intention, therefore, those Acts, by treating men and women alike, avoid

the dangers of a benign-discriminatory law described earlier. They recognize that men, as well as women, have been and continue to be victims of sex-based employment discrimination. And they avoid burdening women with any detrimental aspects of those laws that would be felt by them if those laws were not equally applicable to men.

72. See notes 116–22 chapter 3, & accompanying text.

73. *See* L. KANOWITZ, WOMEN AND THE LAW: THE UNFINISHED REVOLUTION. note 10.

74. 416 U.S. 351 (1974).

75. Weinberger v. Wiesenfeld, 420 U.S. 636 (1975). See notes 35–41, chapter 3, & accompanying text.

76. Califano v. Goldfarb, 430 U.S. 199 (1977). See notes 42–45, chapter 3, & accompanying text.

77. Orr v. Orr, 440 U.S. 268 (1979). See notes 46–57, chapter 3, & accompanying text.

Chapter 5. The Equal Rights Amendment and the Overtime Illusion

1. L. KANOWITZ, WOMEN AND THE LAW: THE UNFINISHED REVOLUTION, University of New Mexico Press, Albuquerque, 1969.

2. *Id.* at vii–viii.

3. *Id.* at 195.

4. *Id.*

5. *Id.* at 154.

6. *Id.*

7. *Id.* at 195.

8. *Id.* at 100.

9. Kanowitz, *Women and the Law: A Reply to Some of the Commentators,* 4 FAM. L. Q. 19, 29 (1970).

Chapter 6. The New Mexico Equal Rights Amendment

1. 404 U.S. 71 (1971).

2. *See, e.g.,* L. KANOWITZ, WOMEN AND THE LAW: THE UNFINISHED REVOLUTION, University of New Mexico Press, Albuquerque, 1969.

3. 16 Wall. 130.21 L.Ed. 442 (U.S. 1872).

4. 208 U.S. 412 (1908).

5. 335 U.S. 464 (1948).

6. 368 U.S. 57 (1961).

7. White v. Crook, 251 F.Supp. 401 (N.D. Ala. 1966).

8. 281 F.Supp. 8 (D.Conn. 1968).

9. Miskunas v. Union Carbide Corp., 399 F.2d 847 (7th Cir. 1968), *cert. denied* 393 U.S. 1066 (1969).

10. Williams v. McNair, 316 F.Supp. 134 (D.S.C. 1970). *aff d* 401 U.S. 951 (1971).

11. Note 1 *supra*.

12. *See* Loving v. Virginia, 388 U.S. 1. 9 (1967); McLaughlin v. Florida, 379 U.S. 184, 191–92 (1964); Korematsu v. United States, 323 U.S. 214, 216 (1944).

13. Eisenstadt v. Baird, 405 U.S. 438 (1972). Mr. Justice Brennan, in footnote 7 of his opinion, made the following observations: "Of course, if we were to con-

clude that the Massachusetts statute impinges upon fundamental freedoms under *Griswold*, the statutory classification would have to be not merely *rationally related* to a valid public purpose but *necessary* to the achievement of a *compelling* state interest. *E.g.*, *Shapiro v. Thompson*, 394 U.S. 618 (1969); *Loving v. Virginia*, 388 U.S. 1 (1967). But just as in *Reed v. Reed, supra*, we do not have to address the statute's validity under that test because the law fails to satisfy even the more lenient equal protection standard."

14. 341 F.Supp. 217 (D.C. Ala. 1971): *aff'd* 407 U.S. 970 (1972).

15. Note 2 *supra* at 43–45.

16. Note 11 *supra*.

17. Note 10 *supra*.

18. *See also* Stanley v. Illinois, 405 U.S. 645 (1972), deciding on due-process rather than equal-protection grounds that a father of an illegitimate child cannot be bypassed in awarding custody of a child to strangers. Though the father in the case had urged a violation of the equal-protection clause because mothers of illegitimate children were not accorded this kind of treatment, the court decided the case primarily as a due-process violation because the child could be taken from him without a hearing.

19. 5 Cal.3d 1, 485 P.2d 529, 95 Cal. Rptr. 329 (1971).

20. For a recent example, *compare* People v. Anderson, 6 Cal.3d 628, 493 P. 2d 800. 100 Cal. Rptr. 152 (1972) *with* Furman v. Georgia 40 U.S.L.W. 4923 (1972).

21. But *cf.* Chief Justice Burger's recent observation: "Some lines must be drawn. To challenge such lines by the 'compelling state interest' standard is to condemn them all. So far as I am aware, no state law has ever satisfied this seemingly insurmountable standard, and I doubt one ever will, for it demands nothing less than perfection." Dunn v. Blumstein. 405 U.S. 330 (1972) (dissent).

22. *See* Brown, Emerson, Falk & Freedman, *The Equal Rights Amendment: A Constitutional Basis for Equal Rights for Women*, 80 YALE L.J. 871, 893 (1971).

23. PA. CONST. art. I, § 27 reads; "Equality of rights under the law shall not be denied or abridged in the Commonwealth of Pennsylvania because of the sex of the individual." Adopted May 18, 1971.

24. *See* A Report on Possible Effects of the Equal Rights Amendment (April 5, 1972).

Chapter 7. The ERA: The Task Ahead

1. *See* S.J. Res. 8, 92d Cong., 2d Sess. (1972), H.R.J. Res. 208, 92d Cong., 1st Sess. (1971), 86 Stat. 1523.

2. *See* Note, *The Amending Process: Extending the Ratification Deadline of the Proposed Equal Rights Amendment*, 10 RUT.-CAM. L.J. 91 (1978).

3. As of the date this speech was given, thirty-five states had ratified the ERA. Only one state, Indiana, has given its ratification within the last four years, while five states, including Indiana, have "rescinded" their ratifications.

States ratifying the ERA are:

Hawaii	March 22, 1972
Delaware	March 23, 1972
New Hampshire	March 23, 1972
Idaho	March 24, 1972
Kansas	March 28, 1972
Nebraska	March 29, 1972

Tennessee	April 4, 1972
Alaska	April 5, 1972
Rhode Island	April 14, 1972
New Jersey	April 17, 1972
Texas	April 19, 1972
Iowa	April 21, 1972
Colorado	April 21, 1972
West Virginia	April 22, 1972
Wisconsin	April 26, 1972
New York	May 3, 1972
Michigan	May 22, 1972
Maryland	May 26, 1972
Massachusetts	June 21, 1972
Kentucky	June 26, 1972
Pennsylvania	September 26, 1972
California	November 13, 1972
Wyoming	January 26, 1973
South Dakota	February 5, 1973
Oregon	February 8, 1973
Minnesota	February 12, 1973
New Mexico	February 28, 1973
Vermont	March 1, 1973
Connecticut	March 15, 1973
Washington	March 27, 1973
Maine	January 18, 1974
Montana	January 25, 1974
Ohio	February 7, 1974
North Dakota	February 3, 1975
Indiana	January 18, 1977

[1979]U.S. CODE CONG. & AD. NEWS 349.

States "rescinding" ratification are Idaho, Indiana, Nebraska, Tennessee, and Kentucky, although Kentucky's rescission was vetoed by the state's acting governor.

For the position that rescissions are invalid, *see* Appendix. *But see,* Rhodes & Mabile, *Ratification of Proposed Federal Constitutional Amendments— The States May Rescind,* 45 TENN. L. REV. 703 (1978). The question of the constitutionality of rescission has generated much discussion. *See generally,* Burke, *Validity of Attempts to Rescind Ratification of the Equal Rights Amendment,* 8 U.W. LA. L. REV. 1 (1976); Heckman, *Ratification Of A Constitutional Amendment: Can A State Change Its Mind?,* 6 CONN. L. REV. 28 (1973); Note, *The Equal Rights Amendment: Will States Be Allowed to Change Their Minds?,* 49 NOTRE DAME LAW 657 (1974); Comment, *Constitutional Amendments —The Justiciability of Ratification and Retraction,* 41 TENN. L. REV. 93 (1973).

4. *See generally* L. KANOWITZ, WOMEN AND THE LAW: THE UNFINISHED REVOLUTION (1969) [hereinafter cited as KANOWITZ, WOMEN AND THE LAW]; Brown, Emerson, Falk & Freedman, *The Equal Rights Amendement: A Constitutional Basis for Equal Rights for Women,* 80 YALE L.J. 871 (1971).

5. *See* cases discussed at note 60 *infra.*

6. *See, e.g.,* California Fair Employment Practices Act, CAL. LABOR CODE § 1411, et seq. (West 1978). Section 1411 prohibits discrimination in employment on

the grounds, inter alia, of sex. The law was upheld as a valid exercise of the state police power in Northern Inyo Hosp. v. Fair Employment Practice Comm'n, 38 Cal. App. 3d 14, 112 Cal. Rptr. 872 (1974).

7. For discussions of the constitutional aspects of sex-discriminatory laws, *see, e.g.*, Ginsburg, *Sex Equality and the Constitution*, 52 TUL. L. REV. 451 (1978); Ginsburg, *Gender and the Constitution*, 44 U. CINN. L. REV. 1 (1975); Lombard, *Sex: A Classification in Search of Strict Scrutiny*, 21 WAYNE L. REV. 1355 (1975); Note, *Sex Discrimination and Equal Protection: The Question of a Suspect Classification*, 5 N.Y.U. REV. L. & SOC. CHANGE 1 (1975).

8. U.S. CONST. art. IV, [2, cl. 1 provides: "The citizens of each State shall be entitled to all privileges and immunities of citizens in the several States." U.S. CONST. amend. XIV, § 1 provides, in pertinent part; "No State shall make or enforce any law which shall abridge the privileges or immunities of citizens of the United States."

9. U.S. CONST. amend. V, provides, in pertinent part: "Nor shall any person . . . be deprived of life, liberty, or property, without due process of law." The due-process provision of this amendment has been held to embody an equal-protection guarantee as against the federal government, Mathews v. De Castro, 429 U.S. 181, 182 n.1 (1976); Bolling v. Sharpe, 347 U.S. 497, 499 (1954).

10. U.S. CONST. amend. XIV, § 1, provides, in pertinent part: "Nor shall any State deprive any person of life, liberty, or property, without due process of law."

11. U.S. CONST. amend. XIV, § 1, provides that no state shall "deny to any person within its jurisdiction the equal protection of the laws."

12. *See, e.g.*, former CAL. CIV. CODE §§ 156, 172, and 172a. § 156 provided: "The husband is the head of the family. He may choose any reasonable place or mode of living, and the wife must conform thereto." § 172 provided: "The husband has the management and control of the community personal property, with like absolute power of disposition, other than testamentary, as he has of his separate estate; *provided, however*, that he can not make a gift of such community personal property . . . without a valuable consideration . . . without the written consent of the wife." § 172a similarly gave the husband management and control of the community real property. (West 1954).

§ 156 was finally repealed effective Jan. 1, 1975. CAL. CIV. CODE § 5101. Sections replacing § 172 and § 172a now provide for common control of community property. CAL. CIV. CODE §§ 5125, 5127 (West Supp. 1978) (effective Jan. 1, 1975).

13. *See, e.g.*, Forbush v. Wallace, 405 U.S. 970 (1972), *aff g*, 341 F. Supp. 217 (M.D. Ala. 1971). Based on Alabama's common law rule that the husband's surname is the wife's legal name, the district court upheld an unwritten regulation of the Department of Public Safety which required each married female to use her husband's surname in applying for and obtaining a drivers' license. The court found that the state's interest in preserving the integrity of identification and drivers' records through licenses was a significant state interest. Requiring married females to use the husband's surname was found to be reasonably related to that end. *Id.* 221–22. The Supreme Court affirmed without opinion.

14. *See, e.g.*, Juri v. Juri, 69 Cal. App. 2d 773, 160 P.2d 73 (1945). Upholding the custody award of the former marriage's two offspring to the wife, the California court of appeal cited former CAL. CIV. CODE § 138(2) (West 1954), which provided, in pertinent part: "other things being equal, if the child is of tender years, custody should be given to the mother; if the child is of an age to require

education and preparation for labor or business, then custody should be given to the father." Former § 138 was replaced by CAL. CIV. CODE § 4600 (West Supp. 1978) (amended 1970), which abolishes both statutory preferences. The *Juri* court observed: " 'it is not open to question, and indeed it is universally recognized, that the mother is the natural custodian of her young. This view proceeds on the well known fact that there is no satisfactory substitute for a mother's love.' " 69 Cal. App. 2d at 779, 160 P.2d at 76 (quoting Washburn v. Washburn, 49 Cal. App. 2d 581, 588, 122 P.2d 96, 100 (1942)).

The bias toward awarding custody to the mother remains where the children are illegitimate. Recently the United States Supreme Court upheld a Georgia statute that recognizes the mother as sole parent and gives to the mother all the "paternal" power. The father challenged the statute, claiming it violated equal protection by denying him visitation rights if his child were adopted without being legitimized. *See* Quilloin v. Walcott, 434 U.S. 246 (1978); GA.CODE ANN. § 74–203 (1973).

15. *See, e.g.,* Childs v. Charles, 46 Ga. App. 648, 168 S.E. 914 (1933) (accrued rent held not payable to wife's estate, although title was in wife and wife contracted with the boarder, because husband as head of the household had superior power to make contracts regarding the property).

16. *See, e.g.,* State v. Costello, 56 N.J. 334, 282 A.2d 748 (1971) (where females were subject to indeterminate sentence of up to five years not reducible for continuous orderly deportment, while males were subject to sentencing by judge for less than maximum term and reduction for good behavior for same offense, disparate sentencing treatment impinged on fundamental interests and state would be required to show a substantial justification for sentencing scheme on remand).

17. *See e.g.,* State v. Hall, 187 So.2d 861 (1966) (exclusion of women from jury service pursuant to statute did not deny woman defendant her right to equal protection of the law under the Fourteenth Amendment).

18. Among these were maximum hours laws for women, or women and minors, only, *see* KANOWITZ, WOMEN AND THE LAW, *supra* note 4, at 117-24, 182–88 (1969); weight-lifting limits in employment that were applicable only to women workers, *id.* at 114-17; and women-only minimum-wage provisions, *id.* at 188-92.

19. *See* United States v. Reiser, 394 F. Supp. 1060 (D. Mont. 1975), *rev'd,* 532 F.2d 673 (9th Cir. 1976) (court of appeals reversed decision wherein defendant male draftee's motion to dismiss an indictment against him for failure to submit to induction was granted. The district court found the sex-based classification suspect and held that the government failed to demonstrate a compelling interest in the distinction. The draft law that inducted only males and not females was held violative of equal protection). [But see Postscript, *infra,* discussing U.S. Supreme Court decision in Rostker v. Goldberg, 49. LW 4798 (1981) upholding male-only draft-registration law.]

20. *See* Weinberger v. Wiesenfeld, 420 U.S. 636 (1975) (Social Security Act provision that granted survivors' benefits based on earnings of a deceased husband and father to both widow and minor children in her care, but granted benefits based on earnings of a deceased wife only to the minor children and not the widower, violated the equal-protection clause. The Court held that both widows and widowers should receive support to enable them to care for young children at home, and noted that women's earnings contribute to a family's support as do men's, and that benefits accruing from earnings should be equal).

21. *See* KANOWITZ, WOMEN AND THE LAW, *supra* note 4, at 154–92; Note, *Are Sex-Based Classifications Constitutionally Suspect?*, 66 NW. U.L. REV. 481 (1971); and sources cited at note 4 *supra*.

22. 208 U.S. 412 (1908).

23. 335 U.S. 464 (1948).

24. *Id.* at 467.

25. 368 U.S. 57 (1961).

26. *Id.* at 69. In 1975, relying on the defendant's Sixth Amendment right to a jury trial in criminal cases, the Court held it unconstitutional to exclude women or give them automatic exemptions from jury duty based on sex. Taylor v. Louisiana, 419 U.S. 522 (1975).

27. 83 U.S. (16 Wall.) 130 (1872).

28. *Id.* at 139.

29. *Id.* at 141.

30. *Id.* at 141–42.

31. In re Bradwell, 55 Ill. 535, 539 (1869).

32. *See, e.g.*, Williamson v. Lee Optical Co., 348 U.S. 483 (1955); Lindsley v. Natural Carbonic Gas Co., 220 U.S. 61, 78 (1911); *see generally*, Tussman & tenBroek, *The Equal Protection of the Laws*, 37 CAL. L. REV. 341 (1949).

33. Hoyt v. Florida, 368 U.S. 57 (1961).

34. *See Forum, Equal Protection and the Burger Court*, 2 HASTINGS CONST. L.Q. 645 (1975); *see generally*, Note, *Developments in the Law—Equal Protection*, 82 HARV. L. REV. 1065 (1969).

35. *See, e.g.*, Loving v. Virginia, 388 U.S. 1 (1967) (state antimiscegenation laws that discriminate on the basis of race violate the equal-protection clause); Korematsu v. United States, 323 U.S. 214 (1944) (statutes that discriminate against a class of persons because of their national origin must be strictly scrutinized).

36. Interference with a "fundamental" right triggers a more stringent standard of review. *See, e.g.*, Zablocki v. Redhail, 434 U.S. 374 (1978) (marriage is a fundamental right); Shapiro v. Thompson, 394 U.S. 618 (1969) (right to travel is fundamental); Harper v. Virginia Bd. of Elections, 383 U.S. 663 (1966) (right to vote is fundamental).

37. *Cf.* Dunn v. Blumstein, 405 U.S. 330, 363–64 (1972) (Burger, C.J., dissenting): "Some lines must be drawn. To challenge such lines by the 'compelling state interest' standard is to condemn them all. So far as I am aware, no state law has ever satisfied this seemingly insurmountable standard, and I doubt one ever will, for it demands nothing less than perfection." *But cf.* Regents of the Univ. of Cal. v. Bakke, 438 U.S. 265 (1978) (opinion by Justice Powell: state's interest in achieving racial diversity in governmental educational programs is compelling).

38. *See, e.g.*, Note, *Are Sex-Based Classifications Constitutionally Suspect?*, 66 NW. U. L. REV. 481, 493–95 (1971); Note, *Developments in the Law—Equal Protection*, 82 HARV. L. REV. 1065, 1173–77 (1969); and note 5 *supra* and sources listed therein.

39. *See* Note, *Sex Discrimination and Equal Protection: Do We Need A Constitutional Amendment?*, 84 HARV. L. REV. 1499, 1507–08 (1971); sources cited at note 4 *supra*.

40. 188 CONG. REC. 9598 (1972).

41. *See* S. J. Res. 8, 92nd Cong., 2d Sess. (1972), H.R.J. Res. 208, 92nd Cong., 1st Sess. (1971), 86 Stat. 1523 (1972), 118 CONG. REC. 9598 (1972).

42. *See Hearings on S. J. Res. 61 and S. J. Res. 231 Before the Senate Comm. on the Judiciary*, 91st Cong. 2d Sess. 165 (1970) (testimony of L. Kanowitz) [hereinafter cited as 1970 Hearings].

43. *See id.* at 298–99 (testimony of T. Emerson).

44. *See* Hale & Kanowitz, *Women and the Draft: A Response to Critics of the Equal Rights Amendment*, 23 HASTINGS L. J. 199 (1971); Note, *The Equal Rights Amendment and the Military*, 82 YALE L. J. 1533 (1973).

45. *See* chapter 2, *supra.* The court in United States v. Reiser, note 19 *supra*, at 1062 noted that women "will never accomplish total equality unless they are allowed to accept the concomitant obligations of citizenship," (i.e., compulsory military service). *See also* Brown, Emerson, Falk & Freedman, *The Equal Rights Amendment: A Constitutional Basis for Equal Rights for Women*, 80 YALE L. J. 871, 873–74 (1971).

46. *See, e.g.*, McGuire v. McGuire, 157 Neb. 226, 59 N.W.2d 336 (1953).

47. UNIFORM MARRIAGE AND DIVORCE ACT. § 308 (1973).

48. California has adopted a version of the Uniform Act. CAL. CIV. CODE § 4801 (West Supp. 1978) (amended 1976), for example, provides that the following circumstances shall be considered by the court in determining whether, and in what amount, support payments shall be ordered: "(1) The earning capacity and needs of each spouse. (2) The obligations and assets, including the separate property, of each. (3) The duration of the marriage. (4) The ability of the supported spouse to engage in gainful employment without interfering with the interests of dependent children in the custody of the spouse. (5) The time required for the supported spouse to acquire appropriate education, training, and employment. (6) The age and health of the parties. (7) The standard of living of the parties. (8) Any other factors which it deems just and equitable."

49. The Uniform Act indirectly discourages maintenance awards by preferring allocation of property to the parties to provide necessary support. Maintenance payments may be awarded only if the Court finds that the spouse seeking maintenance: "(1) lacks sufficient property to provide for his reasonable needs; and (2) is unable to support himself through appropriate employment or is the custodian of a child whose condition or circumstances make it appropriate that the custodian not be required to seek employment outside the home. (b) The maintenance order shall be in such amounts and for periods of time as the court deems just, without regard to marital misconduct, and after considering all relevant factors including: (1) the financial resources of the party seeking maintenance, including marital property apportioned to him, his ability to meet his needs independently, and the extent to which a provision for support of a child living with the party includes a sum for that party as custodian; (2) the time necesary to acquire sufficient education or training to enable the party seeking maintenance to find appropriate employment; (3) the standard of living established during the marriage; (4) the duration of the marriage; (5) the age and the physical and emotional condition of the spouse seeking maintenance; and (6) the ability of the spouse from whom maintenance is sought to meet his needs while meeting those of the spouse seeking maintenance." UNIFORM MARRIAGE AND DIVORCE ACT § 308, 435–36 (1973). *See also* Goodman, Oberman & Wheat, *Rights and Obligations of Child Support*, 7 SW. U. L. REV. 36 (1975).

50. Orr v. Orr, 47 U.S.L.W. 4224 (1979).

51. This attitude was formerly embodied in statutory law. *See* former CAL. CIV. CODE § 138(2), note 14 *supra*.

52. *See* comment on Georgia law preferring unwed mothers to unwed fathers, note 14 *supra*.

53. *See, e.g.*, Watts v. Watts, 350 N.Y.S. 2d 285 (1973) (presumption that mother should have custody of children of tender years violated state law and was unconstitutional). *See also* Foster & Freed, *Child Custody*, 39 N.Y.U.L. REV. 423 (1964); Podell, Peck & First, *Custody—To Which Parent?*, 56 MARQ. U. L. REV. 51 (1972).

54. *See, e.g.*, CAL. CIV. CODE § 4600(a) (West Supp. 1979), *as amended by* 1972 Cal. Stats., ch. 1007, § 1, deleting the former language, which stated: "but, other things being equal, custody shall be given to the mother if the child is of tender years." *See* note 14 *supra*.

55. *See,e.g.*, Ridinger v. General Motors Corp., 325 F. Supp. 1089, 1093–94 (S.D. Ohio 1971). State statutes restricting employment of females in factories were held in conflict with, and superseded by, equal employment opportunities provisions of 1964 Civil Rights Act, which prohibit discrimination in employment unless sex is a bona fide occupational qualification reasonably necessary to normal operation of business.

56. *See* U.S. DEPT. OF LABOR, WOMEN'S BUREAU, ANALYSIS OF COVERAGE AND WAGE RATES OF STATE MINIMUM WAGE LAWS AND ORDERS, *passim* (Bulletin 291, Aug. 1, 1965).

57. *See, e.g.*, Ridinger v. General Motors Corp., 325 F. Supp. 1089, 1092–94 (S.D. Ohio 1971).

58. *See* KANOWITZ, WOMEN AND THE LAW *supra* note 4, at 192–96.

59. *See* 1970 *Hearings, supra* note 42, at 161, 172–74. That research apparently contributed, along with pressure from rank-and-file women members of the organized labor movement, to a dramatic turnabout in the position of the AFL-CIO leadership who, for these last six or seven years, have been among the most active and influential ERA supporters.

60. *See, e.g.*, Katzenbach v. McClung, 379 U.S. 294 (1964). Title II of Civil Rights Act of 1964, § 201, 42 U.S.C. § 2000a (1964), which prohibits discrimination in places of public accommodation, was held to be within the congressional power to regulate interstate commerce as applied to a small restaurant that served mostly local patrons. The *Katzenbach* Court held that the restaurant was sufficiently connected with interstate commerce to justify congressional exercise of power because a substantial portion of the food served in the restaurant had moved in interstate commerce. *See also* Perez v. United States, 402 U.S. 146 (1971), where sufficient connection was found between purely local "loan-sharking" and interstate crime to sustain regulation and prohibition by Congress of such activities in Title II of the Consumer Credit Protection Act, § 201, 18 U.S.C. § 891 *et seq.* (Supp. V 1964). The law is based on the Congressional finding that local extortionate credit transactions adversely affect interstate commerce.

61. *See, e.g.*, U.S. CONST. amend. XIV, § 5.

62. A 1975 Gallup Poll revealed that 58 percent of those interviewed favored the Amendment, while only 24 percent were opposed. A 1976 Gallup Poll produced similar results, with 57 percent in favor and 24 percent opposed. THE GALLUP POLL: PUBLIC OPINION 1972–77 447, 684 (G. GALLUP ed. 1978).

63. The amending process of the federal constitution is set forth in art. 5: "The Congress, whenever two thirds of both Houses shall deem it necessary, shall propose Amendments to this Constitution . . . which . . . shall be valid . . . as Part of this Constitution, when ratified by the Legislatures of three fourths of the several States. . . ."

64. Alabama, Georgia, Florida, South Carolina, North Carolina, Virginia, Arkansas, and Oklahoma are among the southern states that have not ratified. Utah, center of the Mormon Church, has not ratifed. Tennessee, Nebraska, and Idaho have purported to rescind. *See* note 3 *supra.*

65. *See* notes 59 and 42 *supra.*

66. *See Hearings on H.J. Res. 35 & 208 and H.R. 916 Before the House Comm. on the Judiciary,* 92d Cong., 1st Sess. 343 (1971) (testimony of L. Kanowitz).

67. *See* W. Barnett, Sexual Freedom and the Constitution (1973). Attacks against statutes prohibiting homosexuality and homosexual acts have been raised on several constitutional grounds: under the right to privacy stemming from the Bill of Rights, Buchanan v. Batchelor, 308 F. Supp. 729 (N.D. Tex. 1970), *vacated and remanded for reconsideration on constitutional grounds sub nom.* Wade v. Buchanan, 401 U.S. 989 (1971); that criminal statutes proscribing sodomy are void for vagueness, Hogan v. State, 84 Nev. 372, 441 P.2d 620 (1968); and that sodomy laws are an establishment of religion in violation of the First Amendment establishment clause, State v. Rinehart, 70 Wash. 2d 649, 424 P.2d 906 (1967), *cert. denied,* 389 U.S. 832 (1967).

68. Ill. Const. art. 14, § 4.

69. 404 U.S. 71 (1971).

70. 411 U.S. 677 (1973).

71. *Id.* at 682, 688.

72. Justice Powell, concurring in the judgment and joined by Chief Justice Burger and Justice Blackmun, interpreted the meaning of the proposed Equal Rights Amendment in the opposite sense from that adopted by the plurality opinion in *Frontiero. Id.* at 691. The plurality cited passage of the Equal Rights Amendment resolution as support for its finding that classifications based on sex are inherently invidious. *Id.* at 687. In his concurring opinion, Justice Powell stated that the court should defer categorizing sex classifications as suspect due to the pendency of the Equal Rights Amendment. He expressed the view that the amendatory process is the proper manner in which to embody proscription of sex classifications as "suspect": "By acting prematurely and unnecessarily, as I view it, the Court has assumed a decisional responsibility at the very time when state legislatures, functioning within the traditional democratic process, are debating the proposed Amendment. It seems to me that this reaching out to pre-empt by judicial action a major political decision which is currently in process of resolution does not reflect appropriate respect for duly prescribed legislative processes.

"There are times when this Court, under our system, cannot avoid a constitutional decision on issues which normally should be resolved by the elected representatives of the people. But democratic institutions are weakened, and confidence in the restraint of the Court is impaired, when we appear unnecessarily to decide sensitive issues of broad social and political importance at the very time they are under consideration within the prescribed constitutional processes." *Id.* at 692.

As noted in the discussion of Craig v. Boren, 429 U.S. 190 (1976), see notes 73–77 and 82–83 and accompanying text *supra,* members of the plurality in

Frontiero subsequently retreated from their view that sex classifications are "suspect."

73. 429 U.S. 190 (1976).

74. The standard of scrutiny was formulated as follows: "To withstand constitutional challenge, previous cases establish that classifications by gender must serve important governmental objectives and must be substantially related to achievement of those objectives." *Id.* at 197. For a discussion of "middle tier" analysis from its inception in *Reed, see* Gunther, *The Supreme Court, 1971 Term— Foreword: In Search of Evolving Doctrine on a Changing Court: A Model for A Newer Equal Protection,* 86 HARV. L. REV. 1 (1972).

75. 429 U.S. 190 (1976); *see also* Orr v. Orr, 47 U.S.L.W. 4224 (1979).

76. 416 U.S. 351 (1974); *see also* Califano v. Webster, 430 U.S. 313 (1977); Schlesinger v. Ballard, 419 U.S. 498 (1975).

77. "While doubtless some widowers are in financial need, no one suggests that such need results from sex discrimination as in the case of widows." 416 U.S. at 360 (Brennan, J., dissenting); *see also,* Craig v. Boren, 429 U.S. 190, 219 (1976) (Rehnquist, J., dissenting): "There is no suggestion in the Court's opinion that males in this age group are in any way peculiarly disadvantaged, subject to systematic discriminatory treatment, or otherwise in need of special solicitude from the courts."

78. Regents of the Univ. of Cal. v. Bakke, 438 U.S. 265 (1978). Technically, *Bakke* was not a constitutional decision, since only Justice Powell held that a numerical quota based on race, even if aimed at correcting the present effects of past societal discrimination, violated the Fourteenth Amendment's equal-protection guarantes. The Court's invalidation of the quota was achieved, however, because four other members of the court held that it violated Title VI of the 1964 Civil Rights Act.

79. 416 U.S. 351 (1974) (widows could constitutionally be granted property tax exemption, but not widowers, because loss of husband imposes greater financial impact than loss of wife).

80. 430 U.S. 313 (1977). *Webster* held constitutional a statute allowing women to subtract three more lower earning years than males, as it helped remedy the effects of past discrimination when women applied for social security benefits.

81. *But see* Marchioro v. Chaney, 47 U.S.L.W. 2090 (1978) (Washington Supreme Court) (A Washington statute that requires that both sexes be equally represented on political party state committees, and the chairman and vicechairman of state committees be of opposite sexes, does not violate the state constitution's equal rights amendment.)

82. 429 U.S. at 197. *See* note 74 *supra.*

83. 429 U.S. at 197 (emphasis added).

84. *See, e.g.,* Stanton v. Stanton, 421 U.S. 7, 14–15 (1975); Taylor v. Louisiana, 419 U.S. 522, 537 (1975).

85. *See* Justice Powell's concurrence in the judgment in Frontiero v. Richardson, discussed at note 72 *supra.*

86. *Id.*

87. *See* 1970 Hearings, *supra* note 42, at 164.

88. *See* text accompanying notes 38 and 39 *supra.*

89. ALAS. CONST. art. I, § 3; COLO. CONST. art. II, § 29; CONN. CONST. art. I, § 20; HAWAII CONST. art. I, § 4; ILL. CONST. art, I, § 18; MD. CONST. DECL. OF RTS.

art. 46; Mont. Const. art. II, § 4; N.H. Const. Pt. I, art 2d; N.M. Const. art. II, § 18; Pa Const. art. I, § 28; Tex. Const. art. I, § 3a; Utah Const. art. IV, § 1; Va. Const. art. 1, § 11; Wash Const. art. 31, §§ 1, 2; Wyo. Const. art. I, §§ 2, 3. *See* Kurtz, *The State Equal Rights Amendments and Their Impact on Domestic Relations Law*, 11 Fam. L.Q. 101 (1977).

90. *See generally Symposium: The New Mexico Equal Rights Amendment– Assessing Its Impact*, 3 N.M. L. Rev. 1–135 (1973).

91. Publ. L. No. 88–38, § 3, 77 Stat. 56 (codified at 29 U.S.C. § 206(d)(1)(1963)).

92. Pub. L. No. 88–352, 78 Stat. 253 (codified at 42 U.S.C. § 2000e *et seq.* (1964)).

93. Exec. Order No. 11,246, 30 Fed. Reg. 12,319 (1965), *as amended by* Exec. Order No. 13,375, 32 Fed. Reg. 14,303 (1967); 30 Fed. Reg. 12,935 (1965), *as amended by* Exec. Order No. 11,375, 32 Fed. Reg. 14,303 (1967).

94. Education Amendments of 1972, Pub. L. No. 92–318, tit. IX, § 901, 86 Stat. 373 (amending 20 U.S.C. §§ 1681–86 (1970)). Section 901(a) of Title IX (20 U.S.C. § 1681(a) (1976) provides: "No person in the United States shall, on the basis of sex, be excluded from participation in, be denied the benefits of, or be subjected to discrimination under any education program or activity receiving federal financial assistance . . . ." *See* Bueck & Orleans, *Sex Discrimination —A Bar to a Democratic Education: Overview of Title IX of the Education Amendments of 1972*, 6 Conn. L. Rev. 1(1973).

95. 15 U.S.C. § 1961 *et seq.* (1976).

96. *See* note 62 *supra.*

97. The validity of the 39-month extension will undoubtedly be the subject of future litigation in view of the conflicting opinions of constitutional-law experts expressed during congressional hearings on the extension. *See* Report of the Judiciary Committee on the Proposed Equal Rights Amendment Extension, 95th Congress, 2d session, House of Representatives, Report No. 95–1405 (August 1, 1978). The principal arguments by the opponents of the extension have been that it required a two-thirds vote of Congress, rather than a mere majority, even if Congress had the power to change the required time limit. The opponents of extension further argued that, in any event, the original seven-year limit for ratification was immutable. More persuasive to Congress, however, were the arguments of the advocates of extension that since the original time limit was not contained in the body of the Amendment itself, but appeared only in the proposal, Congress retained authority to review the limit should circumstances warrant, and that for the same reasons, only a simple majority vote, rather than a two-thirds vote, was required on the extension question. Regardless of the ultimate determination of this question as a matter of law, it is clear that the extension will be perceived by many people as a species of rule-changing after the game has started, thereby presenting an additional obstacle to ratification during the extended period.

98. *See* 1970 Hearings, *supra* note 42, at 166.

99. *See* L. Kanowitz, Women and the Law, *supra* note 4, at 197.

Chapter 8. The Equal Rights Movement: Shortcomings and Future Prospects

1. Missouri v. NOW, 467 F.Supp. 289 (W.D. Mo. 1979).

2. Missouri v. NOW, 620 F.2d 1301 (8th Cir. 1980).

3. 101 S.Ct. 122 (1980).

4. See p. 00 *supra*.

5. *See, e.g., 9 Women Arrested in 5-Hour Sit-in at Grove Press,* NEW YORK TIMES, April 14, 1970, at 55, col. 3; *cf. 5,000 Join Feminist Group's Rally in Times Sq. Against Pornography,* NEW YORK TIMES, October 21, 1979, at 41, col. 1 reporting, inter alia, that feminists protesting "pornography" refused to permit another group, carrying placards that read "Protect our Children" to join their rally, on the ground that this was an antihomosexual slogan. According to the *Times,* "a man holding an anti-abortion, anti-homosexual poster was tackled by three of the women members, who grabbed the sign and ripped it up." *Id.* at col. 2.

6. PRESIDENT'S COMMISSION ON OBSCENITY AND PORNOGRAPHY, REPORT, Bantam Books, New York, 1970, p. 29.

7. *Id.*

8. *Id.*

9. *Id.* at p. 32.

10. Roth v. United States, 354 U.S. 476 (1957).

11. 100 S.Ct. 1540 (1980).

12. 95 Cal. App. 3d 506, 157 Cal. Rptr. 260 (1980); *cert. granted,* 100 S.Ct. 3055 (1980).

13. 25 Cal. 3d 608, 159 Cal. Rptr. 340, 601 P.2d 572 (1980), *cert. granted,* 100 S.Ct. 2984 (1980).

14. 49 LW 2066 (USDC E. Pa. 1980), *cert. granted,* 49 LW 3401 (1980).

Appendix. Can a State Rescind Its ERA Ratification

1. 188 CONG REC. 9598 (1972).

2. "*Resolved by the Senate and House of Representatives of the United States of America in Congress assembled (two-thirds of each House concurring therein),* That the following article is proposed as an amendment to the Constitution of the United States, which shall be valid to all intents and purposes as part of the Constitution when ratified by the legislatures of three-fourths of the several States within seven years from the date of its submission by the Congress:

"Article—

"Section 1. Equality of rights under the law shall not be denied or abridged by the United States or by any State on account of sex.

"Section 2. The Congress shall have the power to enforce, by appropriate legislation, the provisions of this article.

"Section 3. This amendment shall take effect two years after the date of ratification." S.J. Res. 8, 92d Cong., 2d Sess. (1972), H.R.J. Res. 208, 92d Cong., 1st Sess. (1971), 86 Stat. 1523.

3. 117 CONG. REC. 35815 (1971).

4. For a legislative history of the ERA up to 1971 see Brown, Emerson, Falk & Freedman, *The Equal Rights Amendment: A Constitutional Basis for Equal Rights for Women,* 80 YALE L. J. 871, 981 (1971). For recent legislative action on the amendment see S. REP. NO. 689, 92d Cong., 2d Sess. (1972) (report from the Committee on the Judiciary presented by Senator Birch Bayh for vote in the Senate).

5. The thirty-five states that have ratified are Alaska, California, Colorado, Connecticut, Delaware, Hawaii, Idaho, Indiana, Iowa, Kansas, Kentucky, Maine,

Maryland, Massachusetts, Michigan, Minnesota, Montana, Nebraska, New Hampshire, New Jersey, New Mexico, New York, North Dakota, Ohio, Oregon, Pennsylvania, Rhode Island, South Dakota, Tennessee, Texas, Vermont, Washington, West Virginia, Wisconsin, and Wyoming.

6. LEG. RES. NO. 9, 83d Leg., 1st Sess., 1973 NEB. LAWS 1547, TENN. S.J. RES. 29, 88th Gen. Assembly (1974); N.Y. Times, February 10, 1977, at 18, col. 6.

7. Idaho and Kansas have contemplated rescission as of 1973. Note, *Reversals in the Federal Constitutional Amendment Process: Efficacy of State Ratifications of the Equal Rights Amendment,* 49 IND. L.J. 147 n.3 (1973).

8. During his presidential campaign, Jimmy Carter sent telegrams to Democratic leaders in the sixteen states that had not yet ratified the Amendment on August 23, 1976. He stated: "I am committed to equality between men and women in every area of government and in every aspect of life. . . .

"The Carter-Mondale team will make it clear to the American people that, despite charges to the contrary, the ERA is not an elitist issue but one that affects the economic and social well-being of all Americans.

"While we have seen some progress in changing our laws to prevent discrimination against women, these steps must not be used as an excuse to withhold from women the full guarantees of the Constitution." N.Y. Times, August 28, 1976, at 13, col. 3.

9. Although the issue, presented here with specific reference to the ERA, may be mooted by events, the underlying constitutional questions of the efficacy and justiciability of ratification and attempted rescission of constitutional amendments will be before the nation until they are finally resolved. Many of the underlying considerations of this article can be applied to future amendments.

10. *See* N.Y. Times, November 5, 1975, at 1, col. 5.

11. "The Congress, whenever two thirds of both Houses shall deem it necessary, shall propose Amendments to this Constitution, or on the Application of the Legislatures of two thirds of the several States, shall call a convention for proposing Amendments, which in either Case, shall be valid to all Intents and Purposes, as Part of this Constitution, when ratified by the Legislatures of three fourths of the several States, or by Conventions in three fourths thereof, as the one or the other Mode of Ratification may be proposed by the Congress" U.S. CONST. art. V.

12. For a discussion of congressional attempts to enact ratification procedures binding on state legislatures, see text accompanying notes 145–55 *infra*.

13. U.S. CONST. art. V.

14. All of the constitutional amendments to date have been ratified by the state legislative method except for the Twenty-First Amendment (repeal of prohibition).

15. 5 U.S. (1 Cranch) 137 (1803).

16. *Id.* at 177–78.

17. 3 U.S. (3 Dall.) 378 (1798).

18. The five Justices were William Cushing, James Wilson, James Iredell, Samuel Chase, and Oliver Ellsworth. *See* L. FRIEDMAN & F. ISRAEL, THE JUSTICES OF THE SUPREME COURT: 1789–1969, at 57–70, 79–96, 121–32, 185–98, 223–35 (1969).

19. 253 U.S. 221 (1920).

20. *Id.* at 229–30. The California Attorney General has opined that the Cali-

fornia electorate cannot effectively rescind, by the *initiative* process, the state's legislative ratification of the ERA. 58 OP. ATT'Y GEN. 830 (1975).

21. *Cf.* Burke, *Validity of Attempts to Rescind Ratification of the Equal Rights Amendment*, 8 U.W.L.A.L. REV. 1, 7 (1976).

22. National Prohibition Cases, 253 U.S. 350 (1920).

23. 256 U.S. 368 (1921).

24. *Id.* at 375 (emphasis added).

25. 258 U.S. 130 (1922).

26. The ratifying resolutions of Missouri and Tennessee were allegedly adopted in violation of the constitutions of those two states. Missouri had a provision in its constitution disallowing assent to a federal constitutional amendment if it impaired the right of local self-government. MO. CONST. art. 2, § 3, *quoted in* Leser v. Garnett, 139 Md. 46, 68, 114 A. 840, 846 (1921). Tennessee's constitution prohibited action on a proposed federal constitutional amendment unless the General Assembly had been elected after the amendment was submitted. TENN. CONST. art. 2, § 32, *quoted in* Leser v. Garnett, *supra* at 68, 114 A. 840, 846-47 (1921). The Court rejected a challenge to the ratifying resolutions of these two states on the grounds that ratification is a federal function, transcending state-imposed limitations. Leser v. Garnett, 258 U.S. 130, 137 (1922). Moreover, the resolutions of ratification by West Virginia and Tennessee were challenged as being in violation of those states' rules of legislative procedure, thereby rendering them inoperative. *See* Leser v. Garnett, 139 Md. 46, 71-73, 114 A. 840, 847-48 (1921). The United States Supreme Court rejected this challenge holding that notice by the state to the federal government of ratification was conclusive upon the Court. 258 U.S. at 137.

27. 282 U.S. 716 (1931).

28. *Id.* at 279.

29. The state courts likewise had consistently held that the amending process in its entirety was justiciable. "The authorities are thus practically uniform in holding that whether a constitutional amendment has been properly adopted according to the requirements of an existing Constitution is a judicial question. There can be little doubt that the consensus of judicial opinion is to the effect that it is the absolute duty of the judiciary to determine whether the Constitution has been amended in the manner required by the Constitution . . . ." *In re* McConaughy, 106 Minn. 392, 409–10, 119 N.W. 408, 415 (1909) (judicial resolution of challenge to state constitutional amendment regarding taxes on balloting error grounds). *See also* Rice v. Palmer, 78 Ark. 432, 96 S.W. 396 (1906) (judicially determined whether proposed state constitutional amendment received the majority of votes); Commonwealth v. Griest, 196 Pa. 396, 46 A. 505 (1900) (judicially determined whether the submission of a state constitutional amendment may be by resolution as well as by legislative act approved by the executive).

30. 307 U.S. 433 (1939).

31. 43 Stat. 670 (1924) (originated in the House of Representatives).

32. Coleman v. Miller, 146 Kan. 390, 71 P.2d 518 (1938).

33. Coleman v. Miller, 303 U.S. 632 (1938).

34. 307 U.S. at 447–49. See notes 115–17 *infra*.

35. 307 U.S. at 450 (emphasis added).

36. *Id.; cf.* L. ORFIELD, THE AMENDING OF THE FEDERAL CONSTITUTION 18–19 (1942) [hereinafter cited as ORFIELD.] "It should be carefully noted that [the Court] did

not hold all questions concerning the amending process to be political. The effect of the previous rejection by a state of an amendment and tphe interval of time in which the states might ratify an amendment was . . . held to involve a political question. Thus it is only as to these two questions that the court definitely decided that no justiciable question is involved." *Id.*

37. 48 U.S. (7 How.) 1 (1849).

38. Although the Court in *Luther* was examining the validity of Rhode Island's new government, Chief Justice Taney deviated from the main issue to remark; "In forming the constitutions of the different States . . . and in the various changes and alterations which have since been made, the political department has always determined whether the proposed constitution or amendment was ratified or not by the people of the State, and the judicial power has followed its decision." *Id.* at 39.

39. ORFIELD, *supra* note 36, at 20.

40. [I]t seems an unusual approach for the body recognized as having the power to review acts of Congress to adopt and rely on an act of Congress as precedent . . . ." *Id.* at 20.

41. *Id.* See text accompanying notes 19–28 *supra.*

42. 307 U.S. at 459 (Black, Roberts, Frankfurter, & Douglas, JJ., concurring).

43. *Id.* at 450 (Hughes, Stone, & Reed, JJ.).

44. *Id.* at 474 (Butler & McReynolds, JJ., dissenting).

45. See note 118 *infra.*

46. The dissents of Justices Butler and McReynolds consisted almost entirely of quotations from the *Dillon* case. See text accompanying notes 23–24 *supra.*

47. This discussion pertaining to the *Coleman* case is also applicable to *Coleman's* companion case, Chandler v. Wise, 307 U.S. 474 (1939), in which the Court summarily dismissed the case on the ground that after certification of ratification had been forwarded to the secretary of state there no longer was a justiciable controversy.

48. "Beginning with the proposed 18th amendment, Congress has customarily included a provision requiring ratification within 7 years from the time of the submission to the States." SENATE LIBRARY, PROPOSED AMENDMENTS TO THE CONSTITUTION OF THE UNITED STATES OF AMERICA, S. DOC. NO. 163, 87th Cong., 2d Sess.)244 (1963).

49. 369 U.S. 186 (1962).

50. *Id.* at 209.

51. *Id.* at 210–17.

52. *Id.* at 217.

53. *Id.*

54. *Id.* at 237.

55. 395 U.S. 486 (1969).

56. H.R. Res. 1, 90th Cong., 1st Sess., 113 CONG. REC. 24 (1967). Two years later Congressman Powell was seated and sworn in and a fine was imposed. H.R. Res. 2, 91st Cong., 1st Sess., 115 CONG. REC. 33-34 (1969).

57. "Each House shall be the Judge of the Elections, Returns and Qualifications of its own Members . . . .

"Each House may determine the Rules of its Proceedings, punish its Members for disorderly Behavior, and, with the Concurrence of two thirds, expel a Member." U.S. CONST. art. I, § 5.

58. It is interesting to note that Chief Justice Burger, before he was appointed to the Supreme Court, wrote the court of appeals decision that was reversed by the Supreme Court. In the decision, Burger affirmed the dismissal by the district court, not because of lack of jurisdiction as the lower court had decided, but on political question grounds applying the *Baker v. Carr* test. Powell v. McCormack, 395 F.2d 577 (D.C. Cir. 1968), *rev'd*, 395 U.S. 486 (1969).

59. 395 U.S. at 521–48.

60. *Id.* at 548 (emphasis added).

61. "No Person shall be a Representative who shall not have attained the Age of twenty five Years, and been seven Years a Citizen of the United States, and who shall not, when elected, be an Inhabitant of that State in which he shall be Chosen." U.S. CONST. art. I, § 2.

62. 395 U.S. at 550.

63. *Id.* at 549.

64. *Id.* at 548–49, *quoting* Baker v. Carr, 369 U.S. 186, 217 (1962).

65. See note 68 *infra*.

66. Justice Powell, a leading spokesman for judicial restraint, described it thus: "Due to what many have regarded as the unresponsiveness of the Federal Government to recognized needs or serious inequities in our society, recourse to the federal courts has attained an unprecedented popularity in recent decades. Those courts have often acted as a major instrument of social reform." United States v. Richardson, 418 U.S. 166, 191 (1974) (Powell, J., concurring).

67. Baker v. Carr, 369 U.S. 186, 210 (1962).

68. *See* Wright, *The Role of the Supreme Court in a Democratic Society— Judicial Activism or Restraint?* 54 CORNELL L. REV. 1 (1968). *See also* Mendelson, *The Politics of Judicial Activism*, 24 EMORY L.J. 43 (1975); *Dorsen & Kurland, The Burger Court—A Preliminary View*, 28 RECORD 109 (1973); Kurland, *1970 Term: Notes on the Emergence of the Burger Court*, 1971 SUP. CT. REVIEW 265 (1971).

69. *See* Flast v. Cohen, 392 U.S. 83, 99–100 (1968).

70. *But see id.* at 98.

71. 418 U.S. 166, 180–97 (1974) (Powell, J., concurring).

72. 422 U.S. 490 (1975).

73. "No Money Shall be drawn from the Treasury, but in Consequence of Appropriations made by law; and a regular Statement and Account of the Receipts and Expenditures of all public Money shall be published from time to time." U.S. CONST. art. I, § 9, cl. 7.

74. 392 U.S. 83 (1968). "First, the taxpayer must establish a logical link between [taxpayer] status and the type of legislative enactment attacked. . . . Secondly, the taxpayer must establish a nexus between [taxpayer] status and the precise nature of the constitutional infringement alleged." *Id.* at 102.

75. 418 U.S. at 175.

76. *Id.* at 177–78, *quoting Ex parte* Levitt, 302 U.S. 633, 634 (1937).

77. Justice Powell pointed out the various inconsistencies: "The opinion purports to separate the question of standing from the merits . . . yet it abruptly returns to the substantive issues raised by a plaintiff for the purpose of determining 'whether there is a logical nexus . . . . .' " 418 U.S. at 180–81. "Similarly, the opinion distinguishes between constitutional and prudential [i.e., judicial self-restraint,] limits on standing. . . . I find it impossible, however, to determine whether the two-part 'nexus' test created in *Flast* amounts to a constitutional or a

prudential limitation . . . ." *Id.* at 181. "[I]t is impossible to see how an inquiry about the existence of 'concrete adverseness' [as presented in *Baker v. Carr*] is furthered by an application of the *Flast* test." *Id.* at 182.

78. "[T]he Court's standard for the determination of standing [requisite personal stake in the outcome] and its criteria for the satisfaction of that standard [logical link between status and type of legislation attacked, and nexus between status and nature of constitutional infringement alleged] are entirely unrelated." 392 U.S. at 122 (Harlan, J., dissenting).

79. "While I have joined the opinion of the Court, I do not think that the test it lays down is a durable one for the reasons stated by my Brother Harlan." *Id.* at 107 (Douglas, J., concurring).

80. 418 U.S. at 188 (Powell, J., concurring).

81. *Id.*

82. *Id.* at 189.

83. *Id.* at 196.

84. *Id., quoting* Flast v. Cohen, 392 U.S. 83, 106 (1968).

85. 422 U.S. 490 (1975).

86. Petitioners claimed that the zoning ordinance violated their constitutional rights under the First, Ninth, and Fourteenth Amendments and statutory rights under 42 U.S.C. §§ 1981–83 (1970). Similar claims have since been rejected by the Court in Village of Arlington Heights v. Metropolitan Housing Dev. Corp., 97 S. Ct. 555 (1977).

87. "[I]t is quite clear, when the record is viewed with dispassion, that at least three of the groups of plaintiffs have made allegations, and supported them with affidavits and documentary evidence, sufficient to survive a motion to dismiss for lack of standing." 422 U.S. at 520–21 (Brennan, J., dissenting).

88. 418 U.S. 166, 196 (1974).

89. 422 U.S. at 498, *citing* U.S. v. Richardson, 418 U.S. 166 (1974) *and* Schlesinger v. Reservists to Stop the War, 418 U.S. 208 (1974). *Schlesinger* held there was no standing to bring a class action challenging Reserve membership of members of Congress as being in violation of the Incompatibility Clause of Art. I, § 6.

90. "Unrestrained standing in federal taxpayer or citizen suits would create a remarkably illogical system of judicial supervision of the coordinate branches of the Federal Government." 418 U.S. at 189.

91. "Without such [prudential] limitations . . . the courts would be called upon to decide abstract questions of wide public significance though other governmental institutions may be more competent to address the questions and even though judicial intervention may be unnecessary to protect individual rights." 422 U.S. at 500.

92. Justice Powell's views on the ERA itself may bear on his potential approach to resolving the ratification question. The Court struck down a federal statute according different benefits to male and female members of the uniformed services in Frontiero v. Richardson, 411 U.S. 677 (1973). Significantly, four justices asserted that sex, like race, was a suspect classification and hence triggered close scrutiny. *Id.* at 682. Concurring, Justice Powell argued that the discriminatory government practice could be invalidated on the less rigorous rational-basis standard on the authority of Reed v. Reed, 404 U.S. 71 (1971). More important, he suggested that characterizing sex classifications as "suspect" was inappropriate because the ERA was already making its way through the ratification process. *Id.* at 692. In his view, "this reaching out to preempt by judicial action a major political decision

which is currently in process of resolution does not reflect appropriate respect for duly prescribed legislative processes." *Id.* In expressing this view, Justice Powell may have overlooked the principal impetus behind the ERA—previous inaction by the Court in response to numerous instances of official sex discrimination challenged under existing constitutional provisions. *See* L. KANOWITZ, WOMEN AND THE LAW 1–99, 149–54 (1969). More recently, Justice Powell has conceded that under recent Supreme Court cases, the "relatively deferential 'rational basis' standard of review normally applied takes on a sharper focus when we address a gender-based classification." Craig v. Boren, 97 S. Ct. 451 (1976) (Powell, J., concurring). But this concession by no means undermines the attitude he expressed in *Frontiero* of deferring to Congress in matters related to the ratification of the Equal Rights Amendment.

93. 369 U.S. 186, 217 (1962).

94. "Not only does resolution of such issues frequently turn on standards that defy judicial application, or involve the exercise of a discretion demonstrably committed to the executive or legislative; but many such questions uniquely demand single-voiced statement of the Government's views." *Id.* at 211.

95. *Id.* at 217. An example of this principle occurred during the Reconstruction when the Court, because of the need for solidarity of purpose, refused to rule on whether the Georgia Constitution had been coerced by Congress and was therefore invalid. White v. Hart, 80 U.S. (13 Wall.) 646 (1871).

96. 369 U.S. at 217. *Baker* partially relied on *Field v. Clark* in which the Court, ruling on a challenge to the validity but not the authenticity of a signed United States statute, stated: "The respect due to coequal and independent departments requires the judicial department" to rely on congressional authentication to "determine . . . whether the Act, so authenticated, is in conformity with the Constitution." Field v. Clark, 143 U.S. 649, 672 (1892). *See also* Leser v. Garnett, 258 U.S. 130 (1922). *Leser* relied on *Field* in determining that the ratifications certified by the secretary of state were conclusive upon the Court. *Id.* at 137.

97. *E.g.,* Powell v. McCormack, 395 U.S. 486 (1969). "Such a determination falls within the traditional role accorded courts to interpret the law, and does not involve a 'lack of respect due [a] coordinate [branch] of government'. . . ." *Id.* at 548.

98. 369 U.S. at 217.

99. *Id.*

100. See notes 17–29 & accompanying text *supra.*

101. 369 U.S. at 217.

102. Powell v. McCormack, 395 U.S. 486, 521 (1968).

103. *Id.*

104. *See* J. ELLIOT, DEBATES ON THE ADOPTION OF THE FEDERAL CONSTITUTION 531 (1881).

105. *Id.* at 128.

106. *Id.* at 558.

107. Initially, the framers were reluctant to give Congress *any* power in the amending process. At the Convention George Mason said, "It would be improper to require the consent of the National legislature, because they may abuse their power and refuse their assent on that very account." *Id.* at 182.

108. See text accompanying notes 11–12 *infra.*

109. 395 U.S. at 519.

110. U.S. CONST. art. I, § 5.

111. See text accompanying notes 55–62 *supra*.

112. 307 U.S. 433 (1939). *Coleman* is discussed in text accompanying notes 30–44 *supra*.

113. 307 U.S. at 450.

114. Note, *Proposed Legislation on the Convention Method of Amending the United States Constitution*, 85 HARV. L. REV. 1612, 1637–38 (1972).

115. Upon receipt of Ohio's rescission, the Senate referred it to the Committee on the Judiciary with the effect of killing the resolution. CONG. GLOBE, 40th Cong., 2d Sess. 876–78 (1868). Secretary of State William Seward, in his announcement to Congress on the Fourteenth Amendment, stated: "[I]t is made the duty of the Secretary of State forthwith to cause any amendment to the Constitution of the United States, which has been adopted according to the provisions of the said Constitution, to be published in the newspapers authorized to promulgate the laws, with his certificate specifying the States by which the same may have been adopted, and that the same has become valid, to all intents and purposes, as a part of the Constitution . . . ;

"[W]hereas neither the act . . . nor any other law, expressly or by conclusive implication, authorizes the Secretary of State to determine and decide doubtful questions . . . as to the power of any State legislature to recall a previous act or resolution of ratification of any amendment proposed to the Constitution;

"And whereas it appears from official documents on file in this Department that the amendment to the Constitution of the United States, proposed as aforesaid, has been ratified by the legislatures of the State of. . .New Jersey [and] Ohio . . . ;

"And whereas it further appears from official documents on file in this Department that the legislatures of two of the States first above enumerated, to wit, Ohio and New Jersey, have since passed resolutions respectively withdrawing the consent of each of the said States to the aforesaid amendment; and whereas it is deemed a matter of doubt and uncertainty whether such resolutions are not irregular, invalid, and therefore ineffectual for withdrawing the consent of the said two States. . . .

"Now, therefore, be it known that I, William H. Seward, Secretary of State of the United States . . . do hereby certify that if the resolutions of the legislatures of Ohio and New jersey ratifying the aforesaid amendment are to be deemed as remaining of full force and effect, notwithstanding the subsequent resolutions of the legislatures of those States, which purport to withdraw the consent of said States from such ratification, then the aforesaid amendment has been ratified in the manner hereinbefore mentioned, and so has become valid, to all intents and purposes, as a part of the Constitution of the United States." 15 Stat. 706–07 (1868). Thereafter, both Houses passed concurrent resolutions declaring the adoption of the amendment. The next day the Secretary of State certified the adoption of the amendment. Coleman v. Miller, 307 U.S. 433, 438–39 (1939).

116. Ohio rejected and then ratified the amendment. New York ratified and then rescinded. A joint resolution was introduced in Congress to declare ratification of the Fifteenth Amendment. It was referred to the Committee on the Judiciary and never reached a vote. CONG. GLOBE, 41st Cong., 2d Sess. 1444 (1870). Therefore no formal resolution was directed from Congress when Secretary of State Hamilton Fish proclaimed the Amendment ratified, including Ohio and New York in his list of states that had ratified. 16 Stat. 1131 (1870).

117. West Virginia ratified following rejection and Tennessee attempted to

rescind. Secretary of State Bainbridge Colby simply promulgated the Nineteenth Amendment without any questions directed to Congress. 41 Stat. 1823 (1920).

118. In 1951 Congress substituted the GSA for the Secretary of State: "Whenever official notice is received at the General Services Administration that any amendment proposed to the Constitution of the United States has been adopted, according to the provisions of the Constitution, the Administrator of General Services shall forthwith cause the amendment to be published, with his certificate, specifying the States by which the same may have been adopted, and that the same has become valid, to all intents and purposes, as a part of the Constitution of the United States." Act of October 31, 1951, Pub. L. No. 82–248, § 2(b), 65 Stat. 710 (codified at 1 U.S.C. § 106b (1970)).

119. It should be noted at this point that only in the case of the Fourteenth Amendment were the disputed states necessary to make up the requisite total for ratification. As to the Fifteenth and Nineteenth Amendments, three-fourths of the existing state legislatures ratified notwithstanding the disputed states.

120. *Cf.* BLACK'S LAW DICTIONARY 1428 (4th rev. ed. 1968): "Ratify. To approve and sanction; to make valid; to confirm; to give sanction to."

121. "[T]he function of a State legislature in ratifying a proposed amendment to the Federal Constitution . . . is a federal function derived from the Federal Constitution; and it transcends any limitations sought to be imposed by the . . . State." Leser v. Garnett, 258 U.S. 130, 137 (1922); Hawke v. Smith, 253 U.S. 221 (1920). "[T]he power to ratify a proposed amendment to the Federal Constitution has its source in the Federal Constitution. The act of ratification by the State derives its authority from the Federal Constitution . . . ." *Id.* at 230. *See also* Dodge v. Woolsey, 59 U.S. (18 How.) 331, 348 (1856).

122. J. JAMESON, A TREATISE ON CONSTITUTIONAL CONVENTIONS 632 (1887). *See also id.* at 628–30.

123. *Id.* at 632.

124. 282 U.S. 716 (1931).

125. *Id.* at 731.

126. "[R]atification is but the expression of the approbation of the people . . . ." Dillon v. Gloss, 256 U.S. 368, 375 (1921).

127. Hawke v. Smith, 253 U.S. 221, 229 (1920).

128. D. WATSON, THE CONSTITUTION OF THE UNITED STATES 1317 (1910).

129. United States v. Sprague, 282 U.S. 716, 732 (1931).

130. "Amendment of the Constitution: (let us hope!) will remain a highly unusual thing." Black, *Amending the Constitution: A Letter to a Congressman*, 82 YALE L.J. 189, 195 (1972).

131. "The Constitution made the amendment process difficult, and properly so. It certainly was not the intention of the original Convention to make it impossible." Ervin, *Proposed Legislation to Implement the Convention Method of Amending the Constitution*, 66 MICH. L. REV. 875, 895 (1968) [hereinafter cited as Ervin].

132. ORFIELD, *supra* note 36, at 210.

133. *See* SENATE LIBRARY, PROPOSED AMENDMENTS TO THE CONSTITUTION OF THE UNITED STATES OF AMERICA, S. DOC. NO. 163, 87th Cong., 2d Sess. iv (1963). Five congressionally proposed amendments have not been ratified by the states. In 1789, only ten of twelve proposed amendments were ratified to become the Bill of Rights. The other two were articles providing for the growth of the House in proportion to the population of the country and for the determination of

congressional compensation only when a new House had been elected. In the 11th Congress an article was proposed relating to the acceptance by U.S. citizens of titles of nobility from foreign governments. In 1861, the 36th Congress proposed an article prohibiting a constitutional amendment to abolish slavery, and in 1924 the 68th Congress passed the Child Labor Amendment resolution. *Id.* at 244–45.

134. See note 4 *supra.*

135. See notes 115–17 *supra.*

136. *See generally* Comment, *Constitutional Amendments—The Justiciability of Ratification and Retraction,* 41 TENN. L. REV. 93 (1973).

137. *See generally* H. ASBURY, THE GREAT ILLUSION: AN INFORMAL HISTORY OF PROHIBITION (1950).

138. When Senator Birch Bayh presented the Equal Rights Amendment to the Senate for passage he said: "The women of our country must have tangible evidence of our commitment to guarantee equal treatment under law. An amendment to the Constitution has great moral and persuasive value. Every citizen recognizes the importance of a constitutional amendment, for the Constitution declares the most basic policies of our nation as well as the supreme law of the land." S. REP. No. 689, 92d Cong., 2d Sess. 11 (1972).

139. *See generally* M. DELSMAN, EVERYTHING YOU NEED TO KNOW ABOUT ERA (1975); *Hearings on the ERA Before Subcomm. No. 4 of the House Comm. on the Judiciary,* 92d Cong., 1st Sess., ser. 2 (1971); Brown, Emerson, Falk & Freedman, *The Equal Rights Amendment: A Constitutional Basis for Equal Rights for Women,* 80 YALE L.J. 871 (1971).

140. From our expression of support for the ERA on the merits, some might infer that our analysis of the amending process itself, and its conclusion that the Court can and should decide that a state may not rescind its earlier ratification, is motivated by partisan political considerations rather than by an objective appraisal of the relevant constitutional language. Such an inference would be erroneous. In the years ahead one or more proposed amendments not to our liking (*e.g.*, an antiabortion amendment, an antibusing amendment, an amendment permitting capital punishment, an amendment permitting prayer in schools) may garner the support of two-thirds of each house of Congress and be sent to the states for ratification. Though we would undoubtedly oppose them on the merits, we recognize that everything we have written with regard to the process of ratifying the ERA would apply to such other amendments as well.

141. See notes 115–17 *supra.*

142. *See also* Coleman v. Miller, 307 U.S. 433, 449 (1939).

143. See notes 115–40 & accompanying text *supra.*

144. A bill introduced in 1870 that would have made attempted withdrawal of state ratification null and void was passed by the House. CONG. GLOBE, 41st Cong., 2d Sess. 5356–57 (1870). It died, however, after being reported unfavorably by the Senate Judiciary Committee. CONG. GLOBE, 41st Cong., 3d Sess. 1381 (1871). In the 67th and 68th Congresses, the Wadsworth-Garrett amendment was proposed, which would have left states free to change prior action until the requisite three-fourths majority had ratified or time expired. The amendment never reached a vote. 65 CONG. REC. 3675–79 (1924).

145. S. 2307, 90th Cong., 1st Sess. (1967). *See* Ervin, *supra* note 131, at 879.

146. S. 623, 91st Cong., 1st Sess. (1969); S. 215, 92d Cong., 1st Sess. (1971); S. 1272, 93d Cong., 1st Sess. (1973).

147. S. 2307, 90th Cong., 1st Sess. (1967) arose after the following series of

events. In 1964 the Supreme Court decided *Reynolds v. Sims*, which, on the basis of the Fourteenth Amendment equal-protection clause established the one-person-one-vote requirement: state legislative apportionment on the basis of population. Reynolds v. Sims, 377 U.S. 533 (1964). That same year the Court, in *Lucas v. Forty-Fourth General Assembly of Colorado*, held on the basis of *Reynolds* that both houses of a bicameral state legislature must be apportioned according to population notwithstanding that the state electorate voted in favor of one house being apportioned according to other factors. Lucas v. Forty-Fourth Gen. Assembly of Colo., 377 U.S. 713 (1964). Reacting to these cases, especially *Lucas*, Senator Dirksen proposed S.J. Res. 103, 89th Cong., 1st Sess. (1965), the so-called Dirksen amendment. See Dirksen, *The Supreme Court and the People*, 66 MICH. L. REV. 837, 858 (1968). The amendment would have allowed the electorate to decide the apportionment; as long as one house was apportioned according to population, the other house could be apportioned on the basis of population, geography, or political subdivision. The Dirksen Amendment received a majority vote in the Senate, but fell short of the requisite two-thirds vote for constitutional amendments.

"In December, 1964, following the decision in *Reynolds v. Sims*, the Seventeenth Biennial General Assembly of the States recommended that the state legislatures petition Congress to convene a constitutional convention to propose an amendment along the lines of the Dirksen amendment . . . . Twenty-two states submitted constitutional convention petitions to Congress during the Eighty-ninth Congress . . . and four more during the first session of the Ninetieth Congress . . . . If one counted the petitions adopted by four other states, questionable in regard to their proper receipt by Congress, this brought the total number of state petitions on the subject of state legislative apportionment to thirty-two." Ervin, *supra* note 131, at 877. This was two short of the requisite two-thirds of the states.

148. 117 CONG. REC. 36804 (1971).

149. S. 215, 92d Cong., 1st Sess. (1971).

150. The ERA was passed by Congress on March 22, 1972, so no potential legislation could have affected its ratification. See notes 1–3 & accompanying text *supra*.

151. Black, *Amending the Constitution: A Letter to a Congressman*, 82 YALE L.J. 189, 190 (1972).

152. Ervin, *supra* note 131, at 902. In addition, section 13(b) provided that any state may ratify a proposed amendment even though it previously may have rejected it and that questions concerning state ratification or rejection of amendments were to be determined solely by Congress and its decisions were to be binding on all courts, state and federal. *Id.*

153. "Congress shall have the Power . . . . To make all Laws which shall be necessary and proper for carrying into Execution the foregoing Powers, and all other Powers vested by this Constitution in the government of the United States, or in any Department or Officer thereof."

154. Bonfield, *The Dirksen Amendment and the Article V Convention Process*, 66 MICH. L. REV. 949, 987 (1968). See also Ervin, *supra* note 131, at 879.

155. ORFIELD. *supra* note 36, at 64–65. See also Corwin & Ramsey, *The Constitutional Law of Constitutional Amendment*, 26 NOTRE DAME LAW. 185, 208 (1951).

156. "While in existence [the convention] is a separate arm of the nation, coordinate with Congress in its sphere." Orfield, *supra* note 36, at 47.

157. Moreover, the House of Representatives has never voted on the proposed legislation under discussion. Even the Senate's own rationale for permitting states to rescind the ratification of convention-sponsored amendments is seriously deficient. That rationale is based upon a perceived analogy with the right of the states to rescind their applications to convoke a constitutional convention. S. REP. NO. 293, 93d Cong., 1st Sess. 14 (1973). The report of the Judiciary Committee even states: "An application [to call a convention] is not a final action. It merely registers the state's view . . . . On the basis of the same reasoning, a state should be permitted to retract its ratification. . . ." *Id.* The fact of the matter is, there is no precedent to support the presumption that a ratification is *not* a final action or that it *merely* registers the state's views. As Professor Bonfield has emphasized: "Applications for a constitutional convention . . . are merely 'formal requests' by state legislatures to Congress, requesting the latter to call a Convention for proposing Amendments . . . . [T]hey do not share the same dignity of finality as ratifications . . . ." Bonfield, *Proposing Constitutional Amendments by Convention: Some Problems*, 39 NOTRE DAME LAW. 659, 671 (1964). Professor Bonfield had previously noted that ratification is the "'final act by which sovereign bodies confirm a legal or political agreement arrived at by their agents.'" *Id.*

Postscript

1. _____ U.S. _____, 101 S. Ct. 1200 (1981).
2. Id. at 1206.
3. Id. at 1204.
4. Id. at 1211.
5. Id.
6. Id. at 1215.
7. Id. at 1219.
8. 430 U.S. 313 (1977), *see* text at Chapter 3, n. 33 et seq., supra.
9. 419 U.S. 498 (1975), *see* text at Chapter 3, n. 29, supra.
10. 416 U.S. 351 (1974), *see* text at Chapter 3, n. 24 et seq., supra.
11. 101 S. Ct. at 1204.
12. Id. at 1205, quoting Weinberger v. Weisenfeld, 420 U.S. 636, 648, n. 16 (1975).
13. 101 S. Ct. at 1206, n. 7, quoting United States v. O'Brien, 391 U.S. 367, 383 (1968).
14. 49 LW 4798 (June 25, 1981).
15. Id. at 4802.
16. 419 U.S. 498 (1975).
17. 49 LW at 4804.
18. Id.
19. Id at 4800.
20. 409 U.S. 50 (1972).
21. *See, e.g.*, Schad v. Borough of Mount Ephraim, 49 LW 4507 (1981) (a zoning ordinance that excludes from otherwise broad range of permissible use all forms of live entertainment, including nonobscene nude dancing, violates the First Amendment).
22. 49 LW at 4806.
23. Id. at 4806, n. 2.
24. Id. at 4805.
25. Id. at 4813.
26. Id. at 4806.

INDEX

Case Index

Arp v. Workers' Comp. Appeals Bd., 165*n* 166, 168*n*48

Baker v. Carr, 128, 130, 133, 185*n*58,*n*64, *n*67, *n*77, 187*n*96

Bolling v. Sharpe, 173*n*9

Bradwell v. the State, 77, 88

Buchanan v. Batchelor, 178*n*67

Bunting v. Oregon, 51

Califano v. Goldfarb, 21, 31, 40, 43, 45, 60, 156*n*4, 159*n*45, 160*n*88, 161*n*102, 163*n*134, 164*n*154, 165*n*166, *n*169, *n*170, 166*n*4, 167*n*16, 170*n*76

Califano v. Webster, 20, 31, 34, 38, 43, 46, 100, 146, 148, 155*n*3, 167*n*15, 179*n*76, *n*80

Califano v. Westcott, 18, 47, 51, 54, 167*n*16

California v. Larue, 150

Chandler v. Wise, 184*n*47

Childs v. Charles, 174*n*15

Clem v. Brown, 64

Coleman v Miller, 125–27, 184*n*47, 188*n*115, 190*n*142

Commonwealth v. Griest, 183*n*29

Craig v. Boren, 18, 35, 58, 59, 100, 101, 149, 157*n*15, 158*n*27, 159*n*59, 160*n*83, *n*88, 166*n*14, 178*n*72, 179*n*77, 186*n*92,

DeFunis v. Odegaard, 158*n*26

Diaz v. Pan Am World Airways, 169*n*71

Dillon v. Gloss, 124, 126, 189*n*126

Dodge v. Woolsey, 189*n*121

Duley v. Caterpillar Tractor Co., 39, 165*n*15

Dunn v. Blumstein, 171*n*21, 175*n*37

Eisenstadt v. Baird, 170*n*13

Field v. Clark, 187*n*96

Flast v. Cohen, 131, 133, 185*n*69, *n*77, 186*n*84

Foley v. Connelie, 157*n*19

Forbush v. Wallace, 79, 173*n*13

Frontiero v. Richardson, 19, 33–34, 43, 45, 99, 160*n*79, *n*89, 178*n*72, 179*n*85, 186*n*92

Fullilove v. Klutznick, 155*n*2

Furman v. Georgia 171*n*20

Gaston County v. United States, 163*n*129

Goesart v. Cleary, 67, 77, 87–88

Goldberg v. Rostker, 117

Graham v. Richardson, 157*n*19

Gray v. Sanders, 66

Griggs v. Duke Power Co., 162*n*114

Griswold v. Connecticut, 170*n*13

Harper v. Virginia Bd. of Elections, 175*n*36

Hawke v. Smith, 124, 189*n*121, *n*127

Hays v. Potlatch Forests, Inc., 168*n*40

Hogan v. State, 178*n*67

Hollingsworth v. Virginia, 123

Homemakers Inc. v. Division of Indus. Welfare, 167*n*19, *n*36, 168*n*48

Hoyt v. Florida, 67,77,88, 175*n*33

Juri v. Juri, 173*n*14

Kahn v. Shevin, 19–20, 32–33, 34, 39, 43, 60, 100, 146, 148, 155*n*3, 159*n*57, *n*58, 161*n*97, *n*103, *n*107, 162*n*122, 164*n*154, *n*156

Katzenbach v. McClung, 177*n*60

Korematsu v. United States, 157*n*18, 170*n*12, 175*n*35

193

Subject Index

more "favorable" women's Social Security benefits, 38
more "favorable" women's tax benefits, 39
principle of, impliedly recognized in *Rosenfeld*, 54–55
race and sex classifications compared, 41–42
removing detriment from women by extending benefit to men, 46, 51
sex-based differential in age of majority, 36–37
U.S. Supreme Court's failure to perceive nature of, 38
viewed as separate laws, 36–37, 37–38
due process clauses, 77, 86, 99
education, sex-segregated, 78
education amendments of 1972, 6, 103
Engels, Frederick, 2
Equal Credit Opportunity Act. 103
Equal Pay Act of 1963, 6, 102
equal-protection clause, 86, 99
Equal Rights Amendment
and child custody, 93
and compulsory military service, 91–92
and family-support obligations, 92–93
and federal legislative power over family relations, 94–95
and state protective labor laws for women only, 93–94
effects, generally, 10, 81, 90–91
effects, inconsistent with "benign" discrimination, 18
in state constitutions, 102
need for, 86–91
opponents' fears, 91–95
opposed by Ronald Reagan, 114
ratification campaign
effect on U.S. Supreme Court, 101–2
male participants in, 2
positive results of, 98–103
shortcomings of, 95–98
denigration of homemaker role, 96
occasional antimale manifestations, 96–97
unnecessary association with abortion issue, 98
unnecessary association with homosexual rights, 96–97
ratification deadline extension, 85
ratification rescissions, 121–43 passim
reasons for delay in effective date of, 81–82
text of, 63, 75, 90

Executive Order 11246 (amended by E.O. 11375), 6, 103
Fair Labor Standards Act, proposed voluntary-overtime amendment to, 53
family support and the ERA, 92–93
federal legislative power and the ERA, 94–95
feminist movement, diversity of, 105
Gorer, Geoffrey, 4
Hamilton, Alexander, 138
Hitler, Adolph, 89
homosexual rights
and the antipornography drive, 112–13
and the EAR ratification campaign, 96–97
hours-limitations laws, as "benign" sex discrimination, 37
husband, as "head and master" of the family, 87
Ibsen, Henrik, 2
"invidiousness," Supreme Court definitions of, 26–27, 160n88
Irvin, Sam, 76
judicial extension of legislatively created benefits
distinguished from "restructuring" laws, 48–49
as intrusive of legislative domain as is abrogation of benefits, 47
not feasible in re compulsory military service, 57
state courts' reluctance to engage in, 47
"restructuring" impliedly allowed if simple and equitable, 49
jury service, denial of women's right of, 87
Kennedy, Edward, 115
"Lysistrata," 11
Madison, James, 138
malapportionment of state legislatures, 127–28
males
as "discrete and insular minority," 34–35
discrimination against. See antimale discrimination
Marx, Karl, 2
Mead, Margaret, 4
military benefits, sex-based discrimination in, 19, 20
Mill, John Stuart, 2, 11
New Mexico
community-property laws of, 9
Equal Rights Amendment of, 75–83 passim
O'Connor, Sandra Day, 152